THE QUEEN OF EVERYTHING

Sonya Braverman

DEDICATION

To my late husband whose love opened my eyes.

To my current husband without whose support I could not have written what I might otherwise have chosen to forget.

To my former clients, whose stories taught me about strength, resilience and courage.

DISCLAIMER

This book is a memoir. The events and experiences portrayed here are based on the author's own recall and are presented as truthfully as memory permits and/or through written or transcribed documents as indicated. All persons within are actual individuals.

The author recognizes that the memories or impressions of the events and experiences described here may be different than how any of the characters in the book or other readers may have remembered or experienced them.

Most of the conversations in the book come from the author's own recollections, though they are not written to represent word-for-word transcripts of such conversations unless they are indicated as such. Some dialogue consistent with the situation or nature of the persons speaking has been recreated because it is almost impossible to recall every word of a conversation. The author has retold them in a way that evokes the feeling and meaning of what was said and, in all instances, the essence of the dialogue is accurate.

The material in this book was not intended to harm any individual or the general public's impressions of such persons but rather as a way to present the author's experiences as honestly as possible. The author recognizes that there are particular truths that are essential to the telling of this story and regrets any unintentional harm resulting from the publishing and marketing of *The Queen of Everything*.

CONTENTS

ACKNOWLEDGMENTS

First of all, to my editor and mentor, Josh Langston, an accomplished best-selling author in his own right, this book is a reality only because of your infinite patience.

To Lloyd Blackwell, teacher. Your support, encouragement and enthusiasm throughout this project was invaluable.

To all my writer friends. You've read, discussed, edited, advised, and then read again. Thank you for being there.

To Erica Jong, esteemed author, poet, screenwriter, and novelist. Thank you for encouraging me to tell the truth.

To Kay Simms. Your touching story encouraged me to let go of more than you think.

To Jamie Hanks Nourzad. You have the eyes of a hawk. How do I ever thank you for clarifying, simplifying, and spotting the errors I couldn't see?

To Jody, who endured years of my talking about "the book" and offered suggestions, outstanding design work, and occasionally a piece of her mind. Sometimes your children know better.

Foreword

What Would People Think?

Like shoeboxes full of old photographs, great heaps of long-ago memories accumulated in every tangled channel of my brain. Decade after decade, my shoebox collection grew. Every now and then, I'd sort through the memories hoping they'd make sense, or simply ignore them, wishing they'd go away. I felt compelled to understand, to find some meaning, some sense of *coherence,* in my existence. The *why* of it all.

So, I set about organizing my memories by experiences, all the while searching to understand who I was, identify the events and people that shaped me and figure out how they impacted the person I came to be. What emerged from all that rambling around in the halls of my backstory are the chapters of this book. The ones that describe *me.*

In the years prior to my late husband's death in January, 2014, I nurtured a ferocious desire to write. When I started writing, I felt like I had drilled for oil and hit a gusher; the pages surged out of my hand. He had been sick for a long time and as the illness progressed, the nightmare it unleashed upon our lives provided me with all the material I needed. Or so I *thought.*

But writing about his illness was just the beginning. In 2012, I registered for a week-long memoir-writing workshop led by Erica Jong, an internationally acclaimed author. Our first assignment was to "Write about the worst day of your life."

"That'll be easy," I mused, "I've had a lifetime of bad days!"

It was hard to know where to begin. What *was* the worst day of my life? It wasn't like I had to scramble to find a worst day because, frankly, there were many. But which one was the *absolute* worst?

Was it the day I learned my parents were going to divorce, or when I was attacked by dogs? Maybe when my grandmother died or the day I was arrested? Or one of the many when I wanted to run away or die. Or that single moment when I sensed there was something terribly wrong bubbling up in my ailing husband's brain, or when I came face-to-face with the reality of just how terribly his life would end. Or maybe on the day, months after his death, when the fog started to clear and I began the long journey to understanding?

It was none of those days.

I decided to write about the day before I stopped drinking, over twenty-five years ago. A day that left me profoundly shamed and forever changed.

With my laptop in front of me, the words simply danced out of my fingers. I wrote in circles, pirouetting delicately like a beautiful ballerina near the most unpleasant parts, haloing gracefully around the phrases but never disturbing a thing. Balancing precisely on tippy-toes, I never ventured too close to anything painful. I was pleased with myself; I had created a beautiful composition.

The next day I stood in front of my classmates and read what I had written. Everyone clapped politely when I finished.

"Beautiful writing," Erica said, nodding her head in my direction.

"Thank you," I responded, smiling proudly. I felt like Erica Jong had just presented me with the Pulitzer Prize! I knew I was a pretty good writer and this piece, in particular, was lyrical and elegant.

"Almost like poetry," she continued. Hesitating for a few seconds, she added, "but how would we ever know it was your 'worst' day? What *really* happened on that day, Sonya? What made it the *worst*?"

Her words caught me off guard. I wasn't prepared. *She said it was "beautiful writing," didn't she? What more does she want?*

"You don't need to wrap up the worst day of your life in a tidy package with sparkly paper and a lovely bow. Unwrap it; show us *why* it was the worst day. Paint a picture with words. Let those words make us *feel* something. We want to go back there with you and experience whatever you did on that day. And, above all else, be honest."

"Oh no," I whispered, shaking my head, "I could *never* write that stuff down. It's too awful." I didn't even want to think about it, much less write about it. "It's so embarrassing." I could never let anyone know how agonizing that day was.

"I imagined as much," Erica said, knowingly. "You talked around it, through it and over it. Are you concerned about how others might react?"

"Yes," I replied sheepishly. "I don't want to immortalize my behavior on that day with words I can never retract. What would people think?"

"Well, they'd probably think you were being honest. If you're going to write a memoir, you have to tell the truth. There's no other way to do it. What other people think about you is *their* problem, not yours, Sonya. Tomorrow, why don't you tell us about what *really* happened that day? Make the worst day of your life come alive."

I walked out of the classroom certain I was never

going back. I liked the way I wrote. It was passionate and creative. Soundless scrolling phrases and gentle swirling flourishes, waltzing around the pages with big words and flowery adjectives. It was all so pretty, pleasing and proper.

But it wasn't real. It was lovely and respectable, but it didn't say anything. Never once did I touch on the essence, the innermost core, of *me*.

Now, Erica Jong wanted me to *scream* the truth all over town, to hang out all my nasty little secrets for the world to read. It was obvious that writing honestly in all its unbecoming glory was going to be hard to do. I was torn; I wanted so badly to write about my life as if I were refined and well-bred. Normal.

But it wasn't.

Reluctantly, I reached for my laptop and began to rewrite the story. No pretend bullshit. No more dancing or fancy-schmancy words to soften the drama. Real life. Yep. The truth.

The images tumbled out, unreeling in my head like a horror movie. The painful words emerged as a thick, gluey bitterness. They burned the back of my throat and stuck to me for hours afterward like hot tar sticks to a worn tire. I was desperate to shove everything back inside where it belonged. I realized there were some things I didn't want to relive.

The intensity of those first candid words opened the old wounds, giving rise to a familiar, yet unidentified, feeling. Later in my writing, I described the sensation as a bottomless mourning wrapped around the hardened knots of loss, regret and self-blame. These grief-laden feelings had been gnawing away at my insides like battery acid, keeping me stuck in the past despite my best efforts to escape.

The next day, with a revised copy of the story in front of me, I stood in front of my classmates again. My hands shook and as I stepped up to the podium. With trembling voice I read, feeling unsteady and off balance, like I was walking barefoot through a porcupine den. What would people think?

My rewrite wasn't a long story and when I finished reading it aloud to my classmates the momentary silence was stunning.

They hated it. They hate me. It was too shocking. I just told a room full of strangers what a loser I am. I wish I could disappear!

Then came the enthusiastic clapping. "Bravo," Erica shouted, standing up. "You nailed it. Wow!"

I returned home after the workshop, took more writing classes and joined a writer's group. I followed Erica's advice and let my real self spill out, sharing the most intimate, and sometimes ugly, details of my life. It wasn't a pretty picture, but it was honest and it felt right. And I watched as the material gradually accumulated, transforming itself into a book.

The thing that bothered me most about writing a book was that people might actually *read* it. Yeah, I know that makes no sense, but what would people think of me?

But even more than *that*, I dreaded that by exhuming my past I might ultimately discover that last awful thing lying hidden in the gutters of my memory. I imagined that whatever I might find there would surely be more than I could handle. *Better to let sleeping demons die. I've punished myself enough; dredging up this sludge all over again is just going to make it more painful.*

But that wasn't enough to extinguish the still-crackling desire to write.

Over time, writing has had an unanticipated positive effect. The emotional upheaval created by unearthing the past has been unexpectedly enlightening. With every chapter, I peeled back another layer of who I was. I began to appreciate the rawness, even the fragility, of my situation in an entirely new way. I came to realize that by the time I was in my twenties, my life had become a tangled mess of never-ending dramas.

Yet, by far, the single most astonishing moment of insight that gradually emerged from placing coherent words on paper was the realization that I had been a *childhood alcoholic*!* I remember exactly when this remarkable revelation smacked me between the eyes. It was an ah-ha moment of monumental significance.

Confronting the truth about myself has been an exceedingly difficult task. Despite that, writing has been my way of coming to terms with what I might otherwise have chosen to run away from or try to forget. Seeing my words in black and white has not only helped me to figure things out and more fully understand the events and people who influenced me, but it's also helped me to tie up the loose ends of my life in a way that no amount of psychotherapy has ever done.

It would have been impossible to imagine that writing something as exhausting as this book would be the most healing, restorative thing I've *ever* done. I found that once I had committed a story to paper, I was able to let go of it. It became less damaging in print than it had locked up in my heart and imprisoned in my brain. In the end, writing this memoir has set me free. I no longer pretend to be somebody I'm not.

Like anyone else's story, mine is a work in progress. There will always be more to remember and more to write about. **The Queen of Everything** isn't an account of my life, but rather a cacophony of moments I never left behind. They've been trapped inside me for decades, even though my body has moved on. They represent the times and places in my life when I was most "me." The person I am today is the result of many of those tender and beautiful moments mixed generously with the exquisitely more painful and traumatic ones.

The way I see it, writing this book is a gift I've given myself. It represents my struggle to close the circle of *me.* And if reading it can encourage just one person to feel less alone or to confront their *own* demons, then I'll be that much happier I took the risk of publishing it.

Finally, it all makes sense.

*See Addendum

Chapter 1

The Queen of Everything

I'm seated at the head of the table in the dining room of my home. My guests are settled around me. Each of us has said a few words of thankfulness as we admire the magnificent golden-brown turkey resting on a platter in the middle of the table. The irresistible aroma of the succulently roasted fowl bursting with an apple-sausage stuffing scents the air and holds the promise of a fine meal. With every "Ooh," "Aah," and "Beautiful," I swell with happiness. To think it was *I* who prepared that awesome bird!

The telephone in the kitchen rings, and I'm jolted to attention. *Who would have the gall to call me during Thanksgiving dinner?* The mere idea of it burns me up. Annoyed, I jump up to answer it, ready to eviscerate whomever is on the other end.

Upon rising, my feet become entangled in the wide-set legs of the chair. I lose my balance and fall to the floor, the wine glass in my hand sloshing its contents all over the carpet. Righting myself clumsily, I claw my way to the phone before the caller hangs up. Nothing matters more than telling that person where to go!

"Hello!" I say sharply with the same angry bark in my voice that greets most callers. The phone has become an effective vehicle for spewing my contempt for the world.

The voice on the other end of the line is my former husband.

"Happy Thanksgiving, Sonya. How are you? I was wondering if I could talk to my daughter," he says politely.

I give him no more than a few seconds to speak before I holler drunkenly, "I don't care if today is the Twelfth of Never, asshole. You're not talking to anyone! It's Thanksgiving, for God's sake! What's wrong with you? Why would you call me today? Don't you have any respect at all?"

"Furthermore, your daughter doesn't even *want* to talk to you; she's having a great time, and we have company, you sonovabitch!" I'm shrieking as loud as possible, each word spoken into the phone like a bolt of lightning. I'm vaguely aware that in my inebriated state I may not be entirely coherent. But it doesn't matter. Being heard is the only thing that's important.

His call has unleashed a frenzied storm within me, an inferno whose fires are fed with alcohol. "Why are you trying to ruin my life?" The words roll out of my mouth in a slur. My boozed-up tongue struggles to form clear, understandable speech in what feels like a mouthful of cement. The phrases ooze out in a gelatinous drool of madness. "Don't you ever *think*? Apparently not. I hope you rot in Hell, bastard!"

The words spill out of my mouth uncontrollably, smearing into one another without thought or feeling. I am running on a fuel called blind rage. "Leave us alone and don't call back. If I ever speak to you again, never would be too soon," I bellow slamming the receiver into its cradle.

No one can escape the fury that has burned inside of me for decades. No one.

Trying to regain my composure, I hesitate a moment to steady myself before turning around triumphantly to face my Thanksgiving guests. My head is spinning as I make my way back to the table, stumbling over the threshold between the kitchen and dining room. My legs feel awkward and wobbly, but the rest of me is feather-light, floating, and far away.

Wow, I really showed him who's boss, didn't I! I feel triumphant and am confident that I have just pulled off an impressive coup. Deliriously successful, I'm punch-drunk with glee and almost giddy with power. *Am I wonderful or what!*

Easing back into my chair at the head of the table, I'm oblivious to the hush that has descended over the room. I glance around the table at the assembled guests — several close friends and their daughter, a neighbor, a colleague and his partner, my younger daughter and my new boyfriend. A perfect group of people with whom to share a refined and elegant holiday meal. I hardly notice the obvious discomfort and stunned looks on their faces as they digest the emotional mayhem I just unleashed in the adjacent room.

My daughter studies her lap, her face frozen, all the while folding and unfolding her napkin. My new boyfriend stands speechless in front of the turkey he is preparing to carve and looks at me disapprovingly. I'm clueless and pay no heed. The wine, my antidote to despair, is working its usual magic. *Aren't I the queen of every damn thing!* I'm so pleased with myself.

A carafe of fragrantly lusty cabernet, a French St. Joseph if I remember correctly, makes its way around the table and I pour myself another glass. I raise the crystal goblet to my already intoxicated lips and wrap my mouth around a sloppily executed toast. "To a good meal, family, friends, happy times, good wine and, oh yes, *especially* to good wine, ah, how I *love* that wine..." I ramble on.

A colleague, sensing my difficulty in completing the toast satisfactorily, rescues me.

"Let us all offer appreciation on Thanksgiving Day for the food we are about to eat in the company of friends and family, gratitude for all of our many blessings and fond hopes for a future of good health and world peace," he says solemnly, raising his glass.

As he speaks, I survey the dining room. The tastefully appointed scene is flawless. I smile with pleasure. The silver candelabrum stand tall and majestic in the middle of the table; glowing candles radiate a honey scent into the air; an ivory lace tablecloth lies spotless beneath gleaming silverware and my best china; and a recording of a string quartet plays sweetly in the background. I spy a few small dots of red wine on the tablecloth and carefully move my fork to the left to cover them up.

Everything is perfect. Yes. Absolutely perfect. I am the Queen of Everything!

But nothing is perfect. I am choking to death on my life.

Chapter 2

Early Morning

The bedroom is a balmy cocoon wrapped in the subtle scent of sleep, a musky still life that hangs stagnant in the air, waiting to be disturbed by an unseen force. The muddy shadows of early morning are pierced by tiny snippets of sunlight that squeeze through shuttered windows, fall haphazardly on the sage green carpet and glitter on the biscuit-colored walls.

A squatty, oval wind-up alarm clock leans on four lopsided legs on the nightstand next to the bed. At just the precise moment, it erupts in raucous disharmony. Still asleep, my heavy hand searches for the source of the noxious racket.

Most of the time the old clock emits the barely audible tap-tap sound of passing time in its predictable, monotonous way. It patiently marks the minutes until seemingly, out of nowhere, it fulfills its only purpose, to wake up the comatose with a commotion that sounds like a monkey playing bagpipes. Unlike anything else in my life, I know exactly what to expect from that clock and when; it's the most consistent and comforting presence in my world.

My body rouses with its usual unwillingness. Whenever I go to bed at night I never know what degree of terrible I'll feel when I wake up in the morning. Sleep doesn't come easy or for very long and is often interrupted by vivid nightmares. Some nights I may stare at the ceiling for hours; I'm unable to close my eyes because of the thunder and lightning in my head.

I struggle to shake off the dark mask of dormancy. Layers of sleep gradually unfold and rise upward to evaporate in the stale air. There's not much life in me in the mornings. I usually arise with a profound lethargy that often prevails into the late afternoon. In fact, I may go through an entire day without being fully awake.

I roll wearily onto my side and the almost liquid sound of well-worn, silky-smooth sheets moves with my body. Tugging drowsily at the puffy quilt that covers me, I want to burrow further into my nest for the whole of eternity. Real life has become just as difficult for me as sleep.

Going about my daily activities, I often long for the comfort of a nap, the kind free of worries and responsibilities. Waking up means dealing with a painful past, an unhappy present, and an uncertain future. I cover my head with the sheet to shut out the world.

A dull headache bangs out a familiar tune near my temples like a toddler's incessant pounding on the lowest octave of a toy piano. The inside of my mouth is as parched as a desert floor; I taste the aftermath of too much wine, a punch of bitter sourness like rotten grapefruit. I run my tongue across my teeth trying to scrub away the night before.

In the well of my stomach, little green men lurch and lunge on the trampoline of my guts, begging for a meal that includes more than just alcohol. As I lift my head off the pillow, I'm aware of the heaviness in my face and suspect that it's more bloated than usual.

Arching my back languorously, I stretch my arms and legs until I feel my muscles quiver in response to a night of inactivity. Groggy, I roll over and pour myself into a sitting position. The contents of my stomach gradually move upwards, billowing towards my throat. I sit motionless on the edge of the bed trying to quiet the angry bile and praying that it will not overflow its banks today.

As I slowly rise to a standing position, I become lightheaded. Hesitantly, I cross the room to open the shutters and look out on the front yard. The bright light makes my eyes hurt. Lately, I prefer the dark; it envelops me in a protective shield and muffles the sound of my thoughts.

It's been an exceptionally warm fall; most of the spent leaves have finally shaken loose from the trees in front of my home. The lavender and peach pansies which rest on the front porch strut their blossoms in defiance of the coming winter. The faintest breeze, barely visible in the movement of the naked branches, is just enough to dislodge a stubborn leaf from the maple tree near the front door. It listlessly wags back and forth on a twig and then abruptly loses its grip and breaks loose.

Free at last.

I watch the wine-colored leaf gently float from side to side, and then tumble over itself onto its back as it makes its way to the ground. It skitters lightly this way and that on the sidewalk as if it hasn't decided whether or not it's content to just settle down and die.

Somewhere deep in my racing thoughts familiar tears begin to form. I suddenly become enraged and despairing all at the same time. Drowning in sadness, I'm frequently overwhelmed by life and the growing intensity of my emotions. The simplest of tasks is often a challenge. It's become more and more difficult to push away the hopelessness. I'm gripped by the repulsive sensation that there is a hideous microorganism in my brain systematically eating the life out of me.

As my mind begins to respond to an awakening body, I remember that today is Thanksgiving. I've looked forward to this day for weeks; I'm hosting my first Thanksgiving dinner, and the opportunity has fueled a rare excitement in me. I've planned every last detail with the greatest care. I'll be a model of calm competence; everyone will see how steady and in control I am. After today, I'll have won the love and admiration of all my guests. And they'll spread the word that I've finally gotten my act together. Today will be different. A turning point.

I yearn for this day to be perfect. An intense desire to create an event so meaningful and so memorable that the mere mention of my name in the future will evoke warm recollections of today's Thanksgiving dinner.

Do you remember that Thanksgiving at Sonya's house? Wasn't it glorious? Isn't she the most fabulous hostess? And such an awesome person!

I'm motivated by a cavernous hunger to make my mark, to be adored and remembered for all time. I'm determined to make today the day that will change the course of my life forever.

Chapter 3

I'm Sure Of It

It's almost noon on Thanksgiving Day and I'm frantically making preparations for hosting my first Thanksgiving Dinner. A perfectly proportioned and pleasingly plump butt-naked turkey relaxes on the kitchen countertop. With the hands of a skilled masseuse, I gently massage the bird with softened butter and aromatic seasonings. After a long, slow roast, it will be juicy and succulent.

I'm sure of it.

I fill the turkey's innards with a spicy-sweet apple-cornbread stuffing, and swaddle the exterior in maple-cured bacon. Closing my eyes, I imagine the mouth-watering taste. For most of my life, I've eaten someone else's turkey at someone else's house. This year will be the beginning of a new tradition -- Thanksgiving at *my* house, with *my* turkey. *I am so proud of that bird!*

I've waited a long time for this opportunity -- a Thanksgiving no one will ever forget. Today's celebration will erase every doubt anyone has ever had about me. I will be the Queen of Everything.

I'm sure of it.

The kitchen practically vibrates with the energy of

holiday preparations. I've spent hours planning the meal, turning down any offers from my guests to bring food. Every detail has been executed with meticulous attention. I've done it all by myself. It will be perfect in every respect.

The luscious aromas of Thanksgiving permeate every corner of the house. When my guests arrive, they'll be greeted by the yeasty scent of just-baked biscuits, homemade cakes and pies, pungent green herbs, crunchy apples, roasted vegetables, crisply toasted nuts, potatoes boiled to the perfect stage of mashed tenderness, bathed in butter and sprinkled with a sharp cheddar cheese.

Sweet onions and garlic sizzle away in a fruity olive oil on the stove, and mingle with the earthy scent of mushrooms fresh from the forest. Celery and a spicy pork sausage brown in another pan creating layer upon layer of fragrant scents.

Everyone seated at the dining table will acknowledge how capable I am. "She's really got her shit together," they'll whisper to one another, shaking their heads in the affirmative, "finally."

I'm sure of it.

Later in the meal, frothy mounds of whipped cream flavored with cinnamon will stand in mountainous peaks crowning perfect apple, pumpkin and chocolate bourbon pecan pies, all flaky and warm.

My home is immaculate. All of my prized possessions have been buffed and polished, displayed on gleaming surfaces for everyone to admire. After all, isn't Thanksgiving a day to pull out all the stops?

For weeks, I've thought of nothing except what a superb Thanksgiving I will create. I've dreamed of elegant table settings, flickering candlelight, subtle laughter and the buzz of convivial conversation. Hardly noticeable in the background, a melodic string quartet will simply echo what everyone will be thinking, "She's so sweet, so accomplished and so in control." What a momentous affair it will be.

I'm sure of it.

Over and over, I've imagined myself sitting at the head of the table, guiding the conversation to match the unforgettable food and impeccable setting. I've made a list of possible topics that might spark interesting chit-chat just in case it stalls. It's in my pocket where I can easily pull it out if need be. There will be no uncomfortable silences at *my* table. Politics, current events, holiday plans -- I make notes of them all. It will be the most enjoyable Thanksgiving of all time.

I'm sure of it.

The table, of course, will be worthy of the cover of *Bon Appetite*. I've set it over and over in my head with my best china, silver and crystal. Under it all lies an ivory lace tablecloth. This is the first occasion I've deemed special enough to use it. An intricate web of natural-colored linen, it's just as exquisite as I imagine this evening's meal to be.

A pair of gleaming silver candelabra with luminous, creamy candles will stand in the center of the table to breathlessly await the slightest touch of a just-struck matchstick. The hint of sulfur mingling with the honey aroma of warm bee's wax will herald the beginning of an unquestionably memorable meal.

The wine, of course, will be fragrant, bold and plentiful. After several trips to the liquor store I finally settled on a robust St. Joseph, a stunning Cabernet, and several bottles of a pricey champagne. After all, this is a special event and the spirits have to be superb, not the gallon jugs I'm used to drinking by myself, but something special. The wine will be as outstanding as the meal.

I'm sure of it.

Lately, I've begun to drive further and further away from my neighborhood to buy alcohol just to avoid what I imagine to be the gossip there. "She's the one that buys all that wine by the gallon. Scotch, too." I know they *think* it even if they don't say it.

But this occasion is different. No baseball cap or dark glasses. For the first time in months, I didn't feel the embarrassment of meeting familiar eyes in the local liquor store. No reason to feel guilty or ashamed. I wanted everyone there to know that it wasn't just *I* who was going to drink all that alcohol; it was for a great event. After all, this was wine to be savored as a harmonious accompaniment to a fine meal. "This is for my famous Thanksgiving dinner," I tell the clerk. Well, I *want* it to be famous.

I'll decant the bottles just prior to the meal so the luscious perfume of juicy, purple grapes will fill the room with their seductive bouquet, beckoning all to drink more than they intended, and perhaps, enjoy the evening more than they had expected. *I want everyone to have a good time, an unforgettable time, so I will keep the spirits flowing.*

As I labor on the preparations for the meal, I begin drinking my "everyday" wine. I'm happy and becoming more excited by the minute. By the time my guests arrive, I'm drifting on the air. Or drunk.

Yet, I'm determined to make the day momentous. So special, in fact, that today will be the start of a Thanksgiving tradition my guests will look forward to year after year. They'll think about the evening and wish every Thanksgiving were like mine.

I'll be a model hostess, calm, relaxed and in control of everything. I'll speak quietly and confidently. Nothing will ruffle my tranquility and composure. I'll think about what I want to say and choose my words carefully. I'll be restrained. Today, cursing, screaming and temper tantrums will become a thing of the past. Any negative perceptions anyone ever had about me before today will be erased and gone forever. Today will be a new beginning.

I'm sure of it.

Chapter 4

Under The Table

Giggles billowed up from my belly in waves of unrestrained joy. I closed my eyes and breathed through my nose, but I couldn't stop the wild frenzy of hysteria. I fought hard to quiet the ever-rising sense that my stomach was going to turn itself inside out and heave my guts all over the place, whether I liked it or not.

Everything was hilariously funny. I covered my mouth with both hands and bit my tongue to calm myself. Like the most graceful of reptiles, I slithered effortlessly off my folding chair onto the floor, landing on my ten-year-old bottom. I sat motionless under the goes-on-forever dining table.

All I saw was white tablecloth and a sea of feet and legs. The harder I tried to stifle the giggles, the faster they tumbled out of my mouth. The more amusing the sound of my own laughter became, the louder I hooted and howled.

Think of something sad like being punished or my best friend moving.

My mind scrambled to create a scene of the most miserable, heartbreaking and tragic event I could imagine. That directive only fed the ecstasy bubbling within me.

I sucked in my breath as hard as I could to silence

myself, but this made my cheeks puff out like I had a mouthful of Kool-Aid that in less than five seconds would burst from my face in sugary squirts. Imagining the bright red liquid dribbling all over the white tablecloth was enough to get me going again. I knew the silence from above could only mean one thing.

Oh-oh. I'm going to get in trouble if I don't stop. Big trouble.

I tried to stop. I really did. But I couldn't. I was so happy.

"Sonny! "Get up and sit on your chair," my favorite aunt hissed as she stuck her head under the tablecloth. "Come on now; cut it out."

My uncle paused the service. He sat at the head of the table and led the Passover Seder. "Well, well, well," he exclaimed casually to the others seated around the table. He had an uncommonly good sense of humor, dry and sarcastic. "There seems to be some trouble at the other end of the room."

What followed were whispers and snickers from some, humorous comments from others, but no one took it very seriously. I was sure my cousins were glad for the intermission in the endless Seder. "Let's bow our heads in silent prayer, while we wait for those who are under the table to emerge."

I heard everything from my secret hideaway. I buried my mouth in my forearm to smother the cackles threatening to spill out of me again. One of my cousins, sensing that being a renegade was a good thing, slipped off his chair, too. He was not to be one-upped by my attention-grabbing behavior.

"Queen Sonya must be drinking the Manischewitz," chuckled my father's youngest sister on whose carpet I sat, as she ran back and forth from the kitchen to check on the Seder meal. "Grab her crown and yank her back on her throne," she said to my father, unable to contain her amusement at my entertaining behavior. My cousins thought the scene I had created was deliciously funny, and they were all whooping and whistling.

"How much has she had?" my straight-laced uncle asked my father in a commanding voice. "Kids," he ordered officially, with his head under the table, "this isn't the way we pray at Passover. Get up on your chairs and make it snappy."

I spent most holidays with my father's close and fun-loving family. Passover was no exception. This year's Seder continued in the same monotonous fashion as it always had. We read from the Haggadah, ate traditional Passover foods, and drank Manischewitz, the only thing that made the insufferable Passover service tolerable.

My father peered under the table at me and reached for my arm. "No more wine for you, Sonya," he said sternly. "Get up off the floor right now so we can continue the service."

I couldn't see his face, but I figured he found my behavior funny like everyone else. When I didn't move, he cleared his throat dramatically; then I knew he meant business. I clumsily exited my fortress under the table. Pleasantly woozy and seeing double of everything, I twisted and turned noisily as I retraced my steps back to my chair at the table.

Reality, ugh. The light hurts my eyes. Passover is so boring. I liked it better under the table.

My boozy gaze led me to the head of the table where the officiant-for-life of the yearly Seder stared at his Haggadah and then winked at me. I tried to suppress the laughter rising in the back of my throat, and then let it rip again. He patiently waited, his eyes on me all the while. "Whenever you're ready," he said as I tried to settle myself.

The sight of his face and sound of his voice as he looked at me with a twinkle in his eye, forcing the corners of his mouth to turn down and not join into the silliness, sent me rollicking back and forth in my chair. Enormous heaving swells of belly laughs spilled out of my mouth.

I am embarrassing myself now. Or worse. I was having too much fun to worry about what "the worse" might be.

My father looked at me with an I-am-no-longer-amused expression and I quieted down. The service continued. My wine glass was refilled with grape juice. When I thought no one was looking, I topped it off with a little Manischewitz. But that didn't escape everyone's eyes.

"Oy vey. For a kid, she can really pack it away," another aunt proclaimed. All the adults around the table were speaking in Yiddish now, a combination of Eastern European languages. I didn't understand a word they were saying, but I was sure it was me they were talking about.

The grown-ups were solemn during the service and paid close attention; the children made eye contact with their cousins across the table and drank too much wine until one of them did or said something humorous and then things fell apart. This year it was me who started the trouble.

By the time the Passover meal was served, I was exhausted and queasy. "Maybe a taste of the noodle kugel?" asked my father. I said nothing. My stomach was in my throat. I broke out in a cold sweat. I felt like my skin was turning green. I wanted to puke.

But when I thought no one was looking, I slyly reached for the bottle. My hand was met by that of my father's who glared at me in an unsympathetic way and said more sternly than before, "I said that's all, and I mean that's all! No more wine down here," he announced to everyone.

Cut off. The first of many days of being too drunk to care.

I was ten years old and two sheets to the wind.

Chapter 5

The Invisible Child

As a youngster, I discovered that alone was the best place to be. Alone meant safety. Alone meant security. Alone meant freedom. Alone meant no yelling or hitting and no crying, punishment or threats.

Alone didn't mean frightened and scared or expecting some creature to crawl out from the closet or under the bed. I wasn't fearful of the things that many children were -- the dark, monsters or thunder.

Afraid was when I *wasn't* alone. It meant watching and waiting for the next bad thing that was going to happen to me. Alone didn't mean bored with nothing to do. When I was alone, I was free to let my mind wander, to think whatever thoughts I might and, in my head at least, be whom I wanted to be with the kind of life I yearned to have.

I had a stunningly energetic imagination. By the time I was in elementary school, I had created an elaborate fantasy life about myself, the loving people who shared that life with me and the happy times we enjoyed. Nowhere in my make-believe were any of the figures from real life. There was no place for them in my untroubled pretend world. I suppose the playful hopefulness of the young me believed there was safety only in what could never be.

My small hand clutches the book of matches I grab from the kitchen counter and stuff in my pocket. I step out the front door of my house, the screen door slamming in my wake, and skip across the front lawn. I don't think anyone notices I've left the house. After all, they don't pay much attention to me when I'm *home.*

I cross the street, taking my time and kicking random stones as I go; when I look over my shoulder and can no longer see my house, I begin to walk more briskly through a neighbor's backyard. My eyes glance to the left and then the right, but I see no one. The coast is clear.

I climb over a split-rail fence that separates one yard from another as I make my way to a small grove of trees not far away. I believe it's a secret shelter known only to me. I've never told anyone about this place, even my best friends whom I play with every day. It lies on an empty lot set back quite a distance from the street. It's my private hideout where I'm certain I would never be found. *But is anyone really looking?* It's here where I find peace.

It's a tender fall afternoon, warm and sunny. There's barely a breeze. As I move closer to my secret place, I feel a rush of anticipation as if I'm waiting for a beloved friend that I haven't seen in years step through the sunlight and embrace me with feelings of extraordinary love.

In the center of a group of smaller trees, stands the tree that has become my friend. It's not a towering giant with heavy, bony arms, nor is it a puny runt, scrawny and spare. It stands tall and distinguished. Solid and trustworthy. Its limbs are so broad and curvaceous they could support the whole world.

The air smells like apples and burning wood. Many of the green leaves which hung on the branches just weeks ago cover the dry earth in the seasonal colors of fall. They lie on the ground haphazardly like tattered streamers after a party, their aroma earthy and damp.

Yet the tree isn't naked. Many leaves still dangle from

the branches, stubbornly hanging on despite the forces of nature. Piles of withered leaves crunch underfoot and make a tinny sound similar to the high-pitched shatter of paper-thin slices of glass breaking on the soft ground.

The trunk is thick and sturdy, maybe three feet in diameter. It's large enough to support hundreds of branches and much too wide for me to hug; perhaps it's a two-person hug. The gray-brown bark, ridged and dotted with bumps of various sizes, holds on tightly to the trunk, wrapping it warmly.

On some days I bring a snack and pretend I'm having a picnic under the tree. On other days, maybe a towel and a book. Even homework. When I walk out my front door, no one says, "Where are you going?" or "What are you going to do there?" or "Be home at four o'clock." That's just the way it is.

I like the shape of the tree. Wide and welcoming, the branches seem like they're waiting to hold me snugly and keep me safe. I'm able to tell my friend, the tree, everything. I know my secrets are safe with her.

Removing the book of matches from my pocket, I open the cover and strike one match against the rough surface on the front. I hold the lit match next to the tip of a dried-up leaf whose brown edges have already begun to curl up. I watch as the flames quickly slither up and around the dry leaf.

A sense of release fills my body as the leaf becomes engulfed in fire. The burning leaf finally loosens its grip on the branch and, giving in to the heat of the blaze, drops to the ground trailing a tail of smoke like a spent rocket. I tuck the matchbook back into my pocket.

I am momentarily gripped by dread and fascination. And then the show is over. Finding a comfortable patch of leaves under the tree, I sit down to rest. *I could stay here forever and never be found. I don't know if anyone would even notice my absence.*

I dream about running away to an adoring family, one who would protect and care for me, a home filled with smiles and love where everyone speaks in gentle voices. I imagine walking out the front door of my home with no goodbyes, with nothing but a pillow case filled with a few pieces of clothing and something to eat. And some books. Just marching in a straight line to see where it would lead me.

I rise from my resting place and pull the matchbook out of my pocket again. I strike another tiny stick of wood roughly against the scratchy flint. It explodes in a powerful display, a multi-colored flare of white, blue, yellow and orange. The flame stands up straight, wavering slightly, but yet so sure of itself. I hold the match between my fingers where, just before it burns my flesh, I blow it out and throw it on the ground.

I light another match and then another. I'm mystified by the fire -- how it moves and smells, it's colors and shapes and, most of all, its power. Inching closer to the tree, I reach up and touch a lit match to a leaf right above my head. The flame skitters across the small clump of dried out leaves.

The parched leaves shy away from the flame as if they know, in their thirsty state, a single spark may cause them to shrivel and dissolve into ash. They're helpless.

A huge knot of anger begins to form deep in my stomach. I'm suddenly sad, an ache I've experienced over and over again in my young life. A painful feeling like a straight razor slicing through raw meat, there's an initial pain and then a misery that won't let go.

I hold another lighted match next to one more cluster of dry leaves. Almost immediately, I regret what I've done. I pray the flames will fizzle out again. I wonder if I've run out of chances.

With a dramatic display, there's a bright flash of color, and the neighboring branch catches fire. I can hear the flames, a quiet whoosh and crackle as the blaze moves quickly from one branch to another. As the flames spread, the burning sounds become louder, and the heat intensifies. I shiver with fright. As afraid as I am at that moment, I have an attraction to fire which takes precedence over everything else, including the punishment I may receive when I return home.

My heart pounds against my rib cage; my entire body shakes with each beat. I'm dizzy with fear. Frozen. I hear the rush of blood screaming in my ears. I'm so scared I can barely breathe, and when I do, my breath is hot and burns my chest. I never expected things to end this way. Panicky, I swear to God I've learned my lesson. I'll never play with fire again.

"I'll do anything -- just don't let my tree burn down," I scream silently.

Tears of rage trickle down my cheeks. I'm afraid the blaze, which is threatening to swallow my beautiful tree, will spread, destroying houses in its path and killing the people inside of them.

I imagine the fire engines, and maybe even the police, will arrive soon. I run away as fast as my girl-legs will take me. I never turn around to learn the fate of my beloved tree. The strong, slightly sweet and fruity scent of fire follows me. It saturates the air; it's in my hair, on my clothing, in my blood and rushing through every inch of my body. I'm certain I'll be spanked when I return home, sealed in my room forever, shamed and possibly even sent to jail. I don't believe anybody can help me survive this one.

When I'm near my home, I force myself to slow down and walk calmly, as if I'm just wandering around the neighborhood looking for a playmate. I worry that anyone who sees me running will connect me to the fire, which surely is burning the entire village down by now. I don't want to go home; home is just a house. There are people who live there, but they're not family. I want to die or disappear before anyone finds out what I've done. My mother is right about me, I think; I'm a rotten-to-the-core kid.

The fire goes out. It doesn't spread. No one is hurt. The fire engines don't come. The tree survives. The girl never returns to the tree. And the angry orange-fire screams of the invisible child are never heard.

Chapter 6

Whiskey Sour Hour

Alcohol was a much more insidious and toxic presence on the maternal side of my family. It was here that my alcohol use and abuse was nurtured, encouraged and reinforced from a young age. I liked the taste of just about any alcoholic beverage, straight or mixed. It didn't take but a few delicate sips before the heady spirits unlatched my hinges and made me act silly. Or stupid. I became less anxious, tense and inhibited. A pleasant calm trickled over me. I could be very entertaining when I drank too much; the more I drank, the more attention my family bestowed upon me.

Alcohol, even a small amount, worked like magic. It didn't take much for me to become happy, compliant and agreeable. But the most remarkable aspect of alcohol was that it allowed me to tune out the stress and unhappiness caused by my cockamamie family. These were damaging lessons, of course, but no one ever saw my early drinking as a problem and, therefore, did nothing to intervene and limit its use. By the time I graduated from high school, alcohol was an essential and indispensable part of my everyday life. But no one had a clue how much. Neither did I.

My grandparents lived close to me, and I visited them frequently. I looked forward to sleepovers, dinners and outings. I was especially fond of my grandmother, a beautiful and loving woman. She provided some of the maternal nurturing lacking in my life. In the company of my grandparents, I could enjoy the privileges and freedoms denied me at home in a more relaxed atmosphere.

At the feet of my eccentric and controlling grandfather is where my taste for alcohol grew and later matured into a roaring, full-blown alcoholism. "It's almost five o'clock." he'd say, turning to look at the gold clock sitting on the table next to his black leather armchair in the family room.

"I'm ready for my whiskey sour. How about you?"

Whiskey Sour Hour occurred daily at five o'clock, not a minute before or a minute after. Five o'clock *exactly*. No matter what. It was a ritual. I always looked forward to it.

My grandfather was meticulous in his creation of the perfect whiskey sour, his favorite alcoholic beverage. "Okay," he motioned rising from his chair, "let's go." We walked to the bar where, lined up in perfectly straight rows against the backdrop of a mirrored wall, stood scores of alcoholic beverages. So many shapes and colors — red, green, blue, clear, yellow, brown. It didn't take long for me to become familiar with the names and flavors hidden inside each unique bottle. Some of the bottles were straight and simple. Others were sensuously curved, a few were round, and some carved, fluted, or etched. More than a few wore intricately engraved silver necklaces indicating what was inside.

I liked being in the bar and felt comfortable there. I enjoyed opening the bottles and smelling the unusual aromas. Some of them were so strong they burned my nose. By the time I was thirteen, I could describe the taste of every one of them. I had developed my own list of personal favorites and was free to sample at will. One of my favorite pastimes was creating original cocktails in the basement bar of my parents' home. As long as I wasn't making any noise, no one suspected a thing.

If I tagged along when my grandparents went out for dinner, my grandfather would often order an extra whiskey sour and give it to me. He didn't seem to know (or care) that providing alcohol to an underage child was illegal. And neither did I. I came to associate eating in restaurants with drinking and, until the day I chose sobriety, wouldn't eat at a restaurant that didn't serve alcohol. In fact, to sit at a table and wait for more than a few minutes for my drink to arrive was pure torture. By the time the meal materialized, I was often too drunk to care about eating.

Whiskey Sour Hour became a polished art form. I was an excellent pupil and a quick learner. My grandfather uncapped the heavy glass whiskey bottle and set it on the counter next to the blender. Its scent was rich and syrupy. Simply breathing in the intense fumes was intoxicating. Then came the carved crystal shot glass. One shot per drink. Maybe a shot-and-a-half for him.

He bent down and pulled the whiskey sour mix out of the small refrigerator under the bar and lined it up right next to the shot glass. He grabbed two delicately stemmed glasses off the shelf and polished them with a bar towel until they glittered like stardust. The preparation couldn't continue until he lifted each glass up to the light and deemed it immaculate. Then he held the glasses under cold water and placed them gently into the freezer.

"We can't forget the maraschino cherries," he said, fumbling in the tiny refrigerator. "The Queen loves her cherries." A friend of his once mistakenly referred to me as a princess, and my grandfather's emphatic reply was, "She's no princess, she's a Queen!"

As soon as he had assembled everything he needed, he poured the shimmering brown liquid into the shot glass and then dribbled its contents into the blender along with the other ingredients.

"This has to be done in the correct order. You can't just throw everything into the blender at the same time and expect to make a perfect whiskey sour." Once I had the formula down pat, it didn't take long before I, too, was concocting a perfect whiskey sour. A child.

Ice cubes were the last ingredient to be added. And they had to be removed from the ice tray before they started to melt. A watered-down whiskey sour would never do. "Away we go," he said with a flourish as he dumped the ice cubes into the blender and switched it on. I watched the whirling mixture pirouette noisily around and around. Following it with my eyes made me dizzy.

As the ice cubes turned to slush, the thickened liquid formed a beautiful foaming head. Quickly, but with great ceremony, he took the frosty stems from the freezer. And, with a lovely ceremonial wave, he poured the sudsy syrup into the frozen glasses. Daintily, he placed several maraschino cherries on top of the foam. Four if it was for me.

"Voila!" he said proudly. "Would you like to have one?"

"Sure." Who wouldn't? Liquid candy with a buzz-kick.

What he presented me with was a sweetly-sour concoction with a rush, a slurpy, slushy potion for grown-ups. Surely not a drink for a kid. But it tasted so good. It made me feel sophisticated. The gentle purr it produced was even more delicious.

I was just a youngster. Unworldly. Inexperienced. But at Whiskey Sour Hour I felt grown-up, loved and respected.

Throughout my youth, no one ever questioned the appropriateness of offering a child an adult beverage. Or making an open bar available to a child. Or inviting a child to prepare drinks for adults. It all seemed perfectly normal to me. And harmless.

As the dysfunction in my family intensified, so did my alcohol consumption. The magical properties of the whiskey sour saved my life. As long as the intoxicating liquid was by my side, I could handle the chaotic ups and sorrowful downs just as serenely as can be. As I gently sipped the luscious nectar, everything that bothered or upset me just faded away. The more I drank, the less aware I became of the craziness in my family.

During the school year, I would walk home for lunch. It wasn't unusual for me to sit down at the kitchen table, eat my bologna sandwich and chips, drink my glass of milk and then go downstairs to the bar and take a couple of swigs of, well, uh, anything. It didn't really matter what it was. I would walk back to school for my afternoon classes feeling a lot better than I had earlier in the day.

What an appealing, icy numbness, almost an emotional paralysis. My body was there, but my head was far away. The stress and anxiety just slid off of my shoulders. I observed the lunacy, seemingly from a great distance. It was almost like being behind a one-way mirror. I could see *them*, but they couldn't see me. I was invisible.

I would look right at those people in my family who were arguing, screaming and crying as if there were a glass wall between us. I heard them, but their commotion didn't upset me. I never realized just how much that background noise actually affected me until much later in my life. Everything I experienced, whether I was aware of it or not, was stored on my hard drive, ready to rise up on its hind legs and, years later, with its sharpened claws, slash my heart wide open. The toxic memories leaked their poison all over me.

From a young age, I understood the popular Hebrew toast, "L'Chaim." With goblets of alcoholic beverages held high, it symbolized a toast to long life and good health. But to me, "L'Chaim" meant something entirely different, a phrase whose meaning became even more significant as I matured into adulthood.

I came to associate "L'Chaim" with an opportunity to drink and the welcome release from negative, disagreeable feelings. It meant the chance to burrow down and curl up deep inside myself in the safety of me. I could experience peace, rather than the problems and people in my world, even if for a short while. I can only compare it now to that of a bookworm, ensconced in a sunny alcove and wrapped in a cozy afghan while reading a gripping mystery. I was transported to another world.

Eventually, alcohol became a needful thing. I couldn't live without it. Until the day I chose sobriety, I never thought I had a problem with alcohol. But the direct association between alcohol and relief was a connection established early in my life.

After many years of my own individual therapy, I was more than surprised to find that not one of my therapists ever suggested the possibility that I was a childhood alcoholic. It wasn't until I began to explore my adult alcoholism with the depth and attention required to write this book, that I discovered how young I actually was when I began drinking on a regular basis, and how much I relied on alcohol to shield and protect me from the coarse realities of my life.

This recognition and later acceptance that I began drinking as a child wasn't something that came to me suddenly. In fact, it took months of writing about my adult addiction to open my eyes and lead me to the conclusion that I was hooked on alcohol long before I became a teenager. The more I rifled through my history of dependence, the more I was quite literally blown away. I wanted, needed and abused alcohol as a child. My mouth watered at the mention of an alcoholic drink, my body craved the calm that alcohol provided and my psyche lusted after it.

There was no adult in my life who ever recognized my childhood drinking as a concern or did anything to curtail my use of alcohol. No one identified the roots of its beginning or saw my drinking as a problem that needed to be addressed by professionals.

It was much more likely that they found my drinking funny and entertaining. Accompanied by laughter, my family often referred to me as "the family shikor" ("drunk" in Yiddish). After all, they had many more serious things to deal with than a child who was acting out.

As I grew into adulthood and the complexity of problems with which I had to cope grew with me, my use of alcohol increased. This served to reinforce the use of alcohol as an absolute necessity for my survival. It was the only way I knew how to cope. The physical craving became an emotional craving that only increased over time.

Through decades of alcohol abuse, the manner in which intoxicating beverages affected me changed, as well. Drinking no longer calmed and quieted me; rather, it seemed to do that initially for a while, and then it intensified and released the fires that had smoldered inside of me for years; I became an increasingly "angry drunk," antagonistic, hostile, critical and abusive.

I developed two distinct styles of drinking: slowly sipping (sometimes during the entire day) or throwing the alcohol down my throat as though it were quenching a terrible thirst. It depended on the situation and how quickly I needed to achieve relief. The latter worked faster, of course, but the former was more ladylike and proper and threw anybody who suspected I had a problem off course.

I drank through my second pregnancy. It was after my second child was born that I began to drink more and earlier in the day. The period of my heaviest drinking began when my daughter was under two years old. Sometimes I went about my day half-drunk.

I thought nothing of getting behind the wheel of my car inebriated, believing I was fully in control of myself. I drove the wrong way down one-way streets. I ran stop signs and stop lights and received one speeding ticket after another. I totaled my car twice in a matter of months. I was stopped for reckless driving and, I'm sorry to say, nothing ever came of it. The charges were dropped. I should have heard the wake-up call then, but I didn't. Or didn't want to.

I shopped at the local liquor store on a regular basis and, in the later years of my drinking, was so embarrassed to be recognized there ("back so soon?") that I would drive some distance from my home to purchase my poison. I couldn't eat a meal without wine. I couldn't fly on an airplane without being tipsy. If I ran out of liquor at home, I would panic. My late husband once noted the large quantity of wine missing from a gallon jug I stored in my kitchen.

"Did you drink all that?" he asked.

My response was, "Oh no. My younger daughter must be drinking." Not true. A lie to cover my tracks. That's what alcoholics do.

Alcohol prevented me from knowing who I was. Alcohol allowed me to remain mired in the negative feelings, thoughts and behaviors of the past. Alcohol kept others from getting close to me and impaired many of my relationships. Alcohol hindered my success, whether as a wife, a mother, a friend or a professional.

When I stopped drinking and threw off the mantle of physical and emotional addiction, I discovered that for decades I had gone to bed nearly every night intoxicated to some degree, and awakened every morning with a hangover.

Whether my alcoholism was the result of genetics, a troubled childhood, an intense sadness or a behavior I haphazardly learned, practiced and was reinforced by my family, is hard to say. Perhaps all of the above.

Beset by an overpowering inadequacy and poor self-esteem, I never thought about who I was, but longed to be someone I *wasn't*. I assumed that what others saw were my weaknesses, never my strengths.

I yearned to be noticed, but was convinced I was invisible. Alcohol gave me the power to ignore my disappointment with life.

Chapter 7

There But Not There

I don't think much about my mother any more. At least not in the same ways. Nowadays, memories of her are scattered and ill-defined; she moves gently in and out of my thoughts every so often. Her visits are hazy and indistinct; she doesn't stay with me for very long. She has no face and doesn't speak, yet I can sense a peacefulness and contentment about her. Remembering her is no longer upsetting.

Years ago, thinking about my mother would take an entirely different form. Her face would appear before me thin and drawn, and she would look tired, sick or unhappy. Her voice would sound sharp and hostile. Those memories were always leaden with fear and anger. One unpleasant flashback after another would crowd my mind. By the time I was a teenager, I had built a strong case against my mother in my head. By the time I was a young adult, I had pushed her out of my life almost entirely.

Through decades of grappling with my own demons, I've managed to create a more accurate and realistic picture of who my mother was and the difficulties with which she struggled. It was a laborious and painful journey to reconstruct what I imagined her life to be like and the part I played in it. I can only guess at how difficult it must have been for her to live that life.

There have been countless moments, when reflecting on my childhood and lack of mothering, that I raged against the loss of the mother I never had, or the hunger for a mother who was absent. It's a grief that will be with me until I die. Over and over, I've wondered whether my life would have taken a different turn had my mother been healthy and emotionally connected to me.

But that was not the case. My mother was there, but not really there. And almost never in a nurturing way. Yet, gone are the embarrassment and revulsion that pushed me away from her as I became older, whether her presence was in my thoughts or in my company.

In their place now are empathy, compassion and forgiveness, the creation of which was decades in the making. In the process of learning about myself and the obstacles I faced, I gradually came to see my mother in an entirely different light.

People treated my mother badly. Her children treated her badly. Her relatives and friends treated her badly. She never had more than the most casual of relationships with her grandchildren, nieces and nephews. It was difficult, if not impossible, to relate to her on more than a superficial level, and even that could be arduous.

She was the most inconsistent of individuals; if I had an acceptable interchange with her at nine o'clock in the morning, there was no guarantee that two hours later she might be raving about something that had set her off. I was always waiting for her to explode in rage, manipulate me with guilt, blame and shame, or give me the silent treatment. Marking time for the next seemingly unavoidable incident to take place became the status quo.

Her emotional state was so fragile, unstable and unpredictable that it led her to behave in ways that were inappropriate and difficult to understand. Every relationship she had was damaged in some way. I suppose her mind protected her from dealing with the reality of just how impaired she really was. She didn't see it.

My mother treated people badly, too. She didn't seem to have any insight into how she conducted herself with others. I would often look longingly at her out of the corner of my eye. I yearned to discover who she really was, to touch her, talk to her, know her, understand her and establish some sort of emotional connection with her. Or even try to make her happy. But she was distant, angry, and most of all, self-absorbed.

On the other hand, I eventually realized my mother was not the cold, cruel or uncaring person I thought she was, even though the physical and emotional abuse I suffered at her hand certainly convinced me otherwise. She was ill-equipped for motherhood. She had no healthy role models to look back on, and a simmering mental illness, which blossomed more fully with each successive child she bore. She did the best job she could with the meager tools she had. Those tools, a product of previous generations of poor parenting coupled with a genetic predisposition to mental illness and treated with a variety of prescription medications, were skimpy at best, completely absent at worst.

The product of a disturbed family system that fed on its weakest link, my mother didn't follow the strict set of rules proscribed by her father, primarily: Be seen, not heard and don't make waves. That toxic system squeezed the life out of her and any of the aspirations she may have sought to fulfill. But sadly, it was safer and more comfortable for her to stay a prisoner of that familiar system than open her wings and fly away.

My mother struggled for most of her adult life with the evils of mental illness. Each consecutive psychiatric hospitalization discharged her to a family who was uneducated about mental illness, resistant to change and heavily into denial. The most remarkable characteristic of how poorly my family coped with my mother's mental illness was their lack of empathy.

It was clear that the cost of developing the skills

necessary to cope more effectively as a family was greater than the cost to remain mired in the same old, same old. The adults in the family were more comfortable with, and more invested in, her staying sick. She was expunged, scapegoated and demonized, a spoke in a never-ending wheel of victimization, generation upon generation.

In and out of short- and long-term hospitalizations, several of which lasted a year or more, drug overdoses and suicide attempts, she was never able to function well, least of all maternally. With all the hospitalizations, medications and expensive psychiatrists, she just became sicker. The cycle was endless. In the hospital, out of the hospital, high hopes, crash and back in the hospital. She was generally incapable of dealing with the stresses of life for very long.

Fighting to become a person with a strong identity, my mother wanted nothing more than to be loved and respected. Loved most of all. Unique, valuable and useful, as well. Most of her efforts to develop into such a person failed or backfired. She pushed people away, knowingly or not.

Until I was seventeen, she had a husband, my father, who was a fine and gentle man who loved her. But he was also powerless, weak and ineffectual. There was little he could do to help her. He ignored my mother's madness in ways that didn't protect me from her.

It was my mother's selfish, narcissistic and controlling father, my maternal grandfather, who held all the chips (and wealth, as well) and, because of ignorance or his own emotional problems, managed to dominate and control her. They were enmeshed in an unhealthy relationship for most of her life. Every step forward my mother took was met by him pushing her two steps back. They were entangled with one another in a dance of anger and power that spanned her entire life. He was unable to give her what she needed and instead, gave her money and luxuries in order to appease her.

No matter how much she may have wanted to individuate from him, he was able to keep her under his thumb, needy, dependent and crippled. He ran the show in a way that benefitted him and him alone. There was a large part of her, I'm sure, that was ambivalent about cutting the cord. He provided her with all the luxuries and financial resources she could have needed or wanted: diamonds, caviar, a beautiful home, household help, stylish clothing and vacations. And expensive psychiatric care. Perhaps this was how he showed love. I doubt these were the things she truly wanted, but she knew nothing more. What was missing from this picture was the undercurrent of familial love and support that would have helped her to become independent. A whole person.

Because my mother was unable to earn love and respect in more acceptable ways -- through marriage, parenting, work and friendships -- she became manipulative and shrewd, her character becoming more disturbed and disordered through the years. She discovered early in life that being "sick" served to meet her material needs and provided some of the attention she longed for. Psychiatric hospitals became a place where she would receive the care and support lacking in her personal life. The more hospitalizations, the more tender, loving care. She would refer to a hospital as a place where she could "rest."

My mother could be mean and vindictive. She would spread stories about people that were unseemly and cruel. Many of the tales she dispersed were focused on the salacious details of individuals whom she believed had harmed her or ruined her life. This one had an affair, that one was a drunk, and another had just declared bankruptcy. I suppose she was only doing what she knew how to do.

It's likely that her fabrications were simply a product of her imagination or perhaps just vicious rumors. When I was a child, she often shared these stories with me in great detail. I remember the anxiety and disgust I felt. When she talked about people it wasn't to praise them.

She would make numerous calls to the police station about any manner of events or people. She reported my "unruly" or "uncontrollable" behavior on several occasions. Oblivious to anything more important the police officers had to attend to, she expected them to rush right over and give her delinquent daughter a lecture, threatening to lock me up if I didn't comply, as per her directions.

My mother was demanding, harsh and critical in her relationship with me. I often felt pressured to do something to fix whatever problem she had at the moment, but whatever I did was never good enough. She was given to wild displays of rage, paralyzing bouts of depression, hysterical rampages, threats, suicide attempts and other inappropriate behaviors. She terrified me.

I tried to stay out of her way. She was barely involved in the day-to-day life of her family. It was a beloved housekeeper who ran the show. I never knew what form her bad mood would take when she woke up in the morning. There was no guarantee her mood wouldn't become worse through the day. It never got better.

As she aged, my mother became even less functional. Most of her friends gradually disappeared from her life; her family barely tolerated her. She behaved rudely and inappropriately to other people.

Her world became smaller and smaller; her major focus of attention was herself. Often misunderstood and misjudged, she could never seem to let go of her identification as mentally ill. To my knowledge, she never experienced an "aha moment" or an epiphany that resulted in her seeing herself as she really was and turning her life around. As a result of her psychiatric problems, she became a pariah, and that was how she went to her grave.

My mother's boundaries were poor. After she and my father separated, she frequently spoke unkind words about him and his family, trying desperately to turn me away from them. She was very jealous of any time I spent with my father and would pile on the verbal abuse. It didn't work and only served to distance me further from her. The "sicker" she acted, the more I stayed away from her.

The way she saw it, I "chose" him over her, and for that

she was forever resentful. In actuality, children naturally gravitate towards the parent who is easier to be with and who acts more "normal." My father was loving, but lost. He was a good parent who had a very close-knit family, but he worked long hours and wasn't around much. He was simply unable to pick up the slack.

Privacy wasn't something my mother valued, her own or others. She was known to answer the front door barely dressed and walked around naked. Closed doors were no obstacle for her. She walked right in. Knocking was not a skill she ever mastered. If one of her children did something that upset or annoyed her, she had no problem airing it in public. Feeling shamed and embarrassed in her presence was just the way it was. I never knew what was going to come out of her mouth next.

I seemed to provoke her more than anyone, and if she wasn't screaming or blaming me for countless transgressions, she was hitting me or ripping my clothing. Striking out was one of the ways she dealt with difficult situations. Even more terrifying than being hit, was her verbal abuse and threats to send me away, particularly to "reform school." I didn't know what reform school was, but I suspected it was bad, very bad.

I truly believed that someday I would end up there, whatever and wherever reform school was. One afternoon, angry at me for something I'd done, and determined to teach me a lesson I'd never forget, she ordered me into the car. I had no idea where we were going until she dropped me off on the side of the road about five miles from our home. She said she couldn't wait for the "reform school" van to come for me. As she pushed me out of the car she screamed, "They'll pick you up soon!" Then she slammed the car door and sped off down the road. She had snapped.

When I tumbled out of the car and realized she was actually going to drive away, I became frantic. I ran down the road after her, crying, yelling apologies, and begging for her not to leave me. I began to walk in the direction of home, and not long after, she returned. Her departure was meant to "scare" me into behaving in whatever way she wanted me to behave.

I learned some valuable lessons from that experience. Keep my mouth shut. Apologize for anything and everything. Agree with everybody. Don't rock the boat. My safety and security depended on it. After that, I never trusted her again.

Mealtimes when my mother was present were a nightmare. I was forced to sit at the table until my plate was clean. It didn't matter that I wasn't hungry or didn't like something. I mean, *really* didn't like it. I had to eat it, anyway. Even if it made me sick. After all, there were all those starving children in some country I'd never heard of with a name I couldn't pronounce. "You'll sit here all night, if that's how long it takes," she barked.

Add to that the crying and screaming if I or one of my siblings was sent away from the table for some unforgivable wrongdoing for which no amount of apologizing would excuse. Is it any wonder that as a child I was always underweight? The only time I had an appetite was when I wasn't with my mother.

I would be sent to my room or punished for the smallest infraction. Punishment meant something severe. Not simply a "time-out," but solitary confinement in my room, sometimes for days. There was no such thing as "talking it out" because I was always wrong and my mother was always right. "You're the child and I'm the adult." That said it all. "I make the rules, and you follow them." I had no rights, no power and was supposedly incapable of independent thought, choice or action.

"Children are to be seen and not heard," was her response if I opened my mouth to disagree. My mother held all the chips and ruled like a dictator. "I'm not your friend," she said, "I'm your mother." She struggled so much to be in control of something.

"I hate you," I once said, in striking position, the venom dripping from my bared fangs. "You don't know anything about being a mother," I snarled.

"The next time you open up your big mouth to me" she replied, "I'll make you regret the day you were born!" She ruled with the threat of physical or emotional punishment rather than with love and understanding. Invoking fear was her guiding principle of motherhood.

The most unsettling thing about my mother's illness was that no one in the family talked about it. I never recall any explanations about what was wrong with her or how best to cope with her behavior. The way I explained her problems to myself was like this: I was just a bad kid. A bad seed. It was *my* fault. This is how mothers act when their child is rotten at the core. Of course, that made her behavior even scarier because my actions alone were responsible for her sickness. The harder I tried to be a good kid, the sicker she became.

When I left for college, the insanity continued. In the summer after my first year, I invited a friend home from school for a visit. As we were pulling into the driveway on our way home from the airport, the rescue squad was carrying my mother out the door on a stretcher. She had sliced her wrists. I was sure it was my fault but I didn't know what I did to cause it. All I could think was, "My mother is stark raving crazy." It never occurred to me that maybe, just *maybe* her illness didn't have anything at all to do with me.

When she returned from the hospital, life at home with her and my siblings was rough. She didn't seem any better. She was still unstable and subject to hysteria and shocking displays of emotion. The stresses of living in the real world were just more than she could bear. I remained the victim of her unpleasant moods and short temper. She was constantly on my back. No matter what was wrong, I did it. This was *her* life and I was going to fit into it and make it better, no matter what.

As I grew older, it became clear that I was not her favorite child and, in fact, the target of all her discontent. I was simply adrift; I thought about running away but didn't know where I would go. My ship was sinking and I was lost. I had no compass, no life vest and no lifeline.

Later in the summer, I visited a college friend in New York. My friend's family was warm and welcoming. I felt happy and loved. Every day left me more and more sure that I couldn't return home. I didn't know what I would do or how I would manage, but I had to find a way to escape or the never-ending drama would do me in. It was an unknown challenge but far better than the alternative. I stayed.

I never returned home to live. I never told my mother goodbye. I never turned around and looked backwards, and never grieved what I had left behind. I began a new life in a new city. Running away from home was a desperate bid for freedom, and revolution was the only way to achieve it.

My mother was very angry at me, and began writing me long rage-filled letters about what a terrible person I was and how I had abandoned her. Perhaps she thought that if I read those words, I would ponder them, and be more likely to come to my senses and return for more of her abuse.

The letters continued for years after and became more about what a disappointment I had been and how I had failed her as a daughter. I guess those letters must have helped her, but they pushed me further and further away from her. I was loathe to answer the phone for fear she would be on the other end, blistering me with her scalding words. She would ask me a round of invasive questions that would invariably incriminate me in some way or another, and then she would excoriate me. She had no idea how toxic she was. It wasn't until many years later when I understood that those letters were about her and how she was experiencing her own life, rather than how I had failed as a human being.

My mother continued writing the same vitriolic nonsense to me until I was in my late twenties. She was simply spewing her unhappiness with life to anyone who would listen. I'm sure those letters came with the expectation that the victim would finally do something to make my mother feel better. And that's when I finally set limits with her: "If you ever write or speak those kinds of words to me ever again, that will be the last time you see or talk me." She didn't speak to me for months after, but she got the message.

In those days, the medications used to treat mental illness were quite sedating and not all that effective. She abused them frequently. If one pill made her feel better, calmer or happier, then *two* pills taken *twice* as often would make her feel *four* times as good! She was often heavily tranquilized, sleeping, slurring her words or stumbling.

She acted like a drunk but she didn't drink. In those days, psychoanalysis was the therapy modality of choice. Three to five days a week lying on the couch, year after year, and then progress only occurred if the patient developed insight, the desire to change and the strength to stand up to those who sabotaged her efforts toward individuation. For my mother, that never happened.

I barely remember what my mother looked like. I'm not sure I ever looked at her in a way that would have allowed me to actually *see* her. I have a few photographs of her taken at different times in her life. Yet, I still have so many questions about her. Was she pretty? Did she have smooth skin? Beauty marks? What color were her eyes? What was her natural hair color? Were her eyelashes long? Was she intelligent? Funny? Kind? Do I look like her? Do I have any of her strengths? Or weaknesses? Was she an introvert or an extrovert? What did she contribute to who I was and who I am today? Would she have been pleased with the person I have become? Or did she even bother to think of those things? Was she so wrapped up in herself that she didn't notice anyone else?

Do I owe her a debt of gratitude, or have I succeeded in spite of her?

Chapter 8

Boys Don't Make Passes At Lasses In Glasses

When I look at old photographs of myself from birth through second grade, I look happy. My hair is long, straight and shiny, sometimes braided or bowed on top of my head, but always impeccable.

In third grade, however, there was a shift. I look sad and unhappy in some photos and, in others, even angry. My length of silky hair is cut in a "pixie," a fashionable haircut executed for the convenience of my mother, what anyone today would call a "hatchet job." Or several years later, permed in the tightest possible coils or even worse, bleached to platinum blonde. I believe the unhappy state of my hair reflected the downturn in my mother's mental health.

The way I looked and how I dressed mattered a great deal to my mother. She worked tirelessly to change my image into something more pleasing and acceptable to her. Perhaps she wanted to mold me into what she wished *she* could have been: beautiful, well-dressed and popular, especially with boys. She set out my clothes each night. She insisted I be perfectly coordinated from top to bottom. No mismatched or sloppy clothing, even when I was sitting on the porch reading. When I became old enough to shop for myself, everything I brought home had to meet with her approval. If it didn't, back to the store it went. Never mind that *I* liked it. She didn't, and nothing else mattered.

If my appearance didn't meet the standards she imposed on me, she probably figured it reflected poorly on her. My mother's lack of satisfaction with me mirrored her unhappiness with herself. What was clearly conveyed to me, over and over, was that my looks displeased her.

I don't believe my mother ever thought she was done with my makeover. At an early age, I learned grades and school weren't important to her. But clothes, makeup and hair were *very* important. Her criticism was freely and liberally dispensed. I was never good enough. And I held on to that notion for decades.

I remember how devastated my mother was when, after getting my eyes checked, the doctor told her I needed glasses. Her response to his prescription was, "Boys don't make passes at girls who wear glasses." How could she encourage my popularity and eventually help me make a "good" marriage, if I wore glasses? I came to understand that glasses were "ugly" and I was embarrassed and ashamed to wear them. I wanted to feel loved and feared that wearing glasses would make me unlovable.

For a long time, I struggled to see without glasses just to please her. I didn't want eyeglasses to interfere with the popularity I ached to achieve. In the end, nearsightedness won out. I vowed that as soon as I was an adult and had money of my own I'd buy contact lenses. Same with the dentist. No daughter of hers would get braces, no matter how it might help her in the future.

But it didn't stop there. Over and over, she would bark, "Sit up straight," or "You need to lie in the sun and get yourself some healthy color," or "You'd look better if you wore more makeup." She sent me to modeling school, make-up school, manners school and dancing school. She equipped me with fancy underwear and push-up bras which I hated — they were so uncomfortable! I guess she thought this kind of underwear was what every properly dressed young teenage girl needed.

"I just want to wear my *undershirt*," I protested. Her message wasn't hard to decipher: "You are unacceptable as you are." For decades, those words played over and over again in my head.

My mother was asleep when I left for school, sometimes still asleep when I returned home for lunch, and in her room or at a doctor's appointment when I came home in the afternoon. We didn't play games together and she didn't read to me. We didn't watch TV or go to movies. We didn't go shopping or cook, bake or do crafty things together. She had no interest in what I was learning at school and didn't help me with homework. She didn't go to the school play or visit my classrooms. We didn't talk about my friends, and she never "ooh-ed" and "ah-ed" over my developing creative talents. We never had a girls' luncheon or went for a manicure together. She was unavailable and uninvolved. Unreachable and untouchable.

I often wondered where her cross-eyed parenting information came from. Was it books, movies, her imagination or her own parents' broken style of parenting?

I recall all the years as a child, and later as a grown woman, when I spent trying to escape from those carnivorous beasts we call dogs. It didn't matter whether the mongrel was a teacup chihuahua, fluffy cockapoo or gentle Labrador retriever. *Any* dog in my vicinity would send me out of my mind. I wouldn't visit the home of a friend who had a dog. I couldn't tolerate the idea of having a dog in my house. I wouldn't take walks by myself. It wasn't uncommon for me to climb a tree or stand on the roof of a car if I had to. I would hide behind, above or under any*one* or any*thing* to flee an oncoming dog. Even a stranger. That's how terrified I was.

I was probably ten or eleven years old on the day of the incident. I'd walked to a friend's house after school to play. She had two German shepherds. I didn't pay much attention to them. When it was time to leave, I recall getting my things together in preparation for the walk home. I opened the screen door, oblivious to the two dogs on the front stoop.

And that's when the dogs, in a sudden fury, began to attack. I don't know whether they were attacking me or each other, but nevertheless, I was caught smack in the middle of their spat. I remember screaming bloody murder and trying to escape. And then -- nothing.

I have no memory of how my physical wounds were tended to. The psychological wounds, however, were another story. They cut deep and I suspect they will never heal completely. Nightmares about dogs were a regular occurrence for decades. As a child, I would turn down invitations to play at someone's house if they had a dog.

"Do you have a dog?" I would ask. If the answer was, "Yes," I would decline the invitation, no matter how much I wanted to go. I no longer felt comfortable playing in the neighborhood or walking to or from school and would beg for rides.

Up until the day of the attack, I had no fear of dogs. My family had a dog for a time but I don't remember much about him. I think he was run over by the milkman before the incident. I wasn't an animal lover, but I wasn't a hater, either.

After my physical wounds healed, my emotional scars might have mended had my mother managed the aftermath of the event more appropriately. No one seemed to understand that I'd been severely traumatized, least of all my own mother.

Playing outside in the neighborhood presented a special challenge. That's what we did then. Played outside with our friends. Until it got dark, and sometimes beyond. But I didn't want to be anywhere a dog might be. Unfortunately, dogs were everywhere; there were no leash laws then.

In the days after the attack, my fear of dogs became much more intense. Every day brought with it a new reason why I couldn't go outside and play. I think my mother expected that I would recover quickly and act like a kid again. But it didn't happen that way. The world became a terrifying place. Everywhere I looked I saw the growling, flesh-eating monsters lying in wait to clamp their ravenous, saber-toothed jaws around my thigh. When I slept I dreamed of huge, drooling creatures and, during the day, I imagined them behind every door and around every corner. Waiting to devour me.

My mother was likely frustrated with my fear of dogs that didn't go away. It seemed to be worse with each passing day, to the point where I simply didn't want to go outside and play. I'm sure she felt she was doing the right thing when one day she announced, "Today you're going outside. Get your jacket!"

I made the usual excuses: "I have a sore throat," "My friends are away," "It's too cold," "It's too hot," "I'm too tired," "I want to read my book."

She would have none of it. "It's time you got over this. Get outside and make friends with the neighborhood dogs." With that, she pushed me out the front door and locked it behind me so I couldn't get back in.

I tried to still myself and not let my mind run me in circles. But it didn't work. I became flooded with anxiety. I kicked and cried and screamed and banged on the door. I guess she thought that, deprived of other options, I would have to make peace with my fear. But I became hysterical with fright. I was surely going to be mauled again and, this time, my tissue and organs would be chewed up and my bones left on the lawn as fertilizer. And who would care anyway.

Much later in my life, more than five decades, I spoke of this event to a childhood friend who lived two doors from my childhood home. She and her mother recall sitting in their kitchen that day and listening to my screams and sobs as I pounded on the front door of my house after being locked out. There wasn't anything they could do. In our close-knit community, nothing would have been worse than calling the police on a neighbor. And to report what? Poor parenting? Besides, I'm sure the police wouldn't have considered what my mother did worth responding to anyway. Now it would be called child abuse. Plain and simple.

Decades passed but my fear of dogs didn't. It's still there, and I keep my distance from unfamiliar dogs, but it no longer interferes with my life the way it used to. In fact, I've actually fallen in love with my younger daughter's dogs.

I can hardly believe it myself.

♟

I was the oldest of four siblings, and my mother subscribed to the old adage, "You're older and you should know better." I seemed to get in trouble more than my siblings because, as she often told me, "You should know better; you're the oldest."

My interpretation of this statement was that my responsibility was to have the "sense" to solve whatever problem contributed to the situation, or be smart enough to have avoided it altogether. Or, had the maturity to keep my mouth shut. The way she saw it was, if a difficult circumstance led to conflict, I must not have done what I *should* have done to either resolve it or not get involved in the first place. In other words, I was expected to act like an adult!

I was sent to one doctor after another to "get fixed." I had radiation therapy for acne and a shrink to get "happy." If I recall, the shrink was not at all interested in finding out if my family might be causing my unhappiness. I had nothing to say to him and refused to go back.

At the age of 40, my mother became pregnant with my youngest sibling, and it was during the pregnancy that her mental health seemed to improve dramatically. She was less volatile and more peaceful. She even smiled and seemed cheerful sometimes. My happiest memory of my mother was during this time. She sat on the sofa next to me and hugged me. Once. I was probably fourteen or fifteen. Oh, how I yearned for more. More consistency, more calm. More affection. More happiness.

Soon after my youngest brother's birth, however, her mental state declined even further. She was largely unable to care for her infant son. The majority of his care fell to the live-in housekeeper and my father. I have scoured my memory for images and searched for photographs of her cuddling, kissing, feeding or playing with her new son. I've found only one.

For a long time, I struggled to find a way to explain to myself why I didn't have a "normal" mother in my life. Many years of therapy later, I've concluded that at some point in my early years, mental illness took my mother away from me. Now, I see myself as a woman whose mother died when I was very young.

This knowledge has affected me in ways I never could have imagined. What has been even more difficult to process is that she was present but absent. *There, but not there.*

There were so many unspoken words between my mother and I. So much emotion. So many unmet needs. She must have loved me. Don't all mothers love their children? The feelings sweep through me sometimes. The nagging worry that it was *I* who pushed *her* away. And, of course, I did do that -- she was unreliable and unpredictable. Perhaps it was *I* who was unlovable, but I don't think so. The doubt, the questions and wondering hang pendulous in the air, waiting for answers to questions unspoken. Who was my mother?

As difficult as her absence from my life has been, I believe my mother actually influenced my life for the better. Her legacy forced me, eventually, to raise myself, to discover who I was in order to rebuild my life, to become a better mother to my children, to contribute to society through meaningful work and volunteering and to learn how to mother myself.

I spoke before the mourners at my mother's funeral, yet my relationship with her was almost nonexistent. I was sad. Sad not for the mother I had and lost, but for the mother I *never* had. And even sadder for the person that my mother could have become. Her wasted life. Mostly, however, I was relieved. I never had to struggle to interact with her again.

These days, I feel only enormous sorrow for the life my mother led, the issues with which she grappled and her unrealized dreams. My only regret is that my ability to see her clearer, my sense of humanity, or call it maturity, was so long in the making.

It is with a tremendous sense of relief that I have managed to free myself of childish blame and arrogant judgment. I wasn't the cause of my mother's problems, and had she not been mentally ill, she would never have hurt me emotionally or physically. *She* was the one who was broken, not I.

♔

When I was younger, I worried that I would turn out like my mother. In fact, I went to every extreme to avoid being similar to her in any way. However, that approach just got me in trouble because extremes of anything often yield the result that one has been trying so hard to avoid.

Years before I stopped drinking, a therapist said to me, "I believe you are clinically depressed. You have many of the symptoms of depression." And then he named a handful. "I think you should see a psychiatrist. Perhaps medication would help you."

As soon as I heard the words "depression" and "psychiatrist," I became deaf as a post to anything else he had to say. It wasn't just once or twice that we had this discussion. It was many over a long period of time.

My response to him was always the same, "I am *not* mentally ill and I will *not* see a psychiatrist. I don't need medication and I'm not psycho. I'm definitely not psycho. I'm not my mother."

"Of course, you're not," he responded. "You're you. But life would be a lot easier if you felt better."

I insisted that I felt fine. "The last thing I ever want is to be like my mother," I confided. Becoming the Wicked Witch of the West would have been preferable. But never my mother. I would do anything to avoid any behavior that smacked of her. I was full of explanations for my wildly emotional state --

everything but the depression and alcoholism that it really signified.

The depression talk was not the only one we had. "Do you think you might have a problem with alcohol?" he inquired one day.

"No." I replied curtly. "I like the *taste* of wine, and scotch, and beer and martinis, that's all. Alcoholics drink in the morning. I don't. Alcoholics stumble around and slur their words. I don't. Alcoholics aren't upper middle class, white Jewish females. I am."

I continued to spout the myths I had heard about alcoholism, none of which I believed applied to me. I was lying to my therapist and myself. But I *had* to believe there was nothing wrong. My survival depended on it.

He wasn't going to stop there. "You know, it's possible that you might be using alcohol to treat your feelings of depression." I knew where this discussion was going to end up: psychiatrists, hospitals, medicines, straight-jackets and people thinking I was just like my mother. Crazy. I was having none of it.

It wasn't until the worst days of my drinking, in the year or so before I stopped, that I became more open to discussing the possibility of further treatment. I was miserable. In those days, Prozac was fairly new in the United States and what I'd heard was that it had an effective success rate in the treatment of depression.

I saw a psychiatrist. She was lovely. Kind and sensitive. I didn't lie down on a couch. She wasn't at all weird as I imagined. She seemed to understand about my demons and empathized with my struggles. And prescribed Prozac.

I took the Prozac as described. I saw her for regular medication check-ups. I felt a little better. I didn't feel like my mother. But I didn't heed the psychiatrist's cautions. She said I had to stop drinking, that alcohol would prevent the medication from working effectively. I didn't listen; I continued to drink heavily.

I discovered that life with Prozac was like getting vision correction surgery. And attitude adjustment therapy. Everything seemed clearer. I still wasn't sleeping well but I felt less anxious. My moods still sashayed up and down, depending on how much I drank. And I seemed to get drunk on less alcohol than before.

Several months into treatment, I went to see her for a medication check-up. I was drunk. It was lunchtime. I had taken myself out for sushi and had much more saki than I should have. I was slurring my words. I couldn't walk a straight line. I had driven myself to the appointment.

"You're not doing yourself any favors by continuing to drink when you're taking Prozac," the psychiatrist admonished. "Alcohol and Prozac are a dangerous mix, especially when you drive or operate machinery. Prozac can potentiate the effects of the alcohol. And since alcohol is a depressant, it will be working at cross purposes with the Prozac."

"Did you know that alcohol can interfere with sleep?" she continued after I described my life-long battle to fall asleep and stay asleep, an always-present state of exhaustion and terrifying nightmares.

I was having none of her alcoholic bullshit. "Would you be willing to go to an Alcoholics Anonymous meeting?" she suggested. The thought of sitting around with a bunch of drunks, lower class males, dirty, crude and homeless, was not for me. I was definitely *not* one of them.

"No."

"Well, she said, I can't let you leave the office and get into your car. You'll have to call someone to pick you up. If you don't, I must call the police. You're a danger to yourself and anyone else on the road."

When my boyfriend arrived at the office, he agreed with her. "I've been asking her to stop drinking now for a long time," he said. "She doesn't think she has a problem," he continued.

He drove me home. I told him I didn't want to talk about my drinking ever again. I screamed and shouted at him when he pursued the subject.

"You need help, Sonya," he said. "You're an alcoholic. You were driving drunk, for God's sake! Wake up."

Several more weeks passed and I went to another appointment with the psychiatrist. This time I was careful not to drink beforehand. She asked me if I'd gone to an AA meeting or had any intention of acknowledging my drinking problem. I hadn't and wasn't. "I can't renew your prescription for Prozac," she said. You're still drinking and I worry that Prozac may be making things worse. It's your choice: alcohol or Prozac."

"I'll be fine without Prozac. I don't think I need it anymore."

I was afraid I was turning into my mother.

Chapter 9

The Rules

There were so many rules in my house when I was growing up that remembering all of them would make my head spin. My mother had favorite sayings that I presume were handed down through generations (or she had made up) and gave her the confidence to believe that she was parenting "correctly." None of them made much sense.

If I were lucky enough to remember a rule, it wouldn't be too long before the rule would change, just like the weather. I believed that the rules were created to suit my mother's need for power and varied with her moods. It never failed that the more unhappy she was, the harsher and stricter she became. And then there were the rules that were made up on the spot to serve some emergency or temporary purpose.

My mother probably thought that if I were to follow the rules, I would become a much better person. And the household would be under control. And what better way to judge whether or not someone is a good parent than well-behaved, compliant children? In my case, it was anxiety and fear that masqueraded as "well-behaved."

It was primarily my mother who parented from a set of rules that I'm sure she believed were appropriate. Because there were so many, and the rules were always changing, and new rules were added at whim, I was always on my toes. I was never sure what to expect. Just when I thought I knew exactly what I should or shouldn't do, the rules would change. I had to tread very carefully to avoid the dreaded "punishments" which were always stern and shaming. Most of the time I was dancing on hot coals.

It was always my mother who doled out the punishment if I broke one of her rules. My father was more accepting (or blind or not around) and I don't ever recall him imposing a punishment. The punishments never fit the crimes; there was no "lesson" I learned. I never arrived at some epiphany about my part in whatever caused me to be punished. What I remember most is the anger, shame and rejection.

As a parent myself, sometimes my rules were silly and irrational, too. I didn't know any better. After all, parenting like my own mother was familiar. I knew my mother's rules sounded weird and made no sense, but I didn't know just how illogical they were until I was well into parenting myself. I swore I would never be like my mother in any way. Not knowing anything different, I did some of the same things my own mother did. I'm horrified now just thinking about it.

These are some of the rules which provided the basis of my mother's child-rearing:

"Don't bother me unless you're dying or the house is burning down."

Now that's something that would instill a feeling of safety and security in a young child's heart.

"Eat everything on your plate. There are starving children in China."

How was cleaning my plate going to help the starving children in China? Better to leave some on the plate, wrap it up and slip it into the mailbox.

"Go outside and play. Come home when it gets dark."

These days, a simple, "Go play in the front yard" is

shocking because you can't even let your kids do that anymore. From a very young age, however, I was permitted to walk or ride my bike alone wherever I wanted. I'd be gone for hours. That would probably get a parent arrested now.

"Let her get hurt; she'll learn not to do that again."

Breaking your arm was considered a learning opportunity. A child was supposed to discover what not to do by hurting themselves. When I was a kid that rule made perfect sense. Today it would surely be neglect.

"Eat what's put in front of you or go to bed without any dinner."

So lemme understand this correctly: I had to eat everything even if I wasn't hungry or didn't like it. I mean, *really* didn't like it. If I didn't, I was sent to bed immediately. And then I couldn't eat anything until breakfast the next morning. This rule resulted in my spending hours alone in my room. I suppose my mother didn't expect me to have any food-related likes or dislikes.

"Who cares if she fails math or history. She's just gonna get married and be a mother."

I struggled in school. I don't think either of my parents knew how much. I guess my mother figured that I didn't really need an education. After all, when I left for college, she made sure to tell me that my goal was to find a good husband, preferably a lawyer or doctor, who would support me so I didn't have to work. A college education would help me only if my husband died prematurely and didn't leave a big insurance policy.

"If your kids don't hate you by the time they're teenagers, you're doing something wrong."

My mother used to remind me that "I'm not your friend, just remember that." Or, "I'm not trying to win a popularity contest." I gave up trying to please her. Hopefully, today's parents find the middle ground.

"This won't hurt a bit."

Liar, liar, pants on fire. How does one learn to trust themselves and others if their own parent lies to them?

"You're older so you should know better."

Right. I'm a child, yet I'm expected to have the judgment of an adult. Tell me how that was supposed to happen?

"If you don't stop crying, I'll really give you something to cry about."

Crying and showing emotion were seen as cardinal sins, a sign that boys were weak and girls "whiny." I think my mother thought this saying was "cute," but I was terrified to find out what it really meant.

"If you don't stop touching your brother I'll cut your fingers off and let the doctor sew them back on."

I think my mother was trying to be clever, but I believed her. Just the thought of it freaked me out. You can't say that in public to your kids anymore.

"It's your brother's turn to lay on the floor of the car now."

Car seats? Seat belts? When I was growing up, it was a treat to get to lay down on the floor in the back of the car, especially on long road trips.

"Go outside and kill each other."

The issue was not stopping a fight or helping siblings resolve their differences, but making sure nothing of value in the house was damaged. As a kid, I was expected to solve my own problems, especially with my siblings. The lack of problem-solving skills within the family severely affected my ability to deal with difficult situations as I grew up.

"Children should be seen and not heard."

Maybe my mother learned this from her own parents. She meant it. If I had something of value to say, it was only after the grown-ups were done talking. I had to be polite and *very* brief. It also meant that I couldn't disagree, complain or have an opinion. I learned early on that no one was interested in what I had to say.

"Do as I say, not as I do."

I observed my mother say and do all manner of inappropriate things, and somehow I was supposed to ignore all that. I was simply to hear her words and pretend her contradictory behavior didn't happen.

"Wipe that look off your face or I'll wipe it off for you."

There's nothing that'll wake you up faster than a good slap in the face.

"Believe me, this hurts me more than it does you. And it's for your own good; one of these days you'll thank me."

It's been proven that punishment doesn't work, at least not the kind that is cruel, or causes embarrassment or shame. I believe my mother thought that the harsher the punishment, the quicker and more completely I would learn my lesson. Why didn't she just sit down and have a nice, friendly talk with me? I suppose that wasn't in her repertoire of parenting tools.

Although most of these rules are typical of how some parents in the 1950's and 1960's viewed their role as parents, that doesn't make them right. I know just as many families whose children were raised in the "olden days" with kindness, sensitivity and respect.

I have to presume that parenting by a set of illogical and irrational rules such as the ones I've described above was part and parcel of growing up in a highly dysfunctional family. The rules contributed much to my own lack of trust in myself and others and little to the development of healthy self-esteem.

Chapter 10

Gotta Feel It In Yo' Bones

Ernestine. Ernie to those who knew her well. Around her neck she wore a mustard seed and a sizable chunk of garlic, both embedded in plastic. And a Star of David. Mississippi-born, she spoke with a thick Southern drawl, and proclaimed herself to be Jewish. "I's born a Negro and I's gonna die a Jew. They's only one God, young'un, and she's sho' 'nuff Jewish!"

For many years, Ernie was our family's housekeeper. Her responsibilities went far beyond what any description of a typical "housekeeper" might be. She was a cook, cleaning woman, chauffeur, laundress, doctor, nurse, baby sitter, errand runner, shopper, crisis counselor, handyman, psychiatrist, savior and mother to four children and two adults. She was everything to everyone all wrapped up in one person. She had an impossible job.

A once beautiful woman, age graced Ernie with no favors. Her black frizzy hair, sprinkled with gray, bore a swath of silver white that rose from her forehead and swirled back towards her crown. When she went to church she wore her hair in a stylish French twist. She looked quite elegant. A wide ribbon of freckles danced under each eye and over the bridge of her nose. The skin under her eyes was ridged with lines, almost like the growth rings in a tree, bearing witness to the years of her labor. She had several pairs of eyeglasses; all of them with broad pointy rims encrusted with rhinestones.

Over decades, she became rather plump. She waddled from one side to another as she walked, yet her well-upholstered frame barreled up and down two flights of stairs innumerable times a day. Taking care of her "family" probably stressed her heart just as much as it stressed her body.

The most glorious matzo ball soup I've ever savored was painstakingly prepared by this wonderful woman. Every Friday, a tall, speckled, black metal stockpot sat on the stove all day long, simmering away. Clouds of fragrant steam rose from the pot hour after hour, leaving its indelible mark on the ceiling above the stove. The rich bouquet of long-bubbling flavors permeated every corner of the house.

I watched her as she created her unique brew, belting out those gospel tunes she loved so much as she worked. She sashayed back and forth in the kitchen between the stove and the counter, wiggling her generous backside, and chopping, stirring, adding more of something, tasting and then doing it all over again until she was certain it was the best soup she'd ever prepared.

"I do declare," she would exclaim, shaking her head back and forth with a broad smile on her face, "Lawd, I believes *this* is my best yet!"

When I finally left home, I asked Ernie to give me the recipe. "They ain't no recipe, chile; just gotta feel it in yo' bones."

I've tried to replicate her matzo ball soup for over five decades, but it can't be done. Whatever it was she felt in her bones -- I don't feel it in mine. Not even a *little* bit. The best matzo ball soup on earth departed this life when Ernie did.

As a new bride, I relied on Ernie's expertise in the kitchen, even though we lived 500 miles apart by then. My first meal for the groom was Ernie's famous fried chicken. *That should be easy! After all, I watched her make it all the time.*

I'll call her; she'll tell me what to do and my husband will love it! And I did just that. I bought all the ingredients she told me to at the grocery store, and then prepped the chicken just the way I'd thought I'd seen her do a thousand times.

"Okay, Ernie," I said to her on the phone that afternoon, "I did everything you told me. What's next?"

She double-checked that I had everything I needed on hand, and said, "Y'all made sure dat chicken's washed real good now?"

"Sure did," I responded with pride, "with soap and water — nice and clean!"

"Lawdy mercy, girl, y'all sayin' *what?*" she bellowed into the phone. "Y'all say soap, S-O-P-E?"

"Well, Ernie, you said 'wash' the chicken, didn't you, W-A-S-H?" I responded, confused.

Then she was cackling in that disharmonious way she did when *she* knew the right answer and you didn't. "Girl, didn't y'all watch anything I done in yo' kitchen all them years? Y'all never seed me wash no chicken with soap, S-O-P-E!"

By now she had burst out laughing. I imagined her jumping all over the room, slapping her knees, and waving her hands around like she did when she was nervous, excited or found something too hilarious for words. "Y'all be throwin' dat chicken right out dat window, you listenin' to me, girl?"

I can still hear her hoots and hollers now. I never tried to make fried chicken again, but my cooking did improve.

Nothing kept Ernie from watching her favorite soap opera in the afternoon. She'd pull a dainty straight-back chair up to the large console television in the living room and switch on "The Edge of Night." She was barely six inches away from the set. Spellbound by the actors and actresses and their miserable lives, she talked out loud to them as they went about creating daily dramas for themselves. "Don't *do* dat," she shouted at one, "y'all gonna be *so* sorry!"

Sometimes, I dragged another chair next to hers; I enjoyed watching with her, and I think she liked the company. During the commercials she would turn her hefty body towards me, the chair groaning under her weight. "Well, girl, what y'all think 'bout dat?" She never really expected a response.

Then she'd proceed to evaluate, blow by blow, all the action since the last commercial. When the episode concluded, she would chatter on and on about all the characters and their latest crises as if they were actual people embroiled in real-life turmoil. Her final words would reveal what she thought was going to happen the following day. "Chile, dat boy is headed fo' some deep troubles."

Ernie was the first person I saw in the morning and the last person I saw at night. She talked constantly. And if she wasn't talking to *someone*, she was talking to herself. There was no filter between her brain and her mouth. She carried on elaborate conversations about what she was fixing for dinner, her "to-do" list, problems with her son or with one of us kids. Silence was an unknown state to her.

She thought dispensing advice to anyone, whether it was the milkman, a handyman or me, was her contribution to the human race. She often remarked that she had "seen the light" and wanted to share it with, well, *everyone*. The words she used were the old-school kind, and she didn't mince them. "Don't y'all be wearin' dat damn hat in ma house," she yapped at the electrician. "Don't y'all have no manners?"

"Girl, you turn off dat TV and git yo'self up dos stairs and do yo' studyin' right now. Y'all needs to be makin' somethin' outta yo'self. You hearin' me, Sonya? Listen up girl, right now, or I's not drivin' y'all to school in the mornin', no matter how much y'all be beggin' me to."

She knew precisely how to get me to do what she wanted. I strongly suspected her threats were bluffs, but I didn't test her. Ernie wasn't school smart, but she was very wise.

Ernie saw herself as the ultimate mediator during sibling spats. "Young 'uns, y'all stop hittin' on each other. I's speakin' loud an' clear. Y'all hittin' one mo' time and I's bein' in yo' face! An' y'all ain't gonna be likin' it one little itty bitty!" she thundered. When she was truly exasperated, she would add, "Ah be tellin yo' Daddy when he gits home, and he gonna tan yo' hide sho' 'nuff." She never told Daddy anything of the kind. Ever.

Ernie would always end a difficult day by saying, "Ah's lovin' y'all real good now, but y'all be painin' me." She did love us all and it showed in everything she did, from getting up early to make hot breakfasts to staying up all night if one of us was sick. After all, that's what mothers do.

Following the birth of my youngest brother, Ernie and I became roommates. My mother was too sick to care for her new son except sporadically, so it was important for Ernie to be nearby most of the time. She lived in our home and she and I shared a room. At first, I resented the loss of privacy. But, she didn't spend any time in the room during the day and always rose well before I did in the morning to care for her family. I found that having her close by at night was rather comforting.

Ernie was a vigilant and loving caregiver to my youngest brother. She was the only mother he ever knew. Once he started walking he could race from one room to another in the time it took Ernie to sneeze. Two seconds tops. "Oh, my Lawd have mercy, where in the dickens is ma baby goin' to?" she shrieked as she raced around in a state of pure panic. "Lawd, ah's prayin' now, don' let anything happen to ma baby!"

"Ma baby" was never far away and was always happy to be found, rewarding her with a big smile and giggles. He thought they were playing a game. When she found him, she covered him with kisses like he'd been gone for a week.

One of my most lucid memories of Ernie is not a pleasant one. In a frenzied outburst of juvenile histrionics (I might have been eleven or twelve), probably angry about something that had nothing to do with her, I lashed out. Full of fury, all I wanted to do was hurt her. And did I ever. At the top of my lungs, I shouted, "Nigger!" at her. I didn't actually know what the word meant, I didn't even know where I'd heard it, but I knew it was bad. Very bad. Maybe even the worst kind of hurtful insult. I had no idea how much pain those six letters would cause her. She was devastated. All the life drained out of her face. Her body went limp. She hung her head. *How could one little word do all that to a person?*

I never saw Ernie cry until that moment. "Why y'all say somethin' like that to me? I aint' done no wrong to y'all. Dat's the worse thing y'all *ever* said to me. You my oldest chile. I loves you, Sonya. You should *know* better, girl!" I can still see the fat tears sliding down her cheeks, marking her beautiful dark brown skin.

I never disrespected Ernie again. The memory of how much anguish I caused her has always left me profoundly regretful. I loved Ernie. I don't know what would have happened to me without her. She was a shield and a protector. She shared the best part of who she was with me, and for that I will be forever grateful. She was like a mother to me.

Chapter 11

My Grandmother Didn't Perspire

In my graduate school studies, I learned more about what had been lacking in my life. I marveled in knowing that the essentials of healthy parenting depended on children growing up in a warm and loving environment in which the parents were calm, clear and consistent. It seemed so simple.

I didn't have that. The state of my family was about as calm as an out-of-control tsunami, as clear a bowl of pea soup, and with no more predictability than the weather in March.

I spent most of my young life waiting for the other shoe to drop, which it did frequently. And for the morning that my mother would wake up, spring out of bed, and whatever devil had hold of her mind would magically loosen its grip and she would become, uh, *normal.* It was a nice dream and I never wanted to let it go.

I had no idea what "normal" was but I craved that kind of life. I thought that what I read in books and watched on television might have been it. I'd heard about "normal" and was sure it was much different than the world in which I had lived -- a wondrous land of smiling faces, happy words and hugs all around. Not the manic up and down and back and forth of the milieu to which I was accustomed.

I didn't have an emotionally stable mother who was a dependable, loving presence in my life. But that doesn't mean I wasn't mothered. I was fortunate enough to have a few significant women in my life through my childhood and into adulthood. I call them my "other mothers," each caring and loving in her own way. My life often felt like a piece of Swiss cheese -- there were so many open, gaping holes -- the other mothers filled in some of the gaps as best they could.

I was fortunate. You may wonder how a child without a "good enough" mother could say that. Well, then, I'll say it again: I was fortunate. How might I have turned out had I not had these wonderful women in my life? I imagine that my struggles would have been much more pronounced. The most profound effect left in the wake of my disordered childhood, other than alcoholism and depression, was my inability to trust others and, ultimately, myself; to have the confidence and sufficient ego strength to accomplish the business of living.

It makes perfect sense, doesn't it? If you can't trust the people in your family to love, support and encourage you, than how do you ever learn to trust yourself?

I lacked a dependable role model at home, someone I could watch, talk to and learn from. A person who could show me how to grow up, a constant presence who taught me the skills necessary to manage my life. I never learned how to study, cook, keep house, manage money or what it meant to be a wife or mother, until I was well into adulthood.

Yet, I was lucky.

There were other devoted women in my life who were emotionally present. These wonderful people made a small dent in my mothering void. Besides Ernie, a cherished housekeeper, and my maternal grandmother, I was blessed with several paternal aunts, a beloved cousin, and a loving mother-in-law, all influential role models who bestowed time and attention on me.

My "other mothers" were all very different, but each of them exceptional in their own way. They didn't replace the birth mother who was lost to me, but they provided a framework for loving relationships and innumerable fond memories. I never thought of any of these women as a substitute mother but each one opened their heart to me in extraordinary ways.

With their help, I eventually evolved into emotional maturity, but it was long after my so-called chronological adulthood. It wasn't easy, and the "learning curve" to adulthood was more difficult and took much longer for me than it should have been.

I've often wondered if any of my other mothers had even the slightest idea of how lost and adrift I was or to what extent I struggled. Or the difficulty I had accepting responsibility for the roles for which I was ill-prepared. Or my troubled history as an alcoholic? I'm grateful to all of them for sharing their lives with me. They provided some of the support and nurturing that was painfully absent.

If I'd been a real queen or maybe even an empress, the most precious jewel in my crown would have been my maternal grandmother. There was no one I would rather be with than her. When she smiled, my world became right again. She often referred to me as the Queen, and I always felt like one when I was with her. When we were together, she only had eyes for me. What could be better than that?

As a child, I felt a kinship with my grandmother I never experienced with anyone else. She loved girl talk, card games, needlework and cooking. She was an accomplished artist. I wanted to be wherever she was. As often as I could. Whatever she was good at, I yearned to be the same. I trusted her and felt safe in her presence.

We spent hours together as she trained me in the art and science of card playing. She was sharp and patient. Talking and taking breaks for tea and lunch were always part of the lessons. She prepared my favorite sandwich, what she called a "Marmaduke." A thick layer of cream cheese topped by a covering of sticky cherry preserves, embraced by two cottony slices of Wonder Bread. It made my mouth water, whether I was hungry or not. Sometimes she would mix cream cheese with sliced green or black olives. I loved that, too. And she let me drink coffee with lots of cream. I believed I was something special when I was with her.

Her famous German Chocolate Cake was a renowned treat. Like every kid, I loved licking the batter bowl. And working my tongue into and out of the mixer blades! Closing my eyes even now, I can smell the gooey, oversweet scents. Fresh out of the oven, I would sit as close as I could to the cocoa-colored wonder, inhaling the warmth and delectable aromas of chocolate, coconut and pecans, as she carefully iced the layers. "Would you like some?" she asked, as we both admired her creation.

"No," I said, "I'm not allowed to eat cake before dinner. I'll get in trouble."

"I promise I won't tell, honey. You can even have two pieces, if you want." As I held my face near, she pierced the thick layer of icing and slowly sliced through the spongy tiers, releasing more ambrosial fragrance.

Fortunately for me, I inherited my grandmother's love of cooking. However, all of her efforts to teach me to bake were for naught. Whatever her secrets were, I couldn't make those desserts happen for me, even when I followed her recipes *exactly*. Many a time I threw my homemade creations in the trash, murmuring, "I'm a piecrust screw up, a biscuit bungler and a cake mix klutz." As I did so, I whispered an apology to my grandmother. "It's not you, Grandma, it's me. I can't make anything magical happen with flour. "

It was my grandmother who nurtured my love of all things artistic and handmade. She was an accomplished knitter and painter and because of her, using my hands to create became a lifelong passion. With her help, I knitted my first sweater when I was just a preteen. And, in the process of producing that masterpiece, she sat by patiently instructing and supporting, no matter how many mistakes I made along the way or how frustrated I became. I was so proud of that sweater. I wanted to do everything she did, and most of all, I wanted to please her.

Sometimes she would invite me to go with her to the hair salon. I would be so excited. I loved to watch her hairdresser as he washed, trimmed and wound her hair on bright pink rollers with brushes inside. He would secure each roller with a hair clip on either end. Then he'd place a large light blue hairnet over her head to hold them all in place. She'd sit under the dryer while she had a manicure.

While she was sitting there, she would always give me a quarter or two to spend at the Woolworth's next door. I loved that store! They had an old-fashioned soda fountain, pine plank floors, and kind little old ladies with aprons asking if they could help me. Those magical coins could buy anything I wanted from row after row of carefully organized treasures. I felt so grown up. I walked into the store by myself, made my purchase, and left. Grandma was always intensely interested in what I bought.

Afterwards, we ran errands and ate dinner at Smith's Cafeteria. How I looked forward to that. As I pushed my tray down the cafeteria line, everything looked so delicious. Grandma let me have anything I wanted, even if she knew my eyes were hungrier than my stomach. She never made me clean my plate and she never yelled at me. A far cry from the meals I dreaded at home.

My grandmother had soft, creamy skin. Her short, wavy hair was a burnished, reddish brown. She greeted everyone with a warm and welcoming smile. It was the kind of expression that came from a sunny place in her heart.

Grandma loved perfume, and always smelled heavenly. Every morning after breakfast, she would drink her coffee and work a crossword puzzle. And then she would prepare for her bath. She gathered fluffy, peach-colored towels from the linen closet, all of them tastefully embroidered in snow-white silk thread with her initials. I heard the water gushing into the tub. If I stood close to the door I could inhale the steaming vapors from the scented hot water.

When she finished her bath and dried herself, she would apply fragrant bath powder with a round, white powder puff. She told me the puff was sable, an exotic animal fur. I rubbed it on my arm and inhaled her scent. The powder would fog up the room and coat all the exposed surfaces with a fine dust. The sweet and spicy aroma hung in the air for hours after. "You're welcome to use it after your bath," she reminded me. She also let me try on her clothes and experiment with her make-up, treats I could never experience at home.

I followed her into the bedroom where I sprawled on her bed and watched as she sat at her make-up table and applied lotions, potions, colors and textures, one after another to her lovely skin. I thought she was the most beautiful woman in the world and I longed to look just like her.

Her clothing was simple and well-made from buttery soft fabrics. I never saw her wear pants or dressed sloppily. She was always tastefully attired. Opening her clothes closet was like stepping into the wardrobe of a fairy princess. I loved to touch the fabrics and smell the aromas which filled the closet. Whenever she would wear one of my favorite outfits, I was sure it was just to make me happy.

This beautiful woman cared little for the many luxuries she was privileged enough to own. She permitted me to gallivant around the house in her expensive jewelry, dragging her mink coat along the carpet after me. She didn't "cherish" her possessions nor want for more; she had the extraordinary capacity to cherish *people*, instead, and she loved to make those people smile.

Above all else, my grandmother was a "lady." An elegant lady. Her family was poor and uneducated so she didn't come by this quality through genetics or breeding. Her manners were impeccable and she was quiet, calm and confident. She was a gracious hostess. Everyone liked her. But most of all, I just wanted to be with her. She was the safest haven in my life.

One day after school, I decided to walk to her house rather than go home. I didn't feel well and I needed some tenderness. She made me hot tea with lemon and honey.

"Can I lie down in your bed, Grandma?"

"Of course you may."

I loved the feel of her sheets, sweet-smelling with her perfumes and powders.

"I'm freezing," I said shaking, obviously running a temperature.

"I can fix that," she responded. She opened her closet and pulled out a full-length mink coat and draped it over me. I was warm in so many ways.

I never saw my grandmother perspire. I think she was above such a common human flaw. I never heard her raise her voice or utter an unkind or inappropriate word. If she ever experienced a disagreeable humor, she never let on. I only crossed her once in my life and it wasn't intentional. She delivered some well-deserved admonishment to me, but in a soft-spoken, polite manner. Her quiet words felt like cannons to my ears. I never did anything of the kind ever again.

As the decades passed and I became a married woman with children of my own, living quite a distance from her, my grandmother became more and more like a beloved lifelong friend. We would talk frequently by phone and I returned as often as possible to her home for visits.

My grandmother was young, and even younger looking. When she was only fifty-eight or -nine, she became a great-grandmother. Everyone thought she was my mother; I was so proud of that. I *wanted* her to be my mother. She was a constant presence in my life from my birth until her death in 1978.

I think of my grandmother every day. I've never stopped grieving her loss. I'm grateful for all the joyful times I spent with her and hold those memories close to my heart. She was happy for me when I was happy, caring and supportive when I wasn't. All the things a mother should be.

♚

From the rubble of a motherless life on one hand to the richness of a mother-full life on the other, has emerged one more mother. I've known her since the day of my birth. It took her a long time to finally introduce herself to me, but she's been the one who has made the most difference in my life.

Over the last twenty-five years, she and I have grown steadily closer. She's become a loving and influential companion. I've learned to trust her and allow her to guide me through some very rough times. With her support, I'm stronger and wiser. Steadfastly by my side, she's my closest confidante.

I was introduced to her by a former therapist many years ago. For a long time, she and I didn't have much of a relationship. In fact, I was pretty contemptuous of her. I thought I knew everything, and didn't need any advice or help from anyone. Least of all her. Whenever she offered words of wisdom, I would scoff and admit that I knew better. I wouldn't let her get close to me. And besides, I didn't like her that much. I certainly didn't trust her. To her credit, I didn't scare her away and she hung in there with me; she never once said, "I'm done with you."

In the initial years of our relationship, her voice would materialize out of nowhere as I was about to react inappropriately to something that set me off.

"Step back and think about this before you respond. If I were you, I wouldn't say that. It's just going to make you look foolish; you won't accomplish anything other than feel bad about yourself. And other people will think you're not quite right," she would advise as diplomatically as possible. I imagined her winking at me as she spoke.

This was all stuff I'd heard before. I didn't take her advice. After all, no one was going to tell *me* what to do. Of course not. I wasn't ready. What did she know about me? Her opinions fell on deaf ears. I saw nothing wrong with how I conducted my life. And it was *so* easy. I simply flicked the autopilot switch and reacted (or *over*-reacted). After all, this kind of behavior was familiar and comfortable and I didn't have to learn new ways to cope. I have to admit, though, autopilot never worked very well. But it was the only thing I knew.

It took a long time for me to get to know her. And even longer to believe she had my best interests at heart. Years. As I became more aware of the regret and sadness I experienced when I spoke or acted without thinking about the consequences, I became more open to listening to her — like when the sheer intensity of my emotions drove people away. Or the unpleasant result following an unbecoming response.

"Just because something crosses your mind," she counseled, "doesn't mean it has to come out of your mouth." *Think* it, but don't say it." And another good one: "Just because someone says something, doesn't mean it's true." Over and over she repeated herself. And over again.

At some point, I became desperate for happy endings. I decided to take a chance and be more receptive to her guidance. But it seemed so difficult, so out-of-character for me.

"Slow down, think things through, choose a course of action that will make you feel good about yourself, that preserves your dignity and self-respect," she repeated. "Reflect on what you want to achieve before you act." Maybe the wisest words ever spoken to me. I'd *never* given much thought to my interactions with others. But somewhere, somehow, it all began to make sense. Perfect sense.

One day, I decided to give it a try. Faced with an obnoxious individual and a complicated situation, I behaved with, ah, *self-respect*. I wasn't mean or sarcastic; I didn't explode or act crazy; and I didn't stomp away in anger. I just *handled* it. Gracefully. With words. Kind words. I was surprised at how well it worked. I felt good about myself. Even *proud*. No shame, guilt or regret. I remained in control. I was learning that there were more appropriate ways of managing interpersonal difficulties.

It's been decades now and my friend is still hanging

around. I consider her to be the best mother I've ever had. I'm still taking her advice. She's become skillful at guiding, supporting and encouraging. And I know she loves me. I don't need her as much as I did, but she helps me make good decisions and do the right thing. I nurture her by indulging in whatever makes her feel loved, happy and peaceful. I hear her loud and clear as she whispers in my ear, "Good job," or "I'm so pleased."

This other mother has stood by me and helped me slow down and restrain my tendency to simply react, or "go off" as some might say. In its place I've acquired a new respect for discipline, thoughtfulness and introspection. And sweet patience. I've learned that I don't have to act unless it's an emergency.

I suppose I've developed a valuable commodity -- insight. I've come to know the geography of me pretty well by now. All the majestic peaks, rolling valleys, fault lines and volcanos. I know what's going to trigger an earthquake and what's going to bring about a day at the beach.

But, I almost always defer to her better judgment now. On the infrequent occasions when I simply barrel forth (auto-pilot still raises its ugly head now and then), I *always* regret it. In fact, when I don't heed her, I hear myself saying, "This is not likely to turn out well, but I'm going to say or do it anyway." She's always right. She's kind, sharp-witted, sensible and perceptive. I owe her a great deal.

This special woman has woven her influence over me through a tangled web of ugly behavior patterns, traumatic experiences, unnecessary drama and exquisite successes. She knows me better than anyone. I've come to love her. With her by my side, I've managed to make my way to today, which is a pretty good place to be. Sometimes she's a pain in the neck -- yapping in my ear advice I need but don't want -- but she's the best mother I could ever ask for, a dear friend and my voice of reason. She'll never leave my side.

Chapter 12

Something Is Missing

Have you ever had the feeling that something is missing? An important something. Something *truly* significant, I mean. Not a something you have misplaced or lost like a favorite sweater or cherished trinket, but a missing which is far greater. More like a hunger. No, even greater. A deep-rooted, endless emptiness.

It's the kind of missing you might experience if something uncommonly meaningful to you vanished. Once all efforts to locate it fail, then everything changes. Your heart feels like it has been dredged right out of your chest with a rusty barbecue fork, leaving behind a raw and weeping black hole of . . . nothingness.

When I was a youngster, I often felt sad and lonely. It seemed that I was longing for a "something" with which I imagined I once enjoyed a perfect connection. I didn't know what that something or somebody was, but I knew it was no longer mine. I lost it, it vanished or it was taken from me. The feelings bubbled up out of nowhere and stayed with me for days.

At some point, I discovered, with considerable surprise, that I was a twin. On the day of my birth, I emerged head first into the world, healthy and kicking and wailing in discomfort at the frightening sounds, bright lights, and cold temperatures called life. And then came my brother. The cord was wrapped around his neck. He was silent and still and died following me into the world. One moment he was right next to me, my soulmate. And then suddenly he was gone. Half of me had disappeared forever.

"A twin? A brother? You mean *I* had a twin brother?" I looked incredulously at my mother as she spoke the words. It wasn't sinking in. "How could that be?" "How do you know?" "Why didn't you tell me?" "What happened to him?"

I had so many questions.

"I had no idea I was pregnant with twins. You were born first," she continued, "and he came next. But he wasn't alive. I was asleep during the birth. The doctor said later he was surprised to find another baby in there. That was him. He didn't make it, though. I was worried that you wouldn't live, either. But you turned out to be a healthy baby girl."

I was speechless, and somehow not surprised. It answered so many of my questions.

She couldn't tell me anything further about how it happened. Was he alive when he was born? Was there any glimmer of life in his tiny body? Did he make a sound of objection at the moment we were separated? Or did he die during the birth process? Was he born dead and the nurses dashed away with him, a naked lifeless body, while she was still on the delivery table? Did my mother give him a name, or hold him? Did she see his face? What did he look like? What were the color of his hair and eyes? Did he suffer? Did I do anything to cause his death? Was my mother upset or sad and did she grieve? Did she feel the loss of that child as much as I did?

I wish I knew the answers to these questions and more. But she and I didn't talk much and I think she probably didn't know anything more about what happened. After all, that was more than seven decades ago, and worlds away from the childbirth experiences of today's mothers. It was before sonograms, CAT scans, MRI's and heart and brain wave monitors. In those days, the doctor was in charge of childbirth, and more often than not, the pregnant mom was put to sleep and had no awareness of or control over her child's entrance into the world. And sometimes she awoke to very bad news.

So, who knows, she might have slept right through the birth and death of her new son. That's the way things were then.

It's been said that the body remembers what the mind does not, and holds on to memories long after the brain has buried it in an out-of-the-way chamber never again to emerge into consciousness. For me that is very true. Somehow, I recall the essence of his being, of his tiny body pressing against my own, floating together in our viscous paradise, exquisitely aware of each other's presence.

Before I was born, my days were spent floating around in the hushed warmth of my mother's belly lying skin-to-skin with my tiny twin brother. How could this not be the most unique and profound event of my life? I was closer to him than I've ever been to any other human being. Those nine months were the most intense period of time I have ever experienced.

When I was in graduate school, working towards my Master's Degree in Clinical Social Work, I read about the significance of twin bonding in the mother's womb. I was fascinated by the research which proved that twins develop an intimate relationship with one another before they're born. Each twin, intensely aware of the other's presence, interacts with and responds to the other in special ways.

This information was compelling, and I read all of the literature I could find on the subject. At birth, twins, born with a fundamental "oneness," must separate from their mother, but also from each other, as well. If one twin is separated permanently from the other at birth, due to death or physical separation, the sudden severing of the in utero bond may have a powerful and lasting emotional impact on the surviving twin. It's almost like cutting a whole person in half. Prior to and for several months after birth, twins see themselves as one person.

The surviving twin remembers the other twin, always misses him or her, and longs for the "oneness" they once enjoyed.

Other research on surviving twins demonstrates that they may suffer from anxiety, depression, a poor sense of self, as well as the feeling that something essential is missing from their life! "Were they talking about me?" I wondered.

What I concluded from this was deeply personal: I spent the first nine months of my life as a twin, but I came into the world by myself. I'd been trying to cope with my emptiness and the pressure I felt to find the part of me that was missing for a long time. The impact of being the surviving twin had affected my emotional well-being and my relationships since the day I was born. In almost every connection I made, I sought to re-create the perfect union I'd once experienced with my twin brother. And I never could.

Propelled into psychotherapy to explore the roots of my depression, I began to grasp the importance of my twin brother's death, and process its impact on my life. After many years of feeling something was missing, I eventually came to understand, among other things, that I was born grieving. An infant, with a gnawing, fire-in-the-belly sorrow caused by the abrupt separation from my twin brother.

In Shel Silverstein's charming little book, ***The Missing Piece***, he writes simply and touchingly about an unhappy creature missing a piece of itself. Similar to the dilemma of the surviving twin, the story raises important questions about the nature of identity and happiness. If only the unhappy creature were to find its missing piece it would finally be happy. Those of us who have ever sought a friend or partner who would "complete" us might find this story especially meaningful.

> *It was missing a piece.*
> *And it was not happy.*
> *So it set off in search*
> *of its missing piece.*
> *And as it rolled*
> *it sang this song —*
> *Oh I'm lookin' for my missin' piece*

Sonya Braverman

I'm lookin' for my missin' piece
Hi-dee-ho, here I go,
Lookin' for my missin' piece.

Chapter 13

No Way Out

It was unthinkable that someday I'd hear the clang of a jail cell door closing. Or the metallic grind of a key turning a lock to ensure I wouldn't escape into the free world to commit further mayhem. Me on the wrong side of a locked jail cell? Impossible.

I'm talking about the side of a cell door that seals a person in like a dangerous animal. The side where there's no privacy and no privileges. The side that permits others to gawk like the captive is a rare specimen of human detritus. The side where there's no freedom and many restrictions. Where any autonomy, independence, or protection one might have enjoyed outside of the cell ceases to exist once that door slams shut.

But there I was. The story isn't pretty, but I have to tell it.

♔

I step out the door of a shopping mall in Washington, DC. It's about nine o'clock. I walk briskly. I worked all day, enjoyed a pleasant dinner with several glasses of wine at a nearby restaurant and went shopping. I'm tired and want to go home. Still feeling a bit inebriated, I'm grateful that my home is only a mile from the mall.

As I make my way to the car, I see two police officers approaching off in the distance. They seem to be heading towards me. I think nothing of it. One of the officers is thick and stocky; the other tall and lanky. As they draw closer, I see their hands on their guns. I look around, assuming something bad is going down behind me and I'm right in the middle of it, but I see nothing.

The officers continue to approach me and as they come closer, one of them says, "Excuse me, ma'am, may we speak to you?"

"Sure. What's wrong?" I say. I look around, feeling apprehensive, but I'm certain they're not interested in *me*.

"Ma'am, have you been shopping at that mall?"

"Yes," I respond holding my hand over my mouth. I hope they can't detect that I may have drunk way too much wine at dinner. I feel spacey and hope I'm not slurring my words. I believe I'm still drunk.

"May we see your shopping bag?"

"Why do you want to see my shopping bag?"

"Please open the bag, ma'am," the stocky one with the deep voice demands.

I do as I'm told. I open the shopping bag, showing the officers the contents, a pair of jeans.

"Do you have a receipt for this item?" the taller officer says pointing to the bag with one long, skinny finger. His nails are dirty.

"Of course," I answer. I don't like him.

"May we see it?"

"Well," I respond, "I don't have it with me. It's at home. On the kitchen counter. I meant to bring it, but I forgot to pick it up on my way out this morning."

"So, ma'am, let me understand. What you're saying is that you have no receipt for the item in your shopping bag?"

"No. I *do* have a receipt. And I can easily retrieve it. I bought this a couple of days ago, but I left the receipt at home. I know right where it is. See, the tags are still on it. I can go home right now and get it. I only live a mile or two away from here." I begin to realize that it's me they're interested in. Panic sneaks into my voice.

"Well, ma'am, we have reason to believe you didn't pay for this item," the stocky officer states, moving closer to me. I can smell cigarettes on his breath. His face is greasy and pock-marked.

"Oh, but I *did*, I did," I interrupt. "I bought it a few days ago. I left the receipt at home. In the kitchen," I repeat, hoping the message sinks in and they'll go away, with the knowledge that they've assumed incorrectly. I don't care anymore whether they think I'm drunk. I just want them to go away.

"Is the item in that bag the one you originally purchased several days ago?" he continues.

I ignore the question. I hope that will end the interrogation. I become aware of how exhausted I am. "I only brought this to the store to compare it to the same thing in another size. It didn't fit right. The one I originally purchased. A couple days ago. But I forgot the receipt. I paid for it, I *did*; I just don't have the receipt *with me*." I'm shivering and it's not cold out.

The taller officer moves closer to me and speaks in a booming voice, "Miss, did you steal this item from the store?"

"What? No! I didn't steal it. I was just trying it on in the dressing room. And comparing it to another size. Please let me go home and get the receipt. I'll show it to you! My house is just five minutes away!" I'm agitated and upset. My voice is half-begging, half-squealing. I'm a tiny mouse, and the cat is backing me further and further into the corner. I'm desperately uncomfortable.

"Have you been drinking, ma'am? I believe I smell alcohol on your breath."

"No way," I lie. *Can they smell it on my breath? And what difference would it make anyway?* "I had something to eat at The American Cafe -- and just one glass of wine," I lie.

"*How* many drinks have you had tonight?"

"Just one, I swear. I *swear* to you."

He levels his bony finger at my shopping bag, wiggling it as if he's itching to pull the trigger. "We believe you've stolen this item here and we're going to take you down to the station."

"No! What station? I didn't do *anything!*" Please let me go home and get the receipt, *please*," I plead. My voice is cracking. I'm overcome by fear and teetering on the brink of hysteria.

"Ma'am don't make us handcuff you."

"*Me*? Handcuff *me*? For what?" I scream, "I didn't do *anything* illegal," I insist.

"Well, ma'am, we'll let you explain that to the court."

"Court? Why?" I'm shrieking. This is no joke.

The stocky officer pulls a pair of handcuffs out of his back pocket and dangles them in front of me. As he reaches for my wrists, I beg, "Please, don't."

He asks for my purse and shopping bag. He cuffs me. "You're under arrest for shoplifting," the same officer states. And then he reads me my rights. I don't hear a word except "arrest." A crowd of people has gathered around us and are staring. I'm horrified. I want to die, right then and there. There's nothing in my life that is worth living for.

"*No*," I say sharply. "Don't take my purse. Please," I scream. "Don't take my purse!"

"Police procedures. You'll get your purse back. Let's go. The squad car is over there, he says pointing to his right. We want you to walk with us peacefully."

"Can't you just drive me home to get the receipt, please?" They don't respond. "I have the receipt. I do. I can show it to you! You'll see."

I'm crying. I can tell the officers aren't going to accept my explanation. My tears are not going to move them. I can't believe this is happening. *Please, please, God, let me wake up from this nightmare. Let them reach the patrol car and realize this is all a big mistake. I'll never do anything wrong again. I promise!*

I walk in between the two officers as they escort me to the squad car, my wrists locked behind my back. I'm ushered into the backseat. The handcuffs are removed and the doors are locked.

There is no way out now.

Chapter 14

A Herd Of Elephants

I'm seated in the back seat of the squad car. The two officers sit in front. The two-way radio punctures the silence with the sound of the dispatcher's voice alerting the officers to what's going on in the world of crime. The officers talk in hushed voices. I'm sure that I'm the subject of their conversation. They drive deep into the armpit of Washington, D. C..

My mouth is dry. It feels gluey, and tastes like something is rotting in my belly. The dream-like haze of too much wine has lifted, replaced by excessive stress. Acid is burning through my stomach and rising in my throat. I can't think clearly. If only I could have another drink.

I'm very frightened. I dig my nails into the palms of my hands as if I want to create a pain worse than the reality of what I fear might happen next. I grip the sides of my thighs ferociously. I don't know what to make of the plexiglass shield between the front and back seats. *Is it there to protect the officers from me or me from them?*

Our destination is the Central Detention Facility, the main headquarters of the Police Department. It's not in the best part of town and certainly not in an area with which I'm familiar. It's close to eleven o'clock at night by the time we pull into the parking area. Many other squad cars are parked there, and at least a dozen officers are milling around. Some look like they have somewhere to go, and others look like they're hanging around with nowhere to go.

The stocky officer who rides on the passenger side gets out of the squad car first and unlocks the rear door. I suddenly realize I've been locked inside the car. Hesitantly, I climb out of the car, fearful of what the next step will lead to. The only detail I notice about the building is how well-lit it is on the outside. Blindingly well-lit. I wonder if this prevents criminals (like me?) from thinking they can make a break for it.

I'm unbearably uncomfortable. Someone might recognize me. *Why have I been brought here and what's going to happen to me?* I overhear several police officers shout in my direction and I know they're talking about me.

"Whatcha got there?" one yells to the taller of the officers who stands on my left. Another one is laughing as he says, "What's dat white chick done now?" His tone of voice is painfully sarcastic. I'm embarrassed in a way I've never before experienced.

Another voice whoops, "A fresh one, huh?" I pray the earth will open up, a huge crevice appear right next to my foot. I step in and the earth swallows me whole. One huge mouthful. After that, I don't care what happens next. *I will suffer anything to escape this hell.*

I'm flanked by the officers as we enter the building and walk up a flight of stairs, across a wide lobby and then down another flight of stairs into a large room that appears to be some sort of administrative space. The pipes are exposed in the high ceiling. There aren't any windows. It looks and smells like a basement. Institutional gray metal desks are arranged in a rectangle in the center. On one side, there's a desk built onto an elevated platform. A large black man with sunglasses sits on a chair in front of the desk, barking orders.

The room is crowded. Policer officers, Detention Facility employees and criminals — not the kind of people with whom I usually associate. The officer on my left points to a wooden bench about fifteen feet away and says, "Go over there and sit down." I feel the eyes of the entire room on me, most of them black; all of them are wondering what ghastly crime the white girl committed.

Someone in this place is probably going to ask me more questions and then drive me back to my car. I believe I can handle that. It'll be a relief.

I sit down next to an elderly black man in a shabby, dark green coat. I don't look directly at him but can tell he's very thin. Hungry looking. Maybe he isn't that old. Perhaps he's just life-worn. Or homeless. His coat is dirty, spotted with what looks like grease. Something dark. Could be blood, too.

The man wears a brown knitted cap. It has two large holes in the top of his head and another area on the side looks like it's beginning to unravel. He smells of alcohol. And other bad things. Rancid bad. Like he's rotting from the inside out. He turns towards me and I notice most of his teeth are missing. *Please don't talk to me. Please.* The two that remain in the front have discolored to a deep khaki. Any moment they're likely to fall right out of his mouth and tumble down to who knows where.

"Whadja' do?" he says, looking at me and slurring. He's unshaven, and his breath smells terrible. I know this without even turning to face him. I pretend I don't hear him. I'm dazed and speechless. Me. Sitting next to a homeless derelict. Or hatchet murderer. *Is this really happening? I'm going to wake up soon, the alarm clock next to the bed signaling that it's time to go to work.*

The man continues to look at me, anticipating my answer. He seems to understand there will be no response, and just shakes his head. I imagine that what he would *like* to say, in the most proper Queen's English is, "Madam, if you wouldn't mind, please excuse me for asking this, but what is a white, educated, well-dressed, fully employed and financially comfortable lady like you doing in a place like this?"

I sit there for almost a half hour, waiting, with no understanding of what I'm waiting for. I watch the officers and Detention Facility employees moving around, searching for some clue about what's going to happen next. The anxiety is intolerable; I begin to imagine a prison cell, a trial and death row.

A male voice calls my name. "*Bray*-vah-man," he rumbles deeply. I'm startled and look around for the source of the voice. "Ova' here, ma'am. *Ma'am!*" he repeats more sharply when I don't move. "Come ova' to the desk," he says, enunciating each word as if he were talking to a disabled child.

I rise from the bench and walk to the elevated platform where an obese black man is sitting behind a desk, looking down on me. He hides behind dark sunglasses. Or maybe they're x-ray glasses that permit him to see things that are hidden. I wish I had worn a heavier coat. I don't want to look at him.

Huge globules of sweat trickle down the side of his face. He's surrounded by piles of official looking documents, rubber stamps, pens and pencils. His desk is messy. He's moving papers around with his fat hands. His fingernails are long and pointy like he doesn't care about how he looks. Cringing, I hope he doesn't touch me. I conclude that he's probably going to tell me this ordeal is over and I can go home. *Whew!*

"Hey, ma'am, is this yo' purse?" he says holding up what the officers took from me. I nod, not sure of what my admission to that question might mean for my future. I guess he's going to return it to me. My first thought is to make sure everything's there.

"What are you doing?" I say, surprised to see him dump out the contents on the paper-strewn surface of his desk, feeling around inside of it to make sure he hasn't missed anything. He opens it wide to look inside. He unzips the compartments and then checks the lining. *What's he looking for?*

"*Po*-lice procedures. You wearin' a watch, rings, bracelets, anything like that?" he asks, not waiting for my reply. "Did y'all pat her down, Leroy?" he shouts across the room. "Clean, ain't she?"

"I have a watch," I say, hoping he won't ask to see my gold earrings and bracelet, too.

"Gimme the watch, ma'am," he says as he continues to shuffle papers.

"Why do I have to give you my watch? I *need* my watch. Aren't I going home now?"

"'Cause I says so!" he shouts. "The way you goin' you don't need no watch."

"Going *where*?" I hand my watch to him. He doesn't ask for the earrings or bracelet. I watch as he looks at my personal property, out in the open for anyone to see. A lipstick, hairbrush, car keys, wallet, checkbook, tampons, Tylenol, a shopping list and notes to myself. He opens my wallet and pulls out the credit cards. He logs them in a notebook. He asks me to certify that what is on his list includes everything in my purse.

"Why do you have to *do that*? I want my purse back. It's *mine*. What about my watch and my money?" I ask him sheepishly. I'm afraid that if I make any trouble -- well, who knows what could happen to me.

"Don't worry, y'all get it back."

"I want to add my watch and money to the list."

"No need, ma'am. You think we gonna be stealin' somethin' from y'all? This here's the *Po-lice* Department!" he says laughing.

I decide not to pursue it, hoping he's looking for something he didn't find and I can pack up and leave now.

"Can I have my stuff back now?" I ask.

"When you leave outta' here," he says as he shuffles more papers on his desk, "whenever that's gonna be. It'll be locked up 'til then."

"'Til when? I want to go." I whine.

"Yo' not going anywheres, sweetheart. Nowhere. We's bookin' you."

"*Booking* me? But I want to go *home!*"

My world is coming apart. Not the slow, stitch by stitch unwinding that occurs as a result of the stress of normal wear and tear, but more like an unmitigated full-out unraveling that is ripping me apart more powerfully with each tug. I hope no one sees how much I'm shaking.

The man just looks at me and chuckles. "Ma'am, don't you 'member bein' 'rested a couple o' hours back?" he asks. "I don't have the time to play games with y'all."

"Yes, I do, but I want to go home."

"That's what ever-body says when they walk through them doors. Now y'all gonna tell me you didn't do it, huh? Nevermind. Y'all gettin' booked. And I'm gonna start here by askin' y'all some questions, miss."

I've lost the ability to think clearly. Actually I can't think at all. He asks me all kinds of questions and compares my answers to what he has on a piece of paper in front of him. "Okay, now you go ova' there and get yo' pitcher taken, hear?" When I don't move, he adds louder, "Right over there, see?" he says, pointing angrily to his right.

"Over here, missy," another man's voice calls. "We's gonna take you a mug shot here, young lady." He points to where I should stand. He gives me a yellow sign with a number on it. I hold it across my chest. "Don't move," he says. "Turn to the side, lady. Okay. Now turn to the other side."

He directs me to a woman, a uniformed officer. She's wearing orange rubber gloves and carrying on in some kind of banter I don't understand with two other officers. "Lady," she calls out, "come on." I look around for the source of the voice, and she says shrilly, "Pay you some 'tention, lady, you ain't the only criminal we got in here!"

That's not how people talk to me in my world. *But I'm not in my world anymore. Maybe I was drugged and transported to another planet? It's possible, isn't it? Nothing in this place is familiar.*

She takes me by the arm, grabs my index finger, presses it to an ink pad, glares at me with eyes of fire, and I'm fingerprinted. She hands me a paper towel to wipe my hand. "Go sit back on dat bench," a voice without a face says. "Somebody'll come get y'all."

Ma'am, do y'all have a lawyer?" says an individual who shuffles towards me from across the room. "You need to call your lawyer, if y'all have one."

"A *lawyer*? "For what? Why do I need a lawyer?" I say incredulously. "I don't have a lawyer."

I scour my brain. *I don't know any lawyers. My divorce lawyer? No way. I wouldn't want her to know I'd been arrested. I must know someone I can call?* Somewhere in the back of my mind is a tickle. The vaguest feeling that I know a lawyer; I just can't think of who it is. The thoughts running through my head are a bewildering jumble fed by anxiety, fear and helplessness.

"Then one'll be appointed by the court," he says sternly. "Now, get up and follow that man there, the one with the keys."

The man with the keys scrutinizes me and then leads me down a long hallway. A gaggle of heavy iron keys hangs on a long leather strap from his belt and sways from side to side as he walks. They clatter and clang against his thigh as he moves. Another officer follows behind him. *They've probably looked at the evidence and found they have nothing against me. I'm simply being escorted out the back door to freedom.*

The hallway is damp and dreary. A single naked light bulb barely illuminates the gloomy scene. The gray cinderblock walls are mottled with mold. The shrill metallic sound of jail cell doors clamping shut and people talking becomes louder.

Someone is crying; another yelling. We round another corner and walk directly into a windowless room lined with jail cells on both sides.

The man with the keys grasps one of the keys without even looking at it. He must have done this same thing thousands of times in order to be able to choose just the right key without looking. He holds it up to a dim florescent fixture hanging from the ceiling. He mutters something to himself and, convinced he has found the right key, opens the door of a cell and ushers me in.

"There you go, missy," he says gesturing towards the inside.

I can't move. "*In there?*" I'm pointing to the inside of the cell. "*In the cell?*"

"Ma'm, *what* did I say?"

I take a few hesitant steps inside and turn around. The heavy iron door, swinging on a dozen leaden hinges, thunders shut. It's the kind of racket that makes the floor vibrate under my feet. Like a herd of elephants, maybe? I've never heard any sound quite like it.

Chapter 15

What Yo' White Ass Doin' In Here?

The cell is small, maybe ten feet by ten feet. Fine for one person, even smaller for more. Two women are already in the cell. The bars on the front of the cell are black iron, flecked with brownish patches and shiny where they've probably been touched by thousands of grubby, greasy hands. I think of the many disreputables who may have fondled those bars, even grabbed onto them for dear life — and all the places those hands have been before — and it makes me queasy.

The walls are constructed of concrete blocks painted a medium gray. Dingy and grimy, the walls don't invite a stranger to stand next to them. I imagine having to touch a wall to steady myself. It would probably feel rough and gritty and dirty enough to stain my fingers.

The floor is cement, ice cold and unforgiving. That too, is splotchy with what looks like an oily residue, years of grime and God only knows what else. There's a dirty toilet sitting in a corner. Just a seat, no lid, no toilet paper and no privacy. There's no marble wash basin, delicately perfumed bar of soap or embroidered linen hand towels.

I don't expect to be here long. I'm sure they'll soon discover their error and I'll be on my way. I have to pee so bad it's going to squirt out of my ears. But I won't perch on that toilet, no matter what.

Other than the floor, there's no place to sit down. Nothing would get me to sit on that floor. Not in my beautiful wool coat and new skirt. The cell smells rotten; a combination of urine, body odor, bad breath and mold.

The ceiling, painted a blinding white, is wrinkled with long, zig-zag cracks. Big chunks of plaster hang loosely, just waiting to fall on me. Brown rings surround several of the deepest cracks, and from one of them, a slow drip of some brownish liquid emerges. I can only imagine where that fluid is coming from.

The only light in the cellblock comes from a single florescent fixture attached to the ceiling about twenty-five feet down the hall. If I had to read anything, it would be near impossible.

I feel tainted and unclean, not so much by anything I've done to get myself in this place, but simply by virtue of being here in this cell at this moment. A jailbird.

"What yo' white ass doin' in *here*, girl?" I turn around sharply to face the voice. One of my cellmates, a young black woman, is sitting on the floor, her back to the wall. "You some fancy *white* lady, huh?"

"Leave her 'lone, Bernice. She one scared lookin' bitch. And she rich, Ah *do* declare. A white, rich bitch." Rayetta's slapping her knees and laughing. "What you done to get yo' self in here, hon?"

"Shut yo' face, Rayetta! You better stop tellin' me what to do, hear?"

"You lookin' like you on yo' way to some party, all gussied up in them *fine* clothes. How 'bout you givin' me yo' coat. What d'ya say? It's cold in dis place." She, on the other hand, is dressed skimpily and covered by a minimum of fabric. I never saw a hooker in person, and wonder if Bernice might *be* one.

Rayetta, who is older, is standing in the corner. Her

clothing is shabby and she's slurring her words. Her eyes are so glazed over you can see your reflection in them. "Shut yo' mouth, Bernice, and I ain't tellin' you no mo'." She may be drunk or high. Or both.

I'm transfixed with fright and can't speak to either of them.

"So, whadja doin' that's gettin' you in this place, high lady?" continues Rayetta. "You some rich white lady. You prolly be sellin' yo' body fo' some pocket change, huh? Don't you got no *law*-yur could be springin' yo' white ass outta here? You best be gettin' you someone or you be in here a long time like we is waitin' on that free law-yur. We not goin' nowheres 'til dat judge gets ready to hear us. Some baby law-yur be tellin' us to 'fess up. Then we s'posed to get out. We didn't do nothing 'cept try supportin' ourselves, you hear? You high-fallutin' so you got some cold cash. Dat's the only thing git you home, girl. Green dollars. You don't be callin' yo' law-yur, you be staying in this place fo' a long while, girlie."

Rayetta's soliloquy is over. I don't think she expects a response and I don't have one to give. Bernice is sprawled out on the floor asleep. She groans, mumbles something unintelligible and rolls over.

She scares me. They both scare me. I move to the opposite corner of the cell.

Rayetta's mumbling to herself and pacing around the cell. Bernice gets up off the floor and starts pacing after Rayetta. She's heavily made up and dressed much more scantily than I originally thought. Now both of them are talking at once. I presume they're both mentally ill or addicts. Or I-don't-know-what. Bernice is very dramatic and her voice is loud. She continues to talk to me. I don't want to talk to her. She doesn't seem to notice.

I'm trying to sort this out. I'm in jail. How am I going to get out of here? What's going to happen next? How long will I be here? My mind is itching with the sensation that there is something I should do or someone I should call who will help extricate me from this awful situation, but I don't know what or who it is. My head is spinning.

And then it hits me. I become saturated with the sticky awareness that I know someone who's an attorney. Why didn't I think of that before? Should I call him? Would he help me? No, I can't do it. I wouldn't want him to know. He might say "No" or remind me of my faults or what a terrible person I am. Or tell people my sorry story. Then what will I do? I'm scared and ashamed. Maybe he would know someone who could make all this go away. Or maybe, just maybe, he hasn't given up on me and would help. Or he might decide he hates me so much after what I've done that he'd just hang up on me screaming, "Loser, loser!"

I think I'm sober now. What I need most is a glass of wine. Maybe it would help calm me down so I could figure out what to do. I'm still not sure what I need a lawyer for.

I look up and down the cellblock for the man with the gaggle of keys who I presume is a guard. Eventually, he shuffles by. "Excuse me," I say, "could I make a phone call to my attorney?"

"Haven't y'all made that call yet? You been here already a couple a hours."

"I haven't called anyone. Can I call now?"

"Lemme check."

He takes his time, dragging himself down the hall. No hurry. Not when you're on the right side of the law. He has no idea how humiliating it is to be here. Or doesn't care. Or is enjoying the drama of making me wait. I understand why prisoners kill themselves. The unknown is an agonizing reality.

"Honey, you a lucky *wo*-man that you gots someone to call." Rayetta and Bernice are both standing now and right in my face. "I be sittin' here on dis dirty floor waitin' on dat court lawyer to come on in here and get me outta here. Day after day and no one's a-comin'. I gonna just rot in dis cell, I do declare!" She shakes her head in frustration and starts yelling, "Guard,

guard, you seen dat court lawyer yet?"

Another fifteen or twenty minutes pass and the guard makes his way back down the hallway. Still dragging his feet like he's slogging through wet cement. No rush, of course.

"Ma'm, you got the number?" he says. "I'm openin' this door for y'all to make one phone call. Make it quick now, no long conversating. You hear? *One* call!"

"Yes, thank you." I'm so angry I could cry, but I promise myself I won't shed any more tears in this place.

He unlocks the door and I'm free. I feel like I can breathe again. He seals the door behind me, ignoring Bernice's pleas for help, and escorts me down the hall. He points to a black corded phone sitting on a desk. "Make yo' call now. One call, one minute. That's *it.*"

I dial the number, hoping the attorney is home and will pick up the phone. It must be one or two in the morning, He has to be there. I hope he doesn't sleep through the ringing.

He picks up the phone almost immediately and sounds wide awake. "Can you pick me up?" I ask. "I don't have a car."

"What?" he says surprised. "Where are you? What happened?"

"At the DC jail. I got arrested. I can't talk now. Can you come?"

"Of course. I'll leave in a few minutes." I don't want him to tell anyone else where I am. In jail. A criminal.

"Hurry, please," I beg. I don't tell him how much I want to get out of here. What must he think of me?

"What did you do that got you arrested?" he says. "Never mind. You can tell me later. I'll be there. Should be about an hour or so."

I hang up, relieved that maybe now there is a way out of this mess. The guard escorts me back to my cell, still dragging his feet.

Bernice and Rayetta are still there. Both awake, they're sitting on the floor. Rayetta's legs are crossed under her and her eyes are half-shut. If this weren't a jail cell I'd swear she was in yoga class.

Bernice, the more vocal of the two is right on me as soon as the heavy iron door slams shut. "Did you call yo' law-yur? Is he comin'? A lady like you has no biniss in a place like dis. You think yo' law-yur might be helpin' me get outta here, too?"

Another hour, or maybe more, passes. I don't have a watch. I just stand in a corner of the cell and wait, knowing I'll be free soon. My cellmates get tired of asking me questions and waiting for answers I don't provide. They fall asleep on the floor.

He picks me up. He tells me he's read the police report. He doesn't ask me what I did or want an explanation. He doesn't tell me I'm a criminal, a loser or that now I have a "record." We eat breakfast at a diner at four in the morning. He informs me he'll take care of everything. I'm very grateful. How pathetic I must appear. He takes me back to the shopping mall to pick up my car and I drive home.

I don't hear anything more from him or the court and I don't ask. Several weeks pass and he calls me. "The charges have been dropped. Dismissed. Your arrest record will be expunged," he says matter-of-factly. I don't know what's been done, who's done it, or how it happened. I don't ask. I don't want to know. We never speak of it again.

I breathe a sigh of relief. I promise myself I'll never again do anything that would ever bring me to a jail again. Not ever.

Chapter 16

Time To Choose

I'm standing on the front porch of my home, my purse slung over one shoulder, my briefcase on the other arm. I fumble with my key ring until I find the right key, slide it into the lock and open the front door. I breathe a sigh of freedom. It's almost six o'clock and the day has been a long one.

It could have been any day of the week, in any year, at any season. I walk through the door directly into the kitchen, not spending the time to take off my coat or deposit what I'm toting in the foyer. I open the liquor cabinet, grab the wine bottle, pour myself a glass and let it ease gently down my throat. *Relief. How I need it. I've been waiting all day for this moment.* It's the first thing I do when I walk in the house, any day, every day. "I'll be okay after I have some wine," I say. And then some more . . . .

In 1984, I met my second husband, Larry. I'd been separated for almost five years by that time. A divorce was in the works. I wasn't sure that I wanted a divorce, but I didn't know what to do to fix the marriage. Perhaps it wasn't so much that the marriage was the problem as it was that *I* was the problem.

I initially believed that if I were living alone, I would feel better, but soon found that a separation didn't solve anything. I wasn't any happier by myself than I was with him. In fact, I started to drink even more. I never realized until much later how difficult everyday living had become. I took every opportunity to act out my overwhelming dissatisfaction with life. It was *I* who needed to heal, not the marriage.

I assumed no responsibility for the failure of the marriage. Why should I? I believed it was *his* fault. After all, *I* was the one who was unhappy so he *had* to be the problem.

Five years later, I still hadn't moved forward nor learned anything from the split. I didn't even realize that a person *should* learn anything from a failed marriage. I was stuck in a bad place without the insight necessary to help myself. My drinking increased dramatically, as well, blunting any hope of coming to terms with the separation or myself.

Larry and I met at the home of a mutual friend. It wasn't a set up. "He's not for you," the hostess said to me the day before.

"She's not for you," the host also cautioned Larry.

It wasn't love at first sight, but there was surely electricity and interest. He was handsome, articulate and funny. He read the newspaper from cover to cover and could discuss world politics with the likes of Kissinger. He had an astonishing sixth sense about people; it took him only a minute or two to determine whether a person was decent and caring. He had a thick middle eastern accent, an uproarious sense of humor, a deep-voiced chuckle, and a twinkle in his eye. It was that twinkle that got me at "Hello."

Fourteen years my senior, Larry was a Holocaust survivor. He was a passionate man who saw life as something to be lived as intensely as possible. Extraordinary in many ways, he was an individual of extremes. He was either *very* happy or *very* sad; he knew no middle ground. His life was an unending search to find perfect love, but the only creature with which he ever found love that pure was with his beloved dog.

A self-made man with little formal schooling, he was born in Poland before WWII and miraculously survived the Holocaust. He worked his way up to general manager of a paint company that exported its products around the world. His colleagues and clients knew him as a Chemical Engineer. But he was nothing of the sort. A bogus Ph.D. diploma hung on the wall in his office. He taught himself everything he needed to know throughout his long, successful career.

Our relationship was loving and happy most of the time, tumultuous at others, the see-saw result of our individual demons going head-to-head. We were fiercely in love for years before we married, and it was that love that kept us together even when my alcoholism and depression and, later, his psychosis and Alzheimer's Disease, weakened the bonds between us. Eventually, I began to heal, but Alzheimer's took away Larry's capacity to protect himself from the horrors of yesterday. The two of us were a hotbed of unresolved losses.

Larry had no basis on which to relate to my life, an overindulged Jewish princess from a financially comfortable (but crazy) lineage. The therapist in me wanted to sink my teeth into his troubled past, but in those days talking about the war years wasn't comfortable for him. Later on, his story emerged like a waterfall that wouldn't stop.

I'd never met anyone like him. I was drawn to him in ways that initially were hard to explain. He ignited something in me that I had never experienced, an excitement, a passion to experience life. Over four years after his death, I still feel his dynamic presence all around me.

"Every day it's the same thing," Larry said as we stood across from each other in my kitchen. I had just walked in the house from work. I was still wearing my coat, my purse hanging from my arm. He had left his office and was waiting for me when I returned from work.

"The first thing you do when you walk in the house, whether you're in mine or yours, is pour yourself a drink. And then another one. And then the fireworks start."

"What are you talking about? There's nothing wrong with having a glass of wine after work. It relaxes me. I'm stressed when I come home. I have to deal with people all day, for God's sake!"

"As soon as you start drinking, you get mean and nasty. And then you start picking away at something about me. And then we argue. *That's* why. Alcohol does bad things to you, Sonya, and it's damaging our relationship."

"No, it's not. *You're* damaging our relationship. You're always making some demand on me. You just can't leave me alone. 'Sonya, I need this from you, Sonya, I need that.' I get sick of it. Can't you just back off and stop needing me every once in a while?"

"It's not me, Sonya. It's your *drinking*. You're an angry drunk. Alcohol changes your personality and it's getting worse, much worse. We've talked about this before. When are you going to look at yourself in the mirror? It's time to stop drinking!"

"Are you telling me I have a problem with alcohol?"

"No. You don't have *just* a problem, you're an *alcoholic*!"

"Fuck you. I'm *not* an alcoholic! You can tell me that all you want. *You* are the problem. You're what makes me miserable and angry. Alcohol isn't *my* problem. It's *yours.*"

"Sonya, the same thing happens *every* day. You drink and then you yell at me or your daughter and you don't stop yelling until you've got it all out of your system, and then it starts all over again the next day. You're a bottomless pit of rage. For god's sake, think about it! I don't like you very much when you're drinking."

"There's nothing wrong with me. Do you hear me? Nothing! If you don't like it, you can always leave. In fact, get out! Get out of my house now!"

"When you and I got engaged, you promised me you would cut down on the alcohol. You haven't. You're drinking even more! The way I see it, you have to choose now because your drinking is getting in the way of our happiness. It's either me or the alcohol!

I turned my back to him, and poured myself another glass of wine. *He's giving me an ultimatum. How dare he!* In the time it took me to put the glass to my lips and roll the sweet liquid around my mouth, I had made my decision.

"The alcohol." I said confidently. I had made my choice. "My drinking isn't a problem; *you* are. Get out of my life." I had made my choice.

Larry stood still for a moment and stared at me. He probably thought his intervention would do the trick; now he was processing what I'd just said. "You'd rather have alcohol in your life than me?" When I didn't respond, he walked toward the front door and out of my life.

I was free.

During the months we were apart, I totaled my car twice. I didn't see the connection between impaired judgment and alcohol abuse. In fact, I didn't yet see the connection to *many* negative events in my life and alcohol. It wasn't until months later, when I had finally stopped drinking and began to look more closely at myself and how I'd been living my life, that I was ready to talk with Larry about salvaging our damaged relationship.

Chapter 17

Time To Tell The Truth

Most of my guests depart. I close the front door of my home with the satisfaction that my first Thanksgiving Dinner was perfect in every way. Everything was flawless — the food, the wine, the company and the setting — no one could have done it better than I. It was truly memorable and I felt like a queen.

My eyes race from room to room. I'm horrified by the untidy state of the house. The kitchen, in particular, is in stunning disarray. Simply looking at it exhausts me. The floor is sticky, and the sink is stacked yay high with dishes. Every bit of countertop is covered with plates, bowls, silverware, pots and pans. My elegant dining room is in shambles; the ivory lace tablecloth is mottled with all manner of vividly colored food and drink.

I need to clean it up but I don't have the energy to face it all now. It'll have to wait until morning. I'm worn out and my thinking is fuzzier than ever.

I didn't eat much during dinner, but everyone said it was delicious. I was so nervous; this was the first turkey I've ever prepared. I'm sure I drank more than the usual amount of wine. But, what the heck, it was a special occasion, wasn't it? I was celebrating. I'm still sipping an outstanding burgundy.

I wrap up the leftovers and cram them into the over-stuffed refrigerator. That's all I can manage right now. My new boyfriend stands by waiting to assist me in any way he can. He's a welcome relief from Larry. He doesn't give me any ultimatums and he's much more laid back. Even so, I still miss Larry something terrible.

New boyfriend is clearing the dishes from the dining room and putting them wherever he can find space in the kitchen. It all seems overwhelming. I'm not sure I can face it tomorrow.

"Do you want to stay?" I ask him. I don't know why I invite him. My heart isn't in it and I'd rather be alone. I feel sweaty and unsociable. And I don't feel like talking. I'm numb with fatigue.

"No thanks," he says politely. "I need to get up early and I wouldn't want to disturb you. I have an appointment at eight-thirty tomorrow morning."

Momentarily, I experience some disappointment. There's a part of me that wants him to *want* to stay, even though I need to be by myself.

"Thank you for inviting me for Thanksgiving. The meal was excellent," he adds. "I'll catch up with you sometime next week," he continues. "Maybe we can get together. I'm going to be pretty busy for the rest of this week." He's walking to the door, obviously anxious to leave.

"Is anything wrong?" I ask, finishing my glass of wine and reaching for an open bottle to pour another. I have a feeling there's something on his mind.

"Well, Sonya, I guess there's an issue I'd like to talk to you about," he admits. "But we're both tired now, so let's get together next week and talk."

"Next week? What is it you want to talk about? You can't just walk out of here trailing crumbs without telling me what it is." I'm irritated now and slurring my words.

"Look, Sonya, well, it's your drinking. It's out of

control. We've gone over this before. Let's talk later. I think we both need a good night's sleep."

"My drinking is *your* issue, not mine. I don't think I have a problem with alcohol. I like wine. I enjoy the taste of it. It makes good food better. And I don't want to talk about it again. We've been down this road before and I'm too tired. Get off my back!" Hesitating, I add, "Okay, okay, okay. Maybe I should drink less. Now, will you stop bugging me about it?"

"You should *stop* drinking completely. Period. Not just drink less! But if you don't want to talk about it anymore, we won't," he says reluctantly.

He kisses me goodbye on the cheek and leaves. I lock the door behind him, turn off the lights, and climb the stairs to my bedroom.

I can hardly muster the energy to take off my clothes and wash my face. I ache with a familiar weariness. Every muscle in my body hurts. I worked so hard to make Thanksgiving perfect. I feel a letdown, almost a despondency. The weeks of planning, preparing and anticipation are over. The thought of waking up in the morning and facing the mess depresses me.

I imagine all the beautiful things my guests are saying right now. And tomorrow they'll call others and tell them about the magnificent Thanksgiving they attended.

As I fall into bed, I believe I can hear the sound of my brain sloshing against the sides of my skull.

♚

I sleep fitfully, tossing and turning to find a comfortable position. No sooner do I doze off than I wake up with a start. My body feels rigid and stiff. I try to stretch it out to no avail. I'm wrapped as tight as a jack-in-the-box.

I rarely sleep well and tonight is worse than most. I awaken frequently through the night, and then have difficulty falling asleep again. I'm often teetering on the very edge of deep sleep, but I never quite achieve it. I wake up in the morning as exhausted as when I go to bed at night. Some nights I lie and stare at the ceiling for hours; as tired as I may be, I can't close my eyes. 'Round and 'round, one thought after another fills my mind with anxiety and a never-ending uneasiness. It's almost like I'm riding the fastest horse on the carousel. I reach for the brass ring, but I can never quite grasp it.

Frightening dreams often populate the hours when I'm able to achieve sleep. I dream of creatures without faces. I'm with my younger daughter in a strange land. As the hideous beasts approach us, the brutes roar and growl menacingly. They open their slobbering mouths as if they are intending to devour us whole. They do bad things to me and worse to my daughter.

Looking into their ferocious maws, I punch and kick them, struggling to escape. Sometimes I do. Other times, I'm swallowed whole and find myself screaming hysterically for the child I've left behind.

In one particularly terrifying nightmare, one of the vicious creatures grabs my daughter in its jaws. As hard as I try, I'm unable to wrestle her away. The beast is stronger than I and carries the child away. She cries out pitifully for me to follow and save her, but I'm unable to rescue her. She disappears, but I can hear her screams for help. I run after the savage monster, wailing in pain, tears streaming down my face. I awaken in the middle of the night sobbing for the child I've lost. My waking hours are haunted for days afterward.

In the early morning hours of the day after Thanksgiving, the alarm clock rings at its preset time. I always have the best intentions when it comes to waking up. The idea of greeting the day by springing out of bed with a smile and a sunny mood, and then spending the morning in productive tasks is a goal I can never achieve.

This morning, however, I wake up with more lethargy than usual, gloomier than ever. I feel sick. My head is pounding;

the light hurts my eyes. My stomach is upset.

I rest quietly staring at the ceiling. I don't think I've ever felt so terrible. *My mood is awful and I don't know why. What's causing this — I don't know — despair? Why do I feel on the verge of panic?*

I close my eyes, trying to remember what day today is. Then it hits me. It's the day after Thanksgiving. *Wasn't it a huge success? I feel like a queen!* With that thought, I recall the state of the downstairs but I don't think that's what's causing my misery. An hour or so, and it'll all be cleaned up. I close my eyes again. A feeling of impending doom weasels around in the convoluted channels of my brain.

I'm agitated and distressed, troubled by something I can't identify. I try to relax my body. I stretch my arms and legs, but I'm tied up in knots. I need to get up and take something for this terrible headache. My mouth is gluey and my teeth feel like they're covered in slime. The contents of my stomach fly around and I'm becoming nauseous.

I turn on my side and breathe through my nose to calm down. I pull the covers tightly around myself all the way up to my neck. I don't know what's bothering me. Several minutes pass as I lie quietly. Something obscure and indiscernible is eating away at me. It feels like a million tiny fruit flies are swarming around chaotically in my head. I try to concentrate, but whatever I'm unintentionally brooding over prickles me even more. Like scratching an itch that only itches more.

An icy cold finger traces a line down the middle of my back. The frozen digit moves up and down my spine, the pressure intensifying, becoming colder and more annoying with every pass. I try to move away, but I can't. I have trouble breathing. My guts feel like I've been hit by an iceberg. I can't stop shivering.

I begin to recall the events from Thanksgiving. Like a porcupine wandering around inside my head, the more I remember, the harder it slaps its spiny tail against the inside of my skull, barbed quills jolting me into awareness. The pain is unbearable.

I ache with memories. It's not a physical sensation, but more like an emotional revulsion and loathing of who I've become. I'm flooded with mental images of my drunkenness. On Thanksgiving, no less! I can no longer contain the disgust I feel for my boozed up life.

The dam has burst wide open. For the first time, I see things clearly and I'm horrified. Flooded with images of my life as an addict, I want to puke. What I remember about my conduct on Thanksgiving smacks of the deepest shame, embarrassment and contempt of who I am.

Disgust cascades over me. I can't deny the problem anymore or insist nobody is paying any attention to it. Or blame it on someone else. People are *not* overlooking it. They know. They *must* know. My therapist has talked about it. I have to face the facts of my alcoholism! I roll over hoping I'm dreaming and when I wake up I will have lost any memories of Thanksgiving.

It doesn't work. I'm wide awake. Almost like I've been plugged in to an outlet after years of living in the dark. Perhaps for the first time in decades. This must be how it feels to be told of the sudden death of a much-loved spouse. The horror, inability to believe, paralysis. I'm not afraid of what others think of me; I fear more what *I* think of me. I hate myself and the life I've led. *It's time to tell the truth. To myself.*

I've used alcohol to escape; I've used alcohol to enjoy myself more; and I've used alcohol to relieve my anxiety and depression. I've used alcohol to cope; I've used alcohol to dissolve my rage; and I've used alcohol to disappear and become somebody I'm not. Alcohol has impaired my ability to function in all areas of my life. Alcohol has affected my relationships. Destroyed some. Alcohol has impacted my ability to make decisions and considered choices for myself and my family. Oh, I've made choices, all right, but often the kind that hurt me and my loved ones.

I was a child when I began drinking. Not yet a

teenager. I lovingly nurtured my relationship with alcohol over decades. More than I've nurtured anything else in my life. By the time I was in my early teens, alcohol and I were inseparable. I'm a full-blown alcoholic and I've been a drunken mess for decades. I see it so clearly now. I must stop. I have to stop. My life depends on it. In fact, there will be no life for me unless I do.

Lying in my bed on the morning after Thanksgiving, I become more sickened with every passing minute. *How could I act this way? Why did it take so long for me to see that the walls of my life were tumbling down?*

I make a promise to myself. "I will never, ever bring a single drop of alcohol to my lips at any time or for any reason for the rest of my life." Such a proclamation scares me, but I'm determined to stand by my words. I'm tired of feeling stuck. I'm tired of feeling bad about myself. I need to make a better life for myself.

I'm done with alcohol forever. So help me God.

That very promise changed the course of every day of my life going forward. I was finally telling the truth.

At that precise moment, I thought I had the disease licked. The decades of drinking were over. What I didn't realize was that not drinking alcohol was only a small part of being sober. That's right. *Not* drinking was the easy part.

It was the rest that was so hard.

Chapter 18

Sober With A Capital "S"

Sober was going to be easy. Just don't drink. Stop. What could possibly be hard about that?

I opened the wine bottles and poured them all down the drain. Even the precious, nut-brown Johnny Walker. The cooking sherry and vanilla, too. I couldn't have any of it in the house.

"Done," I said, as I uttered a soundless promise to myself and wiped my hands clean of alcohol for all time. I was finished drinking. Forever. I told myself that I would never hold a glass of any liquid to my lips that was more toxic than water. I imagined that my battle with alcohol was finally over. I figured I would still want to drink for a while, at least, but the urge would go away. Just like when I stopped smoking. The struggle was over. It was much easier than I thought. Why did it take me so long?

Whoa, horsey, not so fast.

But it wasn't easy at all. In fact, the result of squeezing my life dry of alcohol turned my world upside down. I had mistakenly assumed that if I weren't drinking, I was sober. Cured. End of problem. Well -- I found it didn't work quite that way.

When I gave up cigarettes, I chewed gum, ate carrot sticks and sucked on hard candies. Not a perfect solution, but it worked. Eventually the physical urge to smoke disappeared.

Besides the obvious negative impact on my lungs and general health, the acrid aroma of cigarette smoke that hung on my body, in my hair and my clothing, and the emotional craving for the butts that would alleviate my anxiety, smoking didn't affect my behavior or change my personality.

Alcohol, just like cigarettes, impaired my health. I drank instead of ate. But unlike cigarettes, alcohol impaired my sleep, my immune system, how my brain functioned, my liver and likely a whole host of other organs. I was beset by nightmares and woke every morning with a hangover. You could smell alcohol on my breath and my body. After a bout of heavy drinking, it seeped through my pores for as long as three days after. And it impaired my ability to think and function for up to week after heavy drinking. Because I never took a break from alcohol longer than a day or two, my functional *and* emotional status was always compromised.

Swearing off alcohol was entirely different than nicotine withdrawal. Alcohol caused me to act out in any manner of inappropriate, angry, obnoxious or abusive ways that smoking did not.

Once I was living an alcohol-free life, it was difficult to be around people who were drinking. I hankered for the taste and effects of wine. That meant avoiding restaurants, bars, parties and all places where I had formerly associated alcohol with fun, socializing and relaxation. And avoiding people who drank too much. Living an alcohol-free life changed everything.

Without alcohol, I was lost. I was determined to honor the promise I made to myself; I just wasn't sure how to do it. How would I eat a meal without wine? How would I sleep without a drink? How would I socialize without alcohol? How would I have fun without alcohol? How would I calm down and relax? What would I hide behind if it weren't a liquor bottle?

What would I use as an excuse for my behavior? Even more important, what would I do when I couldn't cope? Little did I know that after my vow to stop drinking, the hardest work was just beginning.

The features of my addiction to alcohol that made it wildly different from an addiction to cigarettes is that I used alcohol as a medicine -- for everything. It worked quicker than pills and lasted longer. And as long as I kept drinking, I could stay sedated and out-of-touch for hours. Not something to be proud of. But how was I going to manage life without alcohol?

The most devastating characteristic about my alcoholism is the behaviors I developed related to alcohol abuse. They were deeply ingrained in my personality over decades of abuse. *Bad* behavior. Angry and mean-spirited. Out-of-control behavior. Inappropriate and boundaryless, without thought or consideration of the consequences. Those responses didn't just magically disappear when I stopped drinking. They were many times harder to eliminate than the urge to drink. That was the hard part of giving up alcohol. No, the *hardest*.

I had to learn to think and *then* act, not the other way around. When I was drinking, risk-taking behaviors like driving under the influence happened all the time. I was unable (or chose not) to weigh the risks of using alcohol against the benefits of being sober.

I had a lack of respect for laws, people, relationships and the standards of social appropriateness. I was plagued by impulsivity and impaired judgment; poor motivation and decision-making; and lack of emotional control and a low stress tolerance. I picked fights just to be heard, prove my point and let off some steam. I held on to fury long after it was time to let it go. I was a walking pressure cooker.

Stopped once for driving the wrong way on a one-way street, the police officer wanted to give me a sobriety test right there on the road. I became enraged and kicked him between the legs. Because my passenger was an attorney, he was able to talk the officer down and he didn't arrest me.

Lucky, you say? No, not at all. I was a danger to myself, my passengers and anyone on or near the road. I should have been arrested and locked up in rehab until I was sober for life.

Sobriety wasn't only about not drinking; *true* (and permanent) sobriety was more about facing and fessing up to the wreck my life had become, and the paucity of insight that alcohol exacerbated. What did I know or care about how I appeared to others or what they thought of me? Did I even think about what I thought of *myself*?

Initially, I believed that sobriety was only about not drinking. It wasn't long before I understood that alcoholism is a symptom of much deeper and more complex problems that must be resolved in order to live alcohol-free forever.

To an alcoholic, *their* bad behavior is always a result of someone else doing something to cause them to react. There's always a reason why they behave the way they do and it's never about *them.* If something goes awry in the life of the alcoholic, it's never *they* who must acknowledge and assume responsibility. It is always "the other guy," the one who did me wrong or *made* me do it. You. It's *you* who made me miserable, unhappy and angry, and you who made me drink. I drink because of you. In fact, *all* of my unhappiness is your fault.

If you would fix yourself, I would be fine.

All part of the lies the alcoholic tells herself and others. One lie on top of another and another. One of the hallmarks of the alcoholic. All designed to cover up the fact that the alcoholic herself is diseased.

Shifting blame and responsibility to the other guy is another feature of alcoholism. The alcoholic may not even recognize their behavior is inappropriate or irresponsible. They live in another reality -- the alcoholic one -- that protects them from the truths that are the source of the drinking.

And then it goes, until the alcoholic finally reaches the stone cold underbelly of their addiction. If they're fortunate enough to do so. Their life is in total disarray, they've alienated countless people and feel like the world is against them and they're fighting on their own.

When the alcoholic hits bottom (some do, many don't), they may come face to face, sometimes for the first time, with the havoc their abuse of alcohol has created. And then, with the force of a tsunami, the inescapable fact of the damage their drinking has done to themselves, their livelihood and the people around them blows up before their eyes.

Missed opportunities, lost opportunities, dead friendships and severed relationships. If nothing else, that smack on the hard granite surface of reality is a wake-up call like no other. Some hear it painfully loud and clear and take it for a message. Others may not, choosing instead to hide behind yet another liquor bottle.

So much for the easy fix. Simply not drinking wasn't enough to solve all my problems.

Drying out was challenging; I marked the days on a calendar. I knew quite a bit about alcoholism; after all, I was a mental health professional. But I didn't know squat about sobriety. Least of all, *true* sobriety. I believed all I needed to do was, you know, not drink. I was so wrong.

Almost everything in my life revolved around alcohol. The first thing I did when I came home from work, even before I took off my coat, was wrap my hand around a large goblet of red wine. And another. I began to eat lunch earlier and earlier, just so I could drink wine. Wine with dinner became wine well before dinner and long after dinner ended.

Abstinence was a small part of sobriety. What was even harder was eradicating the bad habits and behavior patterns I acquired as an alcoholic. Decades of them. Harder still was developing the healthy coping skills I *never* acquired because of drinking! I found that the real work of being sober was far below the waterline, or should I say, the volatile flammable liquid line.

I had so much to learn before I could consider myself a "recovered" alcoholic. The first step, of course, was not to drink. I never drank again, not once, but that doesn't mean I wasn't *desperate* for a drink. Managing day-to-day life without alcohol was tough. Not just *manage,* but manage *well,* get through the day without craving alcohol, without driving to the liquor store, going to a bar and without acting like a *dry drunk.* I heard this had to become a way of life. At first, I didn't know what that meant.

I began to understand that using alcohol to cope was easy, even though it never solved any of my problems. It demanded nothing of me beyond picking up a drink and holding it to my lips for the desired effect. Coping *without* alcohol meant solving complicated problems, dealing with difficult people and working through tricky situations. I was able to counsel my clients, but applying those lessons to myself was damned difficult. Using them consistently even harder.

In the first few years of abstinence, I stumbled and fell many times. I wasn't tripped up by *drinking* alcohol, but by old alcoholic-embedded behavior patterns which persisted long after I stopped boozing. I struggled even more than I did when I was drinking, simply *because* I didn't drink.

Most people drink to become "more" of something: more relaxed, more sociable, or more fun. I drank to become "less," less present mainly. Less responsible and less involved, too. I simply wanted to disappear, to become invisible and untouchable. To become oblivious to whatever problems or demands were waiting for me.

But that isn't what happened. After years of getting tanked, alcohol did bad things to me. Ugly things. I became mean, obnoxious and cruel. I picked fights when I was drinking, and couldn't end those I started. I was impossible to live with. The more I drank, the more I regurgitated all the pain, resentment and anger from decades past; it bubbled up in my throat and exited my mouth in a blazing fury. There wasn't anything invisible about me or my behavior. Just the opposite.

♛

Exploring my own family history has opened up my eyes to the connection between substance abuse and mental illness. There is much written in the literature about this, which answers the question of why substances are often referred to as "medicines" for those who use them. Such was the case in my situation. When I gave up alcohol, I was forced to come nose-to-nose with anxiety, depression and my lack of a strong sense of personal identity.

Both of my parents were addicts. My father drank to excess over a long period of time. My mother couldn't live without her prescription medications, regular visits to the psychiatric hospital and frequent outbursts of anger. Others back down the family tree have been addicted to money, power, anger, working, helplessness, attention, victimization and manipulation.

I used alcohol as a protective shield, a defense against looking inside, getting to know myself and becoming softer, gentler and more loving. As an addict, I held on fiercely to that shield because to let go of it would have made me vulnerable to hurt.

No matter what one is addicted to, the process of "sobering up" is the same. I've seen people "get sober," only to replace their addiction to alcohol with an addiction to something else, for example, hoarding or making money. These folks may consider themselves "in recovery" or cured, but not so. They have simply swapped out one addiction for another one.

Several years after I met my late husband, he gave me an ultimatum: "It's either me or the alcohol." I chose alcohol and we were done. At least for a while. At the time, I couldn't understand why my drinking bothered him so much. The characteristics about the drunken me he pointed out, I couldn't see. Until I *stopped* drinking. And then it became painfully clear.

At an Alcoholics Anonymous meeting, I heard the

expression, "If you're gonna talk the talk, you gotta walk the walk." Not just another foot-tapping phrase, it took some time for the real meaning of this statement to sink in.

"Okay, so you're not drinking anymore," I said to myself. "Fine. Wonderful. Terrific news. Then maybe it's time to stop acting like the self-centered, thoughtless and out-of-control drunk you were when you were drinking!"

Behaving in a way which was consistent with my words seemed to make sense to me, even though I'd never really considered what that meant. The way I applied this to me was this way: I needed to slow down and think things through before I acted. I had to be honest with myself and real with others. No more pretense. I was who I was from the roots of my colored hair to the bunions on my feet. Not only was this a novel experience, it was refreshing. And freeing. I began to drop the mask and simply be *me*.

Honest with myself. That was the hard part. Honest *about* myself. It meant owning up to my bad behavior as a result of alcoholism. And doing the right thing going forward. A friend said something to me I've never forgotten: "When you do the right thing, it's never wrong, even if it doesn't feel good. When you do the wrong thing, it's never right, even though it may feel good." When she said it, I had no idea what she was talking about. More complicated than it sounds, it meant "doing what was right for *me*." The thing that would preserve my dignity and self-respect. I found it took the guesswork out of decision-making.

To be real and live as honestly as possible is a huge part of my sobriety now. Discovering who I am and where I've come from, and deciding where I'm headed is the hardest thing I've ever done. I'm both strong and weak. Loving both parts of me can be demanding. When I look at myself in the mirror now, the face smiling back at me is the person I really am. Perfect? God, no. Do I still make mistakes? Of course. Am I good *enough*. Yes.

During those early years, my therapist said to me, "Sobriety is about progress, not perfection; sober with a small "s" is when you don't drink. We call those folks 'dry drunks.' They're the ones who switch out one addiction for another -- like the man who gave up drinking only to begin having affairs, or the woman who became a compulsive shopper, or the workaholic. Sober with a capital "S" is about being Sober to your core." Sober through and through.

♔

Few people actually believed I was an alcoholic; fewer still knew how serious the problem was. Some folks weren't prepared to deal with me as sober. They were used to the alcoholic me because she was more familiar to them.

Others said, "You're a therapist," so you can't be an alcoholic. Or, "You're middle-class, white and Jewish," so you can't have a drinking problem. Or, "I've never seen you drunk." Or, a few who implied I made up the alcoholism story for attention, and some who said, "One drink won't hurt you," and were insulted when I declined their repeated offers of alcohol. There are those who today, decades into sobriety, still offer me an alcoholic beverage. Somehow, the reality of my disease hasn't hit home for them.

People who don't drink, or people who don't drink to the point of inebriation, have frequently asked me what it feels like to be drunk, "Why couldn't you stop yourself, just put the cork in the bottle, put the bottle back in the cupboard and walk away?"

"Because," I explained, "alcoholism is a genuine medical illness. It's usually not a conscious choice, nor is it a moral, characterological or ethical lapse. There is a strong genetic component and alcohol is often used as a medicine. It involves the inability to control or stop the excessive consumption of alcoholic beverages once it starts."

"People who have never used alcohol or drink in moderation don't understand that the compulsive behavior resulting from alcohol dependency can't be moderated. Alcoholics *cannot* drink in moderation."

"An alcoholic's life is often centered around their drink

of choice. They spend much of their time figuring out how to obtain it, drink it and recover from its effects. They also do this at the expense of pretty much everything and everyone around them, including their work, family and relationships; alcoholics are often in trouble with the law, lie like crazy and are skilled at alienating people."

"Furthermore," I continued, "drinking is an anesthetic and it's easy. Open the cabinet, open the bottle, pour, drink, done. Numb. No feeling, no pain."

I felt very glamourous when I was drinking, sophisticated and grown up. Those slick, classy magazines portray the beautiful woman sitting in a ritzy bar and drinking for hours while chatting with friends as an ideal. Something to strive for. Now that was something I could never achieve. I went from sober to drunk in a few short minutes. By then, I would have been booted out of any high-class establishment.

After years of stuffing myself full of negative emotions, my insides were riddled with the toxic combination of alcohol and negativity. I thought alcohol made all the bad stuff go away, but no, it just tucked it away, deep down, further and further down, until such a time that it would explode from me like projectile vomiting. Then I'd go through the same process again. Open, pour, drink, done. I was dying.

No. I was killing myself.

From the moment I gave up alcohol, I never relapsed. I wanted to. Many times. *What the hell, who'll know?* I missed the taste of wine with food. I missed the buzz. I missed drinking on an airplane to quiet my anxiety, and celebrating on New Year's Eve, wallowing in sorrow when I was sad and celebrating when I was happy. I missed the Manischewitz at Passover and L'Chaim toasts with friends and family. I wanted to drink, but I didn't want to act like a drunk. I couldn't have it both ways. It wasn't possible.

I knew from the start that drinking was not something I could "manage". I was either dry or drunk. I never forgot how profoundly I'd been transformed by the hideous memories of my drinking. I "needed" alcohol and required it to function. Couldn't live without it. And the emotional need fueling the drinking might never go away. That, I found, was the thing to be "managed."

Early in my sobriety, I bought a tee-shirt, the front of which was embroidered in tiny, half-inch tall letters with the following words: Learn to Laugh. You had to get very close to me to read it. It wasn't emblazoned across my chest like a banner, but rather, just a whisper. As if to say, "I'm treading slowly and tenuously through this new world I've created and I'm not yet sure how it's going to turn out." I still wear that tee-shirt. Proudly.

Why am I sharing this unimportant detail? Because the subjects of this memoir are no laughing matter. Yet, in order to emerge on the other side of self-inflicted trauma, and that perpetuated by my family of origin, I've had to learn a number of essential things. The most significant of those was the ability to look honestly at myself and who I had become. However, the most healing tool I developed was laughter -- at situations that were painful or stupid, and most of all, myself.

Now, don't get me wrong, alcoholism, especially childhood alcoholism, isn't the least bit funny. But once I made the commitment to address lifelong issues and turn the course of my life around, I had to learn how to laugh at myself in order to survive. And, at the somewhat quirky, kookie gal I've become. I'm talking here about gaining perspective, reordering priorities and squarely facing who I was and how I behaved. In every facet of my life. If I weren't able to do that, the grief, pain, guilt and despair would have eaten me alive.

I still have moments even now when the regret of how I threw away years of my own life and hurt the lives of others slithers out of my heart and positions itself around my neck like a giant boa constrictor, threatening to squeeze the life from me.

Laughing at myself doesn't mean I don't take the years of ruin seriously, try to push them away or forget the consequences of my actions. Not at all. I take it all *very* seriously. But I still have to laugh. I laugh at my lack of judgment, at the poor decisions I made, at the things I said and didn't say, the things I did and didn't do, the situations I got myself into and the scant awareness I had of who I was and how I was living my life. Even at the length of time it took me to heal.

Those things aren't especially humorous except in a sad sort of way. Raw and unappealing. Similar to the way one would look at an unflattering caricature of oneself from long ago.

In the worst years of my alcoholism, at some level of my awareness, I'm sure I knew I had a problem. A serious one. But I blamed my troubles on *something* or *somebody* outside of, and other than, me. Like so many other addicts, I wanted so much to believe *I* wasn't the problem.

It wasn't until after I was in recovery for several years that I began to discover the person who I've become. Actually, I didn't pay much attention to that person when I was drinking. Nor did I bother to think about the state of the world around me or the people in it. Alcohol gave me the power to hide long after the toxic people in my world lost the power to affect me.

Today, I've made peace with my alcoholism. The guilt and regret for how my alcoholism affected me and the people in my life will follow me to my grave. The struggle to meet the needs that fed the alcoholism is still there, but it's no longer the fierce battle it once was. I know what I need to be at peace and what I must give to be happy. Nothing about my commitment to live a substance-free life has changed since that first morning of sobriety.

Sobriety has changed every aspect of my life. I had no idea how much debris was left in the wake of my alcoholism. I'm still shoveling out from under it decades later.

Of everything I've heard or read about alcoholism, there is nothing that sums up my years of drinking better than one of the characters in Noah Hawley's hauntingly beautiful book, *Before the Fall*:

> I burned it all down, drank myself
> into a stupor, pissed off everyone I knew. . . .
> Sometimes the only way to learn not to play
> with fire is to go up in flames.

Chapter 19

Rocking My Own Cradle

"I friggin' hit the jackpot when I got borned to you."

These exact words, spoken in good humor by my younger daughter when she was in her late thirties, made light of the turmoil she experienced as a child. It's likely that she may have wondered what her life would have been like if she had been born to a different mother. Or a better mother. Or a mother who wasn't an alcoholic. I often wonder the same thing about *myself.*

What might I have done differently with my life had I the benefit of a stable mother?

Long before I was an adult, I wanted a child of my own. When I became pregnant, I didn't realize how the act of giving birth would change my life or what the long-term implications of parenting might be. I simply figured that a child would fit easily into whatever life plan I might create for myself; I had no idea that it was *I* who must live *my* life around the needs and wants of a child.

The only thing I knew for sure about having children was that I needed someone to love me unconditionally. My husband loved me but it wasn't enough. That void could only be filled by a baby who would look at me throughout the day with adoring goo-goo eyes and say, "Mommy."

I never once considered the life-long responsibilities of parenting. Or whether I had what it took to be a *good* parent. Yet, I thought I knew everything about parenting -- diapering, sterilizing, bathing, feeding and buggy rides -- what more was there?

I was the oldest of four, my youngest sibling fifteen years my junior. There were many times when I felt more like his mother than his sister. And then I had my own child and discovered how much I *didn't* know about raising children. And how little time I spent thinking or learning about how to raise happy, well-adjusted children.

Given my own upbringing, how could *I* possibly know anything about *that!*

As a young mom, I had every intention of being a far better mother than my own mother was to me. "I don't *ever* want to turn out like her," I would admonish myself after a long day of parenting.

I tried to avoid what I believed were my mother's mistakes. What I didn't realize was that the pendulum only swings in two directions, the extremes of which always yield the same result. So it wouldn't have mattered whether I parented identical to my mother or the opposite -- too strict or too lenient -- the outcome would have yielded the same result.

I suffered from postpartum depression. "What's wrong with me?" I moaned from my hospital bed. "Why am I crying and feeling miserable? I just had a beautiful baby." The depression came out of nowhere with a rabid fierceness and hit me like a bullet right between the eyes. After a few weeks, it disappeared. Or so I concluded. Hindsight tells me I had been depressed for years before I became a mother. Childbirth just made it worse.

As a young woman, I was suddenly thrust into the roles of adult, wife and mother, yet I could hardly manage *myself.* Now I was responsible for the well-being of another life. Along with those roles came more responsibilities than I could deal with, and then the downward spiral of stress, anxiety and depression. My only relief was drinking, and the more I drank, the more I failed at the roles for which I was so ill-equipped. The more I failed, the more stressed, anxious and depressed I became.

It was the most toxic of roundabouts.

Fortunately, I had a better grip on my alcoholism when my first child was born. Generally, I could handle the tasks of parenthood without coming undone very often. I felt fairly confident about my ability to care for a child. In fact, the young me was pretty competent as a mother. I could cope with life as a parent and even thought I was doing a good job of it. The older I became, the more I struggled.

♟

In my early thirties, life became much more complicated, and with it a growing dependence on alcohol. My second child wasn't an easy baby; she was colicky and would rather do anything other than sleep. With a full head of dark curly hair and brilliant blue eyes, she looked like a little doll.

This beautiful child was born into the arms of a mother whose depression and alcoholism had become more pronounced. It was beginning to appear like motherhood was more than I was capable of handling.

Postpartum depression hit me even harder. I couldn't sleep at night and craved sleep during the day. I alternated between severe anxiety and helplessness. I was always irritable. My daughter cried when I was out of her sight. Playing by herself was not something she did well. She didn't sleep through the night until she was over a year old and rarely had a good nap during the day.

When she finally fell asleep, I would often stand next to the crib and wonder what in the world I was doing wrong. Little did I realize that all she really wanted was to be with her mom. And all I wanted was to peel her off of me.

Wherever I was she wanted to be, permanently

attached to my hip or with her arms around my legs. She seemed to want whatever I couldn't give her. Her needs weren't extraordinary. She was just a baby. As soon as I put her down or walked away from her, she would scream. And keep screaming. I didn't know how to cope with a child who needed me that much. There was nothing wrong with *her*; she was simply expressing herself. It was *I* who needed help.

The more she fussed, the more I yelled at her to stop fussing and the more she cried. The more she cried, the more frustrated I became. And then I drank, lashing out in anger. I felt guilty for being abusive, and then drank even more. Under my skin, the anger rose to overflowing. Anyone who was around me at the time bore the brunt of that. I tried desperately to hold on to whatever bits of normalcy were possible.

But I couldn't contain my rage over something I couldn't explain.

I had no parenting goals, or even a philosophy of parenting. If someone had asked me, "What's your parenting style?" I wouldn't have known what they were talking about. To me, parenting was about getting the children up in the morning, feeding, dressing, bathing and putting them to bed. I didn't have the energy for much more. I found pleasure in being a mom, but flying by the seat of my pants from one chore to another was my style. And it didn't work very well.

As time passed, I became even more miserable. As hard as I tried, I didn't feel my role as a mother was a meaningful one. I couldn't accept it as my job. Rather, it was something I *had* to do while I searched for other, more important ways to distinguish myself.

I was sinking, but ever so slowly; I don't think anyone noticed. I surely didn't. There were days when I was too depressed to get out of bed in the morning. At those times, struggling all the while to wake up and function, I was only able to complete the simplest of tasks.

On a bad day, a very bad day, I might not even get dressed. Feed the baby, change the baby, put the baby in the playpen. Feed the baby, change the baby, put the baby in the playpen. It was all I could do to accomplish those tiny bits of parenting. There were days when I could barely talk. If my younger daughter cried, I would yell at her from the adjoining room where I was lying in bed, too fatigued and depressed to rise. Somehow, I never saw my behavior as abnormal or unusual. In fact, I didn't even think about it. I never imagined there was any other way to *be.*

By the time my younger child was in nursery school, I'd started drinking before lunch to erase the gloominess of the days. The depression persisted and became worse. My marriage was falling apart, I'd gone back to college and I sucked at parenting. I was terribly unhappy.

I loved my children with a passion I'd never known. I was in awe of their very existence. That *I* could have created such lovely creatures! The intensity of my love for them was powerful; and just as powerfully did I push them away from me.

As a young and inexperienced mother, I didn't give much thought to whether or not my children were happy. I started out believing parenthood would be easy, and I could effortlessly fit it into my life. I thought being a mother would heal me and complete me, not drown me in responsibilities I hadn't foreseen. I fought hard against the demands taking over my life. "It wasn't supposed to be like this," I whined, "so hard, so challenging and so time-consuming."

What tripped me up even more than the tasks of parenting was how to handle *myself.* Especially if I was hungry, tired, frustrated, angry or sick. On a routine visit to the pediatrician's office with my younger daughter, I told the doctor that she frequently woke in the night crying. "You could give her some Phenobarbital and that might help," he advised. "Better yet, maybe you're the one who should take it instead."

That says it all.

I was emotionally immature; looking backwards, there were numerous times when I might have said that my children knew more about being children than I knew about being a parent. For instance, consistency was not my strong suit. In fact, I wasn't able to do much of anything consistently. If I made a rule about something on one day, there was no guarantee that I wouldn't change the rule the next. If I was happy and fun-loving one day, there was no guarantee that on the next I wouldn't be wallowing in misery. Walking on eggshells is probably the best way to describe the life of anyone who was close to me.

As the child of a mother not entirely unlike myself, I remember the feelings of almost constant stress. The tiptoeing around so as not to disturb the status quo, never sure of who my mother would be at any given moment.

I would guess that my own children may have had similar feelings. I was disconnected, preoccupied and overwhelmed. There wasn't anyone, least of all myself, who knew just how impaired I was. I was destroying myself and the happy life I desired.

My biggest challenge as a parent came when I didn't know how to cope with "a trying day" or any of the other unpleasant or difficult to manage vagaries of parenting. It wasn't my children who were the problem; they were good kids. It was me; I didn't have the tools to be a good parent. I dealt with every frustration I met in the same way -- with extreme behavior. That never worked and merely left everybody feeling upset and angry.

I believe that the adults in my life were oblivious about how to cope with the fallout of a woman who was unable to negotiate the demands and burdens of her life choices. I was like a sleepwalker, fumbling around in the darkness of an unfamiliar world. I couldn't handle life, and no one could handle me.

What I knew about being a parent came from growing up with a self-absorbed and mentally ill mother who was physically and emotionally abusive. She didn't teach me anything about parenting and simply set the stage for history repeating itself in ways I never anticipated.

I parented the way I was parented: without patience and often without respect or sensitivity. That's all I knew.

I believed parents had to be in control and in charge at all times, and the only way to do that was to become a harsh authority figure. Someone to be feared, just like my own mother. Most of the time I didn't see myself as a friend to my children; I believed that being a friend would compromise my role as their mother. "Letting down my guard" and being easy and relaxed, might permit myself to be taken advantage of. "Soft" didn't apply to how I viewed parenting.

God knows, I could *never* be soft.

I focused on meaningless minutiae, attempting to control much more about the children's lives than was actually necessary just to convince myself I had a grip on my *own* life. Or, I ignored important events like going to soccer and field hockey games or back-to school night. Some days, I was so miserable and adrift (and, at times, so drunk) that I could provide only the barest semblance of stability and security for my children.

I never imagined that *my* lack of a stable mother would affect my own ability to be a mother. At least, not to the extent it did. I believed somehow I would just *know* how to parent. And be a good one, too. No matter what, the strength to get up day after day (or night after night) and do the same thing over and over would materialize out of nowhere. I had no idea of the scope of this undertaking.

I promised myself I wouldn't turn out like my mother. However, with each passing year I found myself becoming more and more like her. I *wanted* to be a good mom; I just didn't know how to actually do it.

Oh sure, there were many times when I was warm, kind, playful and loving. I have memories of carefree, happy days of tenderness and laughter. But, more often than not, I couldn't survive the never-ending, repetitive and often challenging tasks of parenting. And it showed.

My parenting MO was to correct and criticize. I thought that's what mothers were *supposed* to do -- mold their children into perfect little specimens of childhood and later, into proper young adults. I believed that if I were successful at that, other people would see me as a good mom and positive role-model for my children. I didn't see that a kinder, gentler way of parenting would have achieved those same goals quicker and with less drama.

Yes. It was all about me.

And at other times, I was so angry, at myself mostly, that I couldn't contain the fury. And that's when I said and did things that I deeply regret.

"Put your coat on," I barked at my younger daughter.

"Mom, I don't need a coat. I'm not cold."

"You're going to catch a cold, put your coat on *right now.*"

"But Mom, I don't want to wear a coat."

"If you don't put your coat on now, we're going to be late. DO IT RIGHT NOW!"

"It's warm out."

"PUT YOUR COAT ON!" I screamed. "What a brat! I'm going to stand here until you do! And when we get home later you're going to be punished and you're never going to forget it! Next time I tell you to do something, you're going to do it. THE FIRST TIME. I guarantee you'll remember today. You just wait," I growled with rage.

By that time, it would be likely that my daughter would be crying and shouting, "I hate you" over and over at the top of her lungs.

Her words made me livid. They were the same words I said about my own mother.

A scenario like that happened frequently and ended in my losing control. I couldn't figure out how to extricate myself from these meaningless power struggles without permitting them to escalate into something more than they were. And, at the same time, retain my dignity and self-respect as a parent. I couldn't see that it didn't matter whether she wore her coat or not. What mattered more was mutual respect and peace.

The way I saw parenting was this way: An order was an order and it didn't matter if the child was miserable and angry. I, however, gloated in false victory or -- well, there was no *or*. That there might be an "*or*" was never an option. Do it my way. The only way. Period.

This unfortunate drama played out over and over and, I learned much later, was a lose-lose situation for everyone. The battle for "Who's in charge here" had a great deal to do with the downfall of my parenting. The constant push to assert *my* power and my children's efforts to develop *their* power and become separate individuals meant we often went head-to-head against one another.

Running out of steam and having reached my limit, I made an appointment with my pediatrician, the father of eight children. He counseled me wisely. "Give your children choices instead of backing them into a corner." And even more importantly, "Don't fight over the things that don't matter. Save the strong-arm parenting for the things that do matter like drugs, alcohol and sex."

I believed him and often reminded myself of his words. And sometimes I could follow through effectively. But I had to be in a good place, sober and not under unusual stress. I could count those days on the fingers of one hand. But when I practiced his preaching, I felt successful.

One day, in particular, stands out in my memory. "It's time to get dressed," I said to my younger daughter who poked around on school mornings until the very last moment. Or *past* the very last moment. One reminder after another would go unheeded. I would often shovel her into the car, me a shrieking wreck of a mother, warning her about the severity of the punishment to follow and how much I disliked her for forcing me to be late to work again.

The funny thing is, she liked school, so her dawdling wasn't related to an aversion to school. She just had different priorities and her conception of time was unlike mine. I usually worked harder than she did to get us places on time.

One morning, ten minutes before we had to leave for school, I called up the stairs as calmly as possible, "This is your final call. Please be standing dressed with your school bag by the front door at exactly eight o'clock, or I will leave without you. If you're late or absent you'll have to attend detention at school on Saturday morning at seven o'clock. It's your choice."

At eight, I was standing by the front door, coat on, briefcase in hand. "I'm not ready!" she shouted down the stairs.

"Then I guess you'll be going to school on Saturday. Goodbye," I called out as I opened the front door. I was still calm.

"Just one more minute, *please*. I'm still in my pajamas."

"I'm sorry. I'll see you later," I commented, shutting the front door behind me.

I was pulling out of the driveway when she came bounding out the door in her pajamas, school clothes in hand.

"I hate you. It's *your* fault that I have to go to school in my pajamas!"

"I'm sorry you feel that way," I replied, basking in the spotlight of a job well done. I didn't say another word.

She was never late again. How I wish I could have maintained that wonderful detachment. It felt so good.

"Act normal!"

"Don't act crazy!"

"You're psycho!"

I heard all of this and more as a parent. Every time one of these phrases was spoken I was appalled because I didn't believe it applied to me. At least, not then. *What are they talking about? I'm not the one acting crazy and I'm surely not psycho. Whatever psycho is.*

I believed that the way I behaved was perfectly normal and my childrearing practices acceptable in every way. "My children just need to be shaped and guided and that's what I'm doing; I'm the parent and I'm in charge." I would remind myself.

I was well into sobriety before I truly understood what my children meant by "Act normal."

I thought nothing of screaming or throwing a fit in public. Or frightening them with threats of abandonment or abuse. Or hitting them. It didn't matter what the issue was and I didn't care who heard, who I embarrassed or what kind of havoc occurred in the wake of one of my tirades.

I was quick to judgment and even quicker to anger. When that rage kicked in there was no stopping me. Nothing would matter more than getting some relief from whatever I believed was bothering me.

I was driven by a seething fury that was always there, even when I seemed happy. It ate away at my guts, inflamed my emotions and warped my thoughts. I arose in the morning with it, nursed it throughout the day and took it back to bed with me at night. Every day. For decades.

It wasn't the kind of anger that was triggered by a specific situation that would provoke me. It didn't grow over a long period of time and then blossom appropriately in a deserved outburst. No. The trigger was always the same. Something was happening that was beyond my control and I couldn't tolerate it. Or someone was irritating me and they were the cause of my upset feelings. I didn't think the situation through, wouldn't put it on hold and definitely couldn't let it go. I simply erupted. It didn't matter who was in my path.

Usually those eruptions would take the form of verbal abuse and, at others, physical abuse. My children were the usual targets when I detonated. I was usually not upset with *them*; they merely touched off something that had been rotting in the pit of my stomach for decades.

After my outburst, I would feel remorse but I wasn't able to change course. What I discovered after I stopped drinking alcohol was how much of my rage was about unresolved losses and how my drinking simply added more fuel to the blaze.

Both the fury and the alcohol interfered with working through the feelings that bubbled up on a regular basis from long ago. I was aware that I was angry but had no idea that it was rooted in decades past. So, rather than identifying the anger as a problem and developing the skills and insight necessary to work it through, I blamed everyone else for my explosions. Then I didn't have to see myself as the problem.

Off the hook.

I went to bed with alcohol in my body almost every day and woke up that way. There was rarely a day when I didn't drink. It affected my physical, emotional and cognitive functioning whether I was aware of it or not.

It's no wonder then, that my children would tell me to "Act normal." Tanked up on the spirits, there was no telling what I might say or do. The more I drank, the more depressed I became. The more depressed I was, the more I drank and the worse I behaved. It was everybody else who was messing with my world. The alcohol helped me deal with the chaos "they" were creating.

In Hope Edelman's exquisite book, **Motherless Mothers**, she demonstrates how the loss of a mother due to death, abandonment or illness can have a profound effect on how motherless mothers raise their own children. With many obstacles in their way, they attempt to mother their youngsters without a role model or blueprint for parenting. They lack the support of a close, positive maternal guide. Plagued by a unique set of problems, they are besieged with poor choices, fears, and failures. These mothers experience very few triumphs.

With the passing of years, as much as I tried to hold back the tidal wave of anger, it tumbled even more recklessly out of me. I was going down quickly. I wasn't oblivious to the mayhem I created, I just didn't know how to stop it. Even then, I wasn't entirely convinced that it was *I* who had the problem; I believed it was my life and everybody in it who was to blame.

As my children grew, I experienced even more regret at how parented, but I could do nothing to stop myself. In the end, the person I was angriest at was me. The more I wanted and tried to be a better parent, the more I failed. Some days, being a good enough mom seemed so out of reach I considered just walking away. I even contemplated suicide. "My children might be better off," I told myself.

I had nothing left to give. I was empty.

I compared myself to other parents whose behavior I studied. I could identify the qualities that made them good parents, and I tried to emulate what I observed. But I couldn't turn the mirror on myself and look at what made me a *poor* parent. I didn't know where to turn, who to ask for help or how to salvage what remained. How could I stay calm and not overreact? How could I manage my anger? How could I let go of the small stuff and focus on the big ticket items? I couldn't distinguish between the two. Everything seemed hugely important.

I never dwelled for very long on how I perceived myself as a mother. It was too painful. I figured I was just not cut out for parenting. It never occurred to me what the effect of drinking and depression had on me as a mother. And how the accumulation of losses with which I had never dealt eroded the image of the competent person I wanted to be.

Years later, as the dark veil of alcoholism lifted and I finally faced the demons from whom I was running, I began to understand the depth of my depression, one so debilitating that I missed out on decades of my life. Sobriety, therapy and medication gave me the strength to change the course of my life, not only as a person, but as a parent. The long road to recovery meant learning how to parent myself and *then* my children. It took a long time until I could look at myself in the mirror and eyeball who I had become. By then, both of my children were living on their own.

The reality of my alcoholism as it related to family life was like this: Alcoholism was a disease, and it unfairly challenged everyone in my family, including those who never touched a drop. Imagine the fear and stress that life with an alcoholic mother must have caused. It wasn't until I became sober that I could bear the emotional burden of the pain I inflicted on those around me.

Fortunately, long-term sobriety has helped me deal with the long-term damage of my drinking. It may never heal completely. The fact that I'm sober now and have been for over twenty-years cannot undo the past. As George Eliot once said, "That is the bitterest of all, to wear the yolk of your own wrongdoing."

♟

The first Mother's Day following my vow of sobriety, I surveyed the mess I had made of my life and swore I would work as hard as I could until the next Mother's Day to be a better mother. I knew it wasn't going to be easy and I wasn't sure I could do it.

I'll never forget my therapist's words during those early days: "Be patient with yourself. You are emerging from decades of alcohol abuse a wounded warrior and those injuries are not going to heal quickly. In actuality, it may take the rest of your life."

I respected his honesty. I was prepared.

What I longed for most was to behave in a way that

made me feel good about myself. I aspired to be the kind of parent my children respected. First, I had to strip away the lies and face the facts. Doing it required a lot of trial and error those first years. Every Mother's Day from then on, I reviewed my progress from the year before and vowed to work even harder. I've done the same thing now for over twenty-five years. Look myself in the eye, 'fess up to my screw-ups and try to do better. I will never stop aiming to be a better parent.

♟

When I embarked on the journey towards true sobriety, I discovered that I had to grieve the loss of my own mother and understand what her loss meant for me as a mother. My mother left me with a huge hole in my heart. The task wasn't only to grieve the mother I had and lost; it was to mourn the mother I *never* had. In order for me to re-learn how to parent my children, I had to make peace with her legacy. But, first, I had to learn how to mother myself.

Most adults who grow up in relatively happy households with good enough parents, learn how to parent themselves and others based on observing their parents first-hand. Adults who don't have the benefit of well-adjusted parents, don't. And, if you can't guide, nurture and support yourself, it is damn difficult to do that for anyone else. This skill is not automatically implanted in every individual at birth. It is learned. And without those lessons, people like me are at a real loss.

I knew I could never parent my children if I weren't happy and my internal house wasn't in order. It was a tough challenge, but I had to discover who I was and how I got that way. I stopped hating myself and developed some compassion for the little girl who had lost her way and the emotionally mature woman she was yet to be.

At the same time, I swore to remain focused on the present, and do what was best for me. I figured if I did what was best for me, it would be best for my children, as well. I wasn't going back to the past to simply wallow in my backstory. I had to live a different kind of life going forward *in spite of it.*

♛

I will never get over who I was — and who I *wasn't*. Especially as a mother. It's been a painful journey to arrive at the place I am now. There are so many moments I want to forget, but I never will. Sometimes, I force myself to remember the dark days as a reminder that I wasn't always the person I am, and that I cannot ever give up the struggle towards being "good enough." There are still moments when the guilt and regret about parenting eat me up. I believe it's the least of the punishment I deserve.

I worry most about what it is that my children will never forget. I agonize over the rat scramble those years with me set off in their heads as they tried to protect themselves from the chaos of a runaway train they called Mom. The walking on paper thin glass. The fear. The inconsistence. The not *knowing* what was next. I never recognized until I was well into sobriety that, as a child, I lived with the very same feelings.

I've been able to wrap my arms around myself and say, "I did the best I could." I grappled with demons, and they were in charge. I can't go back and fix anything. Apologies don't cut it. I don't expect anyone to forgive me, but I'm working hard on forgiving myself. More importantly, I try to move forward and be a better version of myself every day.

After years of bumbling through ancient history I've come to realize that parenting is being responsible for someone else's happiness and well-being day after day, year after year, forever. It is the most challenging and longest-running job there is.

Today, the wounds of the past are healing. Slowly. My parenting skills have improved and I realize how far I've come to get here. Finding my center as a mother has been a long process and I've made plenty of mistakes.

I'm still learning how to rock my own cradle.

Chapter 20

Gangsters, Movie Stars, Drunkards, Lunatics And My Father

I could write a book about my family. No, *volumes.* They're an interesting bunch, some wackier than others. Actually, a few might be considered "normal." Some I can't figure out at all. And, for the most part, I've given up trying. Fortune has handed me a bunch of characters; why would I bother to make stuff up?

Some alcoholism and quite a bit of mental illness thrown in for good measure make it even more intriguing. There's something for everyone in my family tree. I inherited my best characteristics from a few and the worst from others.

The most colorful people from my family are on my mother's side. Family folklore has it my maternal grandfather ran away from home when he was a teenager. He lived with his family in Cheyenne, Wyoming, immigrants from Eastern Europe. They were very strict, and I suppose he didn't want to follow their rules. Or they threw him out.

Whether they parted ways because *he* was crackers or his *parents* were crackers, I don't know. He grew up to be a successful business man, powerful and manipulative. It's possible he may have originated the phrase, "It's not *what* you know but *who* you know that matters."

Whether or not his affluence was derived from completely legal business activities may never be known for sure. His automobile dealership in Toledo, Ohio was a gathering place for a variety of smarmy-looking characters including the Licavoli brothers from the infamous Purple Gang, an offshoot of the Chicago Mafia. The Licavolis controlled criminal operations in Toledo for many years. 'Nuff said.

My grandfather walked around with a cigarette hanging out of the corner of his mouth, a diamond ring the size of grape, and an impressive wad of greenbacks in his pocket. I often wondered why he carried so much cash around with him. I hear he did some prison time, but no one ever talked much about it.

The self-appointed family patriarch, he would unroll one bill after another from the huge roll of cash he always carried with him, flashing his headlight-sized diamond ring and buying his way into everyone's lives, friends and family alike. As a child, I would be indulged in the most seductive ways. Trips, cash, custom-made clothing, lavish gifts, front row seats at concerts and backstage visits with the performers were usual and customary. I suppose this was his way of loving.

At the age of fifteen, his girlfriend, my grandmother, became pregnant with my mother. She wasn't banished to the hinterlands as they often did in those days but, rather, pushed into a marriage with my grandfather that wasn't a happy one.

He indulged my grandmother in all manner of luxuries she didn't really care about. Beautiful clothes, lovely homes, valuable antiques, travel, furs and jewelry. He wasn't much of a husband to her in the ways that were most meaningful. I think he loved her, but he didn't really know how to show it without spending money on her. He wasn't always faithful. And she knew. My grandmother was gentle and loving and deserved more than he could give her.

Several months before I married, my grandmother gave me some advice: "Go to school, get an education, and build a career for yourself. If the marriage doesn't work out, you'll always be able to support yourself, hold your head up high and not end up a prisoner like me." I never realized at the time how much sadness and regret were behind those words, but I never forgot what she said. I did as she instructed.

My forefathers also included a cousin who was a movie actor. He starred in over two hundred films and TV shows. A character actor, he was best known for playing the tough-guy gangster. I remember him well. In real life, he was a kind and loving man, happily married to a lovely woman, and hardly the fearsome character he played in the flicks.

Another relative was a movie magnate who later owned a hotel and casino in Las Vegas. His wife was my great aunt, my grandfather's sister. She was a platinum blonde, petite and quirky, brittle and blunt. I was fascinated by her. Another one of his sisters, who never left the house without her hat, was known for her sharp words and sour disposition. I was terrified of her. She spoke her mind, whether others wanted to hear or not. Some members of my family would say I resembled her. *Not funny.* No.

Squeaky clean describes my father's side of the family, at least on the surface. Most of my aunts and uncles lives on my father's side were cut short by cancer, strokes and a combination of other more chronic illnesses. From what I remember, most of them were close and their relationships with one another fairly normal.

My father was kind and loving. He was a caring parent and a likable man, but he struggled to make a living adequate by the maternal side of my family, and spent a great deal of time away from home. My grandfather, describing why he couldn't work with my father, remarked, "He's too honest. He doesn't have enough larceny in him."

I've always imagined that at one time my father was a happy man, perhaps when he married my mother, but then something happened. Something gradual and poisonous -- whether it was World War II, the influence of my mother and her family or alcohol -- he spiraled every so quietly down the drain.

I was born in early 1945 while my father was overseas. I don't believe he met me until I was almost a year old. In the many letters he wrote home to his family, he spoke excitedly about my coming arrival, and referred to me as his "son."

On November 23, 1944, fresh out of Camp Shelby and on a ship at sea, he wrote:

> Today is Thanksgiving Day and I can't see a thing different about it. In fact, I can't see any difference from yesterday or the day before yesterday, or the day before that. All I can see around me is water, for miles and miles. . . . Let's hope that I can be home to celebrate next Thanksgiving Day. I'll bring my 'son.'

On December 17, 1944, he tells his sister he sent her daughter a birthday card. "Tell her [my niece] that I expect to celebrate her 2nd birthday. In fact, I'll even bring my 'son' to her birthday party."

On January 28, 1945, he wrote, "What's new with my wife? It won't be long now."

Three weeks later, on February 13, 1945:

> Am now in France and would just as soon give all of it back to the French people. It's almost the middle of February and I still haven't had word from home regarding my 'impending fatherhood.' I'm getting coniptions [sic].

On February 19, 1945, two days prior to my birth, he wrote:

> Yesterday, I received an airmail letter from Ruth [my wife], written on February 6th. That was the date the doctor said she was due on and I've heard nothing since, so I assume that 'Jr.' is holding up on his 'Grand Appearance.'

In the next letter he says:

I'm going to have to take a 'shot' of novocaine [sic] soon if I don't get a cablegram from home. 'Jr.' sure is keeping his old man in suspense. I understand that Irv [Ruth's father] is more nervous than me, if that's any consolation.

On February 28, 1945, a week after my birth, he writes:

<u>Still No Cablegram From Home</u>!! I already thought that I had labor pains the other night myself. Damn! I wish that cablegram would arrive.

And then on March 9, 1945, more than two weeks after my birth, he writes to his sister, "It's A Girl. Just in case you haven't heard -- I'm the Proud Father of a baby daughter."

My father didn't return home until after the War ended. He and his brother were in the same regiment that liberated the Buchenwald concentration camp. His stories about the war, and especially those about the camps and the Holocaust survivors, were almost too painful to hear.

He used to say the war changed him, and when he returned home, he didn't feel he was the same person as when he left. I'm sure there was always a part of him that remained back in those terrible times and places.

He talked about his days in the Army wistfully. It was almost as if he missed them: the shared purpose, the camaraderie, the values he was upholding and fighting for. I often felt WWII was the one time in his life my father felt important, useful, and needed.

♟

The most distinguishing characteristics of the maternal side of my family are mental illness, alcohol abuse, and family dysfunction. These features are deeply rooted in every generation and were probably present long before I learned about my grandmother's brother, an alcoholic who was mentally ill. He lived many years of his life in and out of mental hospitals.

In some cases the mental illnesses in my family are serious like ripples in a pond that affect many others and, in other cases, less so. There aren't many of us in my generation (myself included) and the past two generations it hasn't touched. I'm certain that those problems were part of the reason I became a psychotherapist. Unconsciously, perhaps, I may have believed that it was my insurance policy against mental illness. But I'd rather assume that it was because I had the skills to be helpful.

At some point during the years of my own psychotherapy, a therapist once asked me, "What are the qualities about your family that make it so dysfunctional?"

"Well," I began, "it's the patterns that have developed. Patterns that are handed down from generation to generation. And sometimes, my family members act, well, *crazy*. They say and do things that are unkind and often hateful without thinking about the consequences."

"There's just a lack of respect and no desire to understand and talk things through. Most people have little tolerance for differences, no sense of personal responsibility and rarely apologize if they screw up." I hesitated a moment; "Um-m-m-m -- I'm sure there's more."

"Go ahead," the therapist responded, "take some time to think about it."

"Poor boundaries for one. People become involved in situations that are none of their business. Or that they may not understand. Or about which they have faulty information. There's a lack of courtesy and trust, no resilience, little insight and plenty of teasing, sarcasm and mean-spiritedness."

"Can you give me an example?"

"Well, lemme see. Nasty and mean attempts at humor. Making fun of people. About how they look, for instance. I recall a situation where a family member made a joke about a stroke victim. 'Your face looks funny,' the jokester said. He thought it was hilarious."

"In another situation, someone made a wisecrack to a Holocaust survivor about what they had endured. There was nothing even remotely humorous about what that person had gone through. It should have been painfully apparent that the individual who made the joke was the only one who was laughing."

"These are not children who do this kind of thing either," I continued, "they're full-grown adults."

"Wow," she said, "that's some real unpleasant stuff. Is that all?"

"Oh no! I'm just getting started," I shouted excitedly. "Parents don't set examples for their children. Family doesn't have your back, and they don't follow the golden rule."

"Wait. There's more," I say, coming up for air. I was on autopilot now. "My family doesn't allow people to grow and change or allow for reasonable (and occasionally unreasonable) expressions of feelings. They don't provide emotional safety for one another and they don't forgive."

"But most of all, they cannot show empathy, E-M-P-A-T-H-Y. And they cut people off. Over and over."

"You mean estrangements?" the therapist asked.

"Yeah. All over the place. All the time. And it goes on for years. Decades. I'll bet most of the folks who initiated the estrangement in the first place don't even remember what the original problem was anymore!"

The therapist is shaking her head now. "You probably know that the severing of ties, permanent or not, is *the* single, most toxic dynamic in any family and the hallmark of the *most* dysfunctional families."

I hope she doesn't feel sorry for me. Growing up familially-challenged has made me stronger. Honest.

Most people believe we can rely on our family to keep us safe, physically and emotionally, to love us, watch out for us, support and encourage us. The concept of "family" rests on the belief that people will forgive and love us even when we make mistakes. And, when we lose our footing, help us get back up on our feet. After all, they're *family*. When they fail to do this, it can create deep wounds. Where I come from, they've been butchering each other with their fine-honed Ginza knives for generations.

My family has perfected the art of the cut-off. Talking and working out conflict are unheard of. At least not in a way that solves anything. People rarely communicate directly. They do it by way of another person or the written word. Feelings are expressed passive-aggressively through triangles, skewed communication, gossip and lies.

There's little understanding or compromise; blame, judgment, condemnation and anger is how they operate. "I'll never speak to you again," is commonplace. People dance around the elephant lounging in the middle of the living room as if it were invisible. As a result, my family has always been in a constant state of tension, scapegoating and unspoken hostility.

Not everyone in my family participates in this poisonous ritual, but many do. I'm astonished by their capacity to avoid the truth. Whenever, they are presented with the "truth," it is their "truth" that is always more "truthful." In the end, everybody loses.

The cut-offs are usually fueled by misunderstandings caused by poor communication, misperceptions and incorrect assumptions about facts or intents. The people who believe they're "right" (the righteous) often search for cheerleaders to substantiate their faulty conclusions and support their beliefs. They don't want accurate information and they certainly don't want to be confused by the facts. The more people involved, the quicker the situation snowballs, festers and the offender is "amputated." And scapegoated.

No matter what common sense tells them, the

righteous will ignore the facts and anyone who sees things differently. Nothing will convince them they're wrong. They will never admit there may be sensible explanations for a situation. Being "wrong" is an abomination to them. Wrong is the death of the ego. Right defines who they are.

There's no room for rational and reasonable. This is the way things have worked in my family since I can remember. Like wading into a swamp filled with alligators. At night.

People collude against each other about problems which are none of their business and always someone else's fault. They use fear, intimidation, threats, rage, criticism, abuse, sarcasm and manipulation to control others. This style of coping works well and serves to distract everyone from the real problem. It is widely accepted within the mental health community that people who don't deal with their own pain tend to shift it to others.

Estrangement training is handed down from one generation to another. In my extended family, grandparents, parents and children do it. It's all they know. Occasionally, an individual will try to cope in a healthier way. But often the system will erupt in chaos because it's easier, more efficient and more familiar to simply say, "I'm done with you."

If there is any communication at all, it's often through one-sided "mean mail," a passive-aggressive way to avoid dealing face-to-face with another person. People say words they might not feel comfortable saying in person. Terrible words.

From the time I was a young teenager, my mother wrote "mean mail" to me. Her numerous letters outlined, in great detail, all the ways I had disappointed and let her down, and why everything troubling her was *my* fault.

Her letter writing went on for many years. I believe she thought that if only I would acknowledge her reality about me and permit myself to be "rehabilitated," then our relationship would improve and she would be happier. But mean mail served only to drive me further away. Year after year she pounded away at me. Later on, I understood that her letters were a reflection of the unhappiness within herself.

> I heard from someone else that you're pregnant and I couldn't care less, but you should have told me yourself. You've always been a bitch. You never did have any respect for me, and now you're going to teach that to your child. Someone needs to beat the shit out of you. Frankly, I hope you have a child just like you, and she doesn't give a damn about you either! Then you'll know what it feels like.

Shaking, I folded the letter up and put it away. I always felt sick to my stomach after one of her letters.

My late husband once asked me, "Why didn't you throw the letters away?"

"Maybe there was a part of me at one time that believed she was correct," I responded sadly. "And it's all I have left of her."

"You don't *still* feel that way, do you?"

"No, I don't. But I don't think I'll ever forget how the letters made me feel. It was like being smacked in the face with the underside of a golf shoe. I'll *never* do that to my kids."

It took me a long time to understand that my mother's words weren't about me; they were a reflection of how she perceived herself and the world.

Mean mail didn't end when my mother died. Other people in the family have picked up where she left off. The recipients are people whom the writer feels have caused them (or someone else) distress of some kind. Such commentaries lash out at the imagined transgressions of the recipients in the same angry and hateful way. Perhaps the writers expect their victims to respond positively, but that never happens. Quite the opposite.

Here's a recent example:

Guess what, I don't give a damn what you think. There are too many people in this family who agree that you are manipulative and controlling and want nothing to do with you. . . . At least the aforementioned and many more that I need not mention are on the "same page" concerning you. As I stated in my last email, you have no morals, respect or boundaries. You're vicious, sneaky and I've never trusted you. Money is your G-d and spreading your legs for the next "victim" is your MO. You don't know the meaning of "family" love or loyalty . . . .There is NO ONE left for you and no matter what, you WILL NOT have the opportunity to get us all back! I'M SO HAPPY THAT YOUR "TRUE COLORS" HAVE COME OUT FOR ALL TO SEE! YOU need extensive professional help, plain and simple. You need to understand that no one wants you in their lives. . . . You are not capable of having a relationship outside of being a "therapist" and you're not even good at that.

. . . this last "exercise" in HONESTY, . . . has proven that you are deceptive and dishonest. . . . You never liked my honesty but that's your problem. I'm not angry. I just don't like you.

What mean mail really conveys is how miserable the writer is, how unsuccessful they have been at solving their own personal problems and how disconnected they must feel from the joys of life. The writers use mean mail like cutting, drugs, half-hearted suicide attempts or any other self-destructive behavior: to relieve their anxiety. It works because it shifts ownership and responsibility of whatever the problem is to the other person. It's a tough habit to break.

These days, I simply gasp with horror and disbelief

when I re-read old mean mail. I turn to my husband, a man who has an uncommonly good sense of humor about family dysfunction, both mine *and* his, and ask him,

"Don't some of the people who write that garbage ever take a long, painful look at themselves in the mirror? You know what I mean -- look themselves straight in the eyes and explore the roots of their angry feelings? Might they find they are as much the cause of relationship problems as the other guy?"

My husband cocks his head, looks me directly in the eyes, and with a wide grin on his face just snickers. His lighthearted response is always the same.

"Oh, *sure, sure*, Sonya. I get what you're trying to say. Of *course*. You must mean something like this: Those people wake up one morning, rub their tired eyes, run their fingers through their bedraggled locks, drag their sorry selves into the bathroom, look at their scruffy faces in the mirror and say, 'Hello there, self. Self, you know what? I am an *asshole!*'"

"Yeah. *Something* like that," I respond, laughing at myself.

♚

I've learned about human behavior from the classroom and my clinical practice, but even *more* from my *family*. And, my own bad behavior, of course. Anyone who beats up others verbally or blames them for their own or someone else's misery has a few more dots to connect in the game of life. Even worse are those who hold on to that anger with no hope of letting it go.

I'm used to hanging around people who behave badly. During my decades as a therapist, there was nothing foreign about the problems my clients had; I'd heard it all before. In fact, the majority of my clients were a lot healthier than some of the people in my own family.

The most important lesson I've earned in my struggle to come to terms with my family's dysfunction, is to look inside of *me* for the answers to my unhappiness, *before* I shift the responsibility and blame to someone else for *making* me unhappy, and *before* I say or do something that will make me lose my dignity and self-esteem. Or write mean mail.

Even now, every once in a while, I'm tempted to heap blame on the other guy. "That damn so-and-so," I blather. When that happens, I take a time-out and squirrel down to that ugly place inside of me and just wallow around in the pain, trying to figure out who's responsible for how I feel. I let it wash all over me. And when I come up for air, I always discover that it's *me* who's making me miserable!

The business of dealing with one's demons is an inside job.

Chapter 21

Good Enough

Many years of my earlier life were spent in the drive towards perfection, a state I knew had to be flawless and faultless. That pristine, unblemished and completely spotless way of living. There was no room for anything short of "too good to be true." And surely no room to be the person I really was.

In the early days of me, I cared a great deal about what I believed people thought of me. Chances are, they didn't think about me as much as I imagined they did. They probably didn't think about me at all.

I was convinced that if others held me in high esteem I would have achieved the ultimate prize, a trophy given only to those who were exemplary in every way. It made sense. Who wouldn't adore someone who was at the top of their game?

The realization that there is no such thing as perfect, at least as it refers to adult human beings, came as a complete surprise.

"There are perfect flowers, perfect circles, perfect sunsets, perfect beaches, perfect babies, but no perfect grownups," my therapist stated. It was an absolutely stunning revelation.

I didn't believe him.

"All that effort for nothing," I fretted. "Years and years of wasted time devoted to grooming myself into just what I could never be."

Maybe my therapist is wrong. He doesn't have all the answers. I've known some pretty perfect people in my day.

In spite of his good counsel, I ignored him and forged ahead towards an unattainable ideal. The harder I tried to reach that epitome of humanity, the more frustrated and exhausted I became. How I longed to achieve what I admired most in my friends, their families and their lives. If only I could have a perfect body and flawless skin, a good job, happy marriage and ideal children. The world would be my oyster!

It wasn't until several years into sobriety, true sobriety, when I discovered how far afield I had wandered in my search for perfection. *Who was I trying to please?* I aimed to have every hair in place, impeccable makeup and a designer wardrobe. My home couldn't have a speck of dust nor could anything be out of place. For all the world, the appearance of perfect everything was of prime concern.

My efforts to be accomplished at everything led me so far downstream that I had traveled all the way around the bend in the river and was careening over the falls when I eventually realized all my struggles were for nothing.

I was almost fifty years old when I began to pay closer attention to my therapist. He opened my eyes to the concept of "good enough." The idea that I didn't have to be perfect was intriguing: that I could actually have a fine life as "good enough" was a *huge* surprise.

"Nobody cares if you're not perfect," he advised. "Besides, no other person but you would even notice the difference between good enough and perfect."

"Get used to the idea of being "good enough." It's the only healthy way to live your life. *You're* the only person you have to please. Nobody else will care.

The concept of "good enough" was life-changing; a novel idea that I had never considered. That one could live a life in pursuit of something short of perfection just blew me away. That "good enough" could be good enough was startling.

I'll admit, good enough and I weren't friends from the start. It took a lot of practice to stop trying so hard.

"Would people accept me if I were only good enough?"

"*Only* good enough?" my therapist asked, a tad sarcastically.

"Good enough" meant an entirely new way of living my life. I gave it a try. I left the house one day without every hair in place. *Nothing terrible happened.* I stopped worrying so much about my makeup. *Survived that one, too.* I stopped buying clothes that were uncomfortable, yet stylish, and wore what was comfortable. *And lived to tell about it.*

I lowered my housekeeping standards from hygienically clean and obsessively organized to good enough. My drawers were no longer arranged with a T-square. I stopped ironing every single wrinkle out of everything. *Actually, I stopped ironing.* I ceased cooking meals that looked like the cover of <u>Bon Appetite</u>. *And they were still quite delicious.* I didn't have to go to every store for the perfect outfit for a special occasion. I was embracing good enough and it was quite refreshing.

I edged in even closer to good enough. I explored what it would mean to be a good enough mother, a good enough cook or a good enough wife. I learned that one person's good enough wasn't necessarily another's, and that no one else had the right to judge my good enough by their good enough.

One day I left the house without any makeup and the sky didn't fall. That day I knew I had finally succeeded. Ah. Liberation, sweet liberation!

I had discovered the key to get out of jail free, and found I was no less accepted among my peers for having done so. In fact, now I could relax. The anxiety about trying to achieve the impossible was gone. I figured that if I was good enough for *me*, that it no longer mattered what anyone else thought about me. It only mattered what *I* thought about me. "Good enough for you," that's what my therapist said. I realized that the absurd state of perfection was just a dream.

Maybe even a nightmare.

♛

Many years later, having grown comfortable with good enough, I began to write. As I recorded some of my experiences, I worried about what people would think of me if they knew I was *so* far from perfect. What would they think of me as they read through the pages about a drunken child who grew into an adult alcoholic and even landed up in jail!

In the process of writing this book, I realized that what I truly cared most about was not what people thought of my story, my life and the overweight baggage I was dragging after me, but what they really thought of me *now*. At the present time and place. Today. After all the water had passed under the bridge. Who I *am*, not who I *was*. Would I be good enough?

I discussed the ramifications of writing this book about my imperfect life with professional writers, editors, trusted colleagues, long-time friends and members of my writing group. Should I dance around the issues because I didn't want to shock, offend or watch people drop out of my life? Or did I just not care what people thought of me and how I had lived?

I had so many questions. Why would I want anyone to read about my experiences? How would my book affect the people close to me? Do I really want people to know what I went through? How will they feel about me if they knew the truth? What if they don't want anything to do with me after it's in print?

"It's your story and it should stay locked inside of you," a member of my writing group commanded, "so it doesn't upset or embarrass anyone you know. Remember the old adage, 'First do no harm.'"

The words of another group member went something like this: "At this point in *my* life, I wouldn't care about hanging out my dirty laundry. Especially if it was a good story. There may be some people in my life who would disappear or change their opinion about me. But the people closest to me won't be affected. After all, it's who I am *today* that truly matters, isn't it?"

"I'd like to add something to that," said another member who had recently published a memoir about childhood sexual abuse. "Sonya has a compelling story, with a timely and gripping subject. If she's decided to write a memoir about that part of her life, then she has to be true to herself and honest with her readers. If people decide they no longer want her around after they know the truth, perhaps they weren't worth having in the first place."

I liked her approach better. It spoke to who I am.

The conversation became more animated. Everyone was talking now. The oldest member of the group stood up and said, "With all due respect to those members who believe that she shouldn't tell the whole truth: if the people in her circle don't know her story by now, then perhaps they *should*. They're all well into adulthood. Maybe it's time to take the blinders off. And, if they don't want to take the blinders off, then this book isn't going to change that, is it?"

As she sat down, the room became quiet.

"The truth won't make me look so good," I said, breaking the silence. "But the true test of family and friendship will be in whether the people who read my memoir can accept the person that's emerged from my backstory."

After struggling this way and that for a long time, I finally decided that I cared what people thought, but I had a story that I needed to tell. And it was important for me to write it down. Perhaps sharing this part of my imperfect life slams the door forever on the dream of perfection.

In the end, I sincerely hope that those people who believed I shouldn't commit experiences best forgotten to paper will respect the courage it took to tell the truth.

Who I am now is good enough for me.

Chapter 22

The Caregiver Cracks Up

Nothing could have prepared me for the wild ride I experienced with my late husband the day I married him. I believe in *beshert* or meant-to-be. Whatever you call it, it's the same thing. Fate. I was meant to care for my husband as he languished with Alzheimer's Disease, and he was meant to support my sobriety. A match made in heaven. If you believe in that sort of thing.

Our relationship was loving and happy most of the time, tumultuous at others, the see-saw result of our individual gremlins going head-to-head. We were very much in love, and it was the love that kept us together even when our respective illnesses weakened the bonds between us.

I was drawn to Larry's loving and spirited personality. As fiercely as he loved, just as fiercely did he rage against the ravages of his horrendous past, and the people who caused him to suffer, whether they were in the past or the present. His sleep was troubled by nightmares of those awful times and his days by memories and flashbacks. For decades after the Holocaust he was able to hold back the red tide of psychosis. And then his brain gave up the struggle and the walls came crashing down.

The problems in Larry's brain didn't begin with the

identification of Alzheimer's Disease. In 1992, seemingly suffering from depression, his internist prescribed an anti-depressant. His mood improved. But once he felt better, he stopped it. "I feel fine," he said. "I don't need medicines to make me feel better." And that was the end of that.

In 1998, two years after our wedding, he began to experience more and more periods of becoming "unhinged." He was diagnosed with a depressive psychosis. Medications helped, but after a few months, he refused to continue taking them.

Despite my pleading and the psychiatrist's encouragement, he vehemently declined further treatment. Much to my disappointment, he refused to acknowledge that the symptoms of the illness were a serious problem. For him and for us. Left untreated, those symptoms only got worse. Neither of us handled them well.

In 2004, after a period of time in which Larry's cognitive and emotional state worsened dramatically, I knew there was something else wrong. His thought processes were impaired, and his behavior had become even more unstable, unpredictable and, at times, violent. Larry knew something was wrong, as well, and agreed to a psychiatric consultation.

I wasn't particularly surprised when the diagnosis was Alzheimer's Disease. This time he was open to treatment. The way I see it, my husband's brain was a hotbed of smoldering psychosis onto which the fuel of Alzheimer's Disease was thrown. An incendiary combination.

A week later, I met with Larry's psychiatrist. He explained the diagnosis to me this way: the Alzheimer's was releasing more of the psychosis, and the psychosis was making the Alzheimer's worse. He advised me to be prepared for a gradual decline in all areas of my husband's functioning. His guess at the prognosis was six to eight years, depending on the extent to which Alzheimer's affected his physical health. "However," he noted, "Holocaust survivors with Alzheimer's live longer than the general public. Survival is in their blood."

The physician strongly suggested I consider moving my husband into a specialized memory care facility within the year. "The earlier in the illness you place him, the easier it will be on both of you," he said. "Over seventy-five percent of spouses who care for an Alzheimer's patient at home suffer some type of serious physical or mental illness during the caregiving years."

"Rubbish." That wouldn't be me.

Whenever I mentioned to other healthcare professionals that I intended to care for my husband at home throughout his illness, they usually looked askance at me and shook their heads as if I didn't know what I was talking about. *Was there something I didn't know about Alzheimer's or caregiving?*

A few were so bold to actually say, "That's what you think now."

"What do you mean?" I would say

"Alzheimer's is a two-man, twenty-four-hour-a-day job with lots of overtime, no vacations and zero benefits," one person responded. "I know people like you who've said they were going to do it, but I don't know anyone who has actually been able to do it successfully and then lived to tell about it."

I didn't believe any of them. I wondered if they thought I was weak or didn't love my husband enough to care for him.

In the earliest stage of the illness, I had no inkling of what my husband and I were up against. Not even a hint. Even so, I had every intention of being a model caregiver, understanding and patient, gentle and loving. I assumed my husband would be calm, adoring and appreciative in return, and we would spend lazy, tender days together. I promised him I would care for him at home until he died, and that was where he wanted to be.

I imagined that the course of his illness would be uneventful as he slowly lost his mind and physical health.

Death would be slow, painless and peaceful. Every day, I would sit by his side and whisper words of love. He would slip away from me as I held him gently in my arms.

I recalled one of my conversations with a health care provider. "It couldn't be done," they said.

"I don't know who they're talking about but it's not me," I mentioned to a friend. I loved my husband and he wanted me to care for him at home. And I would. Until the day he died. "How bad could it be? I've taken care of sick people before. I'll be able to manage it, no matter what."

It was the "no matter what" part that did me in.

Nowhere in this preposterous fantasy did I presume Alzheimer's Disease would take down not one, but two lives. Alzheimer's didn't just swoop gracefully out of the sea one day like a shark, its beady eyes fastened on an elusive prey, clamping its jaws around him and spiriting him away. It was no "here today, gone tomorrow" kind of thing.

More precisely, it ate the life out of him, piece by little piece, twenty-four hours a day for ten years. I stood by and watched, helpless.

Alzheimer's hung around my husband's neck like a noose. Year after year the knot drew tighter and strangled more of the life from him. Eventually, his brain just choked to death, taking his body down with it, as well. Years of frightening deterioration. He became a prisoner of an illness that left in its place a helpless child in the body of an adult male, the man I had loved for thirty years.

What I found most stunning about the diagnosis of Alzheimer's is the finality of it all; hope that you can "beat it" is *never* an option. There is no other illness that creates the crushing losses, physically, cognitively, and emotionally, and robs the individual of their identity the way Alzheimer's does. It's damage extends to every person in the individual's close circle, too.

Every week brought a new low. Another task he couldn't do, a skill he couldn't recall, a feeling that was gone, a word he couldn't say, a thought that was no longer there, a memory vanished, a familiar face that became a stranger's. His life became a forgotten past, a fleeting present and an unimagined future.

Debilitating flashbacks during the day came out of nowhere. Later, his doctors labeled them hallucinations, delusions and paranoia.

In the initial phases of the illness, many of the losses came on slowly like forgetting how to read, drive, count, dress himself, shave, shower and tell time. He couldn't remember how to use the telephone, eating utensils or a toothbrush. He no longer recognized familiar places and objects. I couldn't drive with him unless he was sedated. If he felt lost, he would become agitated and try to jump out of the moving car. If we were to go out for a ride, our home would be brand new to him when we returned. It would take him five to ten minutes to recall that yes, it actually was where he lived.

The changes often came on so subtly that I didn't pay much attention until his ability to think about, say or do the particular task was almost gone. He couldn't name a banana, count to ten, and tell the difference between day and night or a child and an adult.

His brain forgot to tell him how to chew and swallow, so he frequently choked when he was eating. I couldn't turn my back on him at mealtimes or he would end up gasping for breath or, worse, choking in silence. I became skilled at using the Heimlich. And calling 911.

Prior to the diagnosis, I didn't pay much attention to his frequent statements about once familiar people, places and things. "This place looks different," he said, or "They've changed things," or "When did we get a new sofa?" or "Who is that person?"

No matter what it was, the decor in our home, our favorite restaurant, the color of my hair, or the well-known route we drove to the grocery store, his memory of it had simply vanished. "The way things used to be" was gone forever. Every familiar thing in his world became new. And every new thing was new again the following day. Or even the next minute.

Every year after the diagnosis, Larry's confusion and disorientation increased and so did his care needs. When he couldn't find the bathroom, he urinated in the foyer. When he forgot what a razor was, I shaved him and then sat on the toilet seat while he was in the shower and told him how to wash himself. When that didn't work, I got into the shower with him. In his final months at home, I wiped his bottom, washed his face, and brushed his teeth.

When something set him off, he would become combative and violent; at other times, delusional, paranoid and suicidal. He saw people only visible to him and heard voices where there weren't any. He accused me of stealing his money, giving him medications that made him "crazy," locking him in a closet or outside the house, or abandoning him altogether.

He packed his suitcase many times, determined to escape. He tried to break windows and climb over the fifth-floor railing. Or he cried uncontrollably. Other times, he was so utterly consumed by irrational fears he became catatonic. "Everything is different!" he would cry in frustration, as he squirted shaving cream onto his hairbrush.

Larry went everywhere with me, including to work. I couldn't go to the bathroom unless he was in the same room with me. If I moved out of his line of sight for just a moment, he would think I was gone forever and panic. He was no better off than a child abandoned in the forest, a hundred miles from home.

There were times when he would sneak out the front door, and I would discover him several floors below, knocking on doors trying to find me. He told the neighbors I had moved out and left him there alone. Or I had thrown him out because I had a new husband. I installed a lock on the front door that he couldn't access.

Sonya Braverman

One day, believing I was the "Gestapo," as he sometimes called me, he put his hands around my neck and tried to choke me. And then he hit me. "Die Nazi!" he screamed.

Who was this person? Not the Larry I married.

Later in the day, we had a conversation something like this.

"Larry, I'm very upset right now. You choked me this morning, hit me and called me a Nazi."

"Me? No! I would never do that to you, Sonya-la. I love you. You're my angel."

"But it happened. This morning. You said you were going to kill me."

"You must have been dreaming. You're the only person in my life I can count on. You know that."

He had no memory of his violent behavior or ugly words just hours before.

A few days later, I found a machete under our bed.

Terrifying nightmares about the horrors of the Holocaust plagued him almost nightly. He would often awaken in the middle of the night screaming and crying, fearful that returning to sleep would bring on more terrors. Or he would lie in bed and mutter aloud to himself for hours. The medicines used to slow down the progression of Alzheimer's made his dreams even more intense; sleeping pills had no effect on him, even when I doubled them. And if he didn't sleep, neither did I.

He needed help with any task requiring more than one step. I would stand next to him in the bathroom and say, "Pick up the tube of toothpaste, take the cap off the toothpaste, spread it on your toothbrush, put the brush in your mouth and brush the top, sides, and bottom. Then, rinse your mouth, rinse the brush, put it back in the holder and cap up the toothpaste." Easy for us. Impossible for him. Labels, lists and signs all over the house didn't help because he couldn't read, understand or remember the written or spoken word.

As the deterioration progressed, Larry's emotional state became more volatile and unpredictable. As the sun went down, he frequently became considerably more agitated, a phenomenon known as "sundowning." He became explosive and violent and was difficult to calm down. You had to experience it to believe it.

It was impossible for him to think about the next minute, hour or next day. The illness, functioning much like a big rectangular eraser, stood in front of the chalkboard of his life and wiped the slate clean of every happiness, heartache, voice and face. The chalk dust fell to the floor in heaps of ancient memories. He was a man who no longer had a past, a present or a future. He couldn't even tell you his name.

Except for the Holocaust. Those memories were as clear as a perfect diamond. For him, the cruelty of Alzheimer's was that he retained the most minuscule detail of every tragedy he endured when most everything else was forgotten and gone. Every face, every horror, every heinous act. It was heartbreaking to watch him rail at the invisible and unknowable. Trying to reason with or comfort him didn't work because he truly believed the Nazis were about to break down the front door and capture him again.

Throughout the illness, Larry saw psychiatrists, psychologists, neurologists and internists. All of them prescribed medications for Alzheimer's Disease, psychosis, sleep, depression and anxiety. He consumed vitamins, minerals, and herbals. He tried medical marijuana, and electroconvulsive therapy (ECT). Almost everything worked. For a day, a week, maybe two. And then it didn't.

There was always something else to try. And on it went. Nothing seemed to elevate his mood, clear his cognitions, ease the anxiety, strengthen his memory, calm the psychosis or hold back the progression of Alzheimer's for very long. No matter what kinds of pills he swallowed, his behavior simply grew more difficult to manage. Alzheimer's Disease was like an erupting volcano, barreling down on him with unimaginable force.

It didn't take long for me to realize how pitifully little can be done to alleviate the manifestations of the disease. *And he is going to live the rest of his life like this. Or worse.* That knowledge was devastating

What all this meant for me was no breaks, no respite and no time to regroup and strengthen my resources to face the next day.

My husband's needs slowly overwhelmed my ability to cope. The process was so subtle in the first year or two I barely noticed the change. In the next two years, the stresses of caring for him escalated, but not once during that time did I consider turning over his care to strangers.

Four years into the illness, exhaustion was a way of life. I was weary in a way I have never before experienced. My husband's needs were endless when he was awake, and he had to be watched every minute. He would nap during the day, but the nights were long and sleepless. It was difficult for me to manage him without sleep. I was irritable to such an extent that if you were to innocently cross my path, there was no guarantee I wouldn't rip your heart out.

In the fifth year, I felt like a dozen bulldozers had been driving back and forth over me for months. I was knocked down and crushed by the responsibilities of caring for the man I loved. I was coming undone at a pretty fast clip. There wasn't anything I could do to hold back, slow down or defeat the illness. It seemed hopeless. Nothing that I did for him seemed to matter. The illness was beating both of us to death.

After six years of caregiving, months of sleepless nights, and serious exhaustion brought about by the stresses of Alzheimer's Disease, I could no longer function effectively. I couldn't continue to provide the increasing level of care he required, even with 'round-the-clock paid help. Larry had deteriorated significantly. Completely worn out, the enormity of my caregiving responsibilities blinded me to the day-to-day challenges I had to overcome to survive. My husband was dying and I was losing faith in my ability to care for him. I didn't know how much more stress I could withstand.

I was in the throes of a nervous breakdown. I wasn't running around with a hatchet looking to chop off heads, but I couldn't function. Not well, anyway. Terribly, in fact. I was as burned out as last winter's fire.

The demands of my husband's care had become physically and emotionally overwhelming: unending stress, weeks of sleepless nights and demanding days. My fuse burned shorter and shorter and my brain was unable to think clearly. Anxiety twisted my guts into a knot. My nerves were shot. Gone.

There was always a thunderstorm of activity in my head. My nervous system was like a tangle of frayed wires. Anything was likely to set me off. My brain, constantly sending out distress signals, was always in a state of high alert. Every feeling I had was enormously exaggerated. It was almost like I was living in the middle of a war zone.

I lost my temper with my husband, and then cried about it later because of the pain I caused both of us, even though he didn't remember from one moment to the next. It seemed like I was *always* crying, even if I made no sound. I cried when I watched the leaves fall from the trees, when my husband remembered my name, when I thought about life, and when I thought about death. I had no idea how I was going to go on.

Despair was all around me like an itchy sweater. Bitter grief stuck in my throat. The tenderness and compassion I felt towards my husband was still there, but the futility of it all ate me away. The feelings of impotency grew; I cared for my husband knowing nothing I did would change the outcome.

Every moment was lost in the moment after. There were times when I began to lose sight of the point of it all — to bring my husband any small bit of comfort and happiness.

Completing one task and moving on to the next became the primary goal.

The empathy I had for my husband began to unravel like a cheap sweater, worn and washed too many times. I cared deeply about Larry and his well-being, but it took too much energy for me to keep going. Just a weak yank on one of my threads was all I needed to come completely undone. And I did, over and over again.

One day, when I thought I couldn't handle any more, I imagined myself putting a pillow over my husband's head while he was sleeping. For a moment, all I wanted was to end it all. To put him and myself out of our combined misery. The thought of it now horrifies me. I was that broken. The spirit-crushing nature of the illness was more than I could bear. It was at that moment that I knew we were *both* in trouble. "Mayday! Mayday!" I screamed silently.

I presented a brave face to the outside world. Only an intimate few knew the extent to which I was sleepless, sick and severely stressed. I was losing it. One day a group of well-meaning friends from my Alzheimer's support group paid me a visit. They all knew Larry well.

"You can't keep doing this. You're coming apart. Larry needs more help than you can give him at home. If you don't move Larry out of the house, you'll die of exhaustion, stress or worse. And if you're gone, what's going to happen to him! Who will care for him? It's time to leave the caregiving to the professionals and concentrate on being a wife." They informed me of an opening at Greyswood, an 8-bed memory care residence for Alzheimer's patients not far from our home.

I called my doctor. "What should I do?" I asked him. He ordered me into his office the following day and put it like this: "You've been wearing out for six years. All of your operating systems are damaged. You have nothing left to give."

He called what was happening to me a "nervous breakdown." He reminded me about the connection between persistent stress and heart disease, strokes and cancer. "I'm surprised you've made it as long as you have. It's time to move Larry to a new home. You'll both be better off. He needs more care than you can provide, and you need to recuperate, be a wife and say goodbye."

I resisted, reluctant to give up or give in. But I knew all of them were right. I had lost the ability to work, nurse my husband or take care of myself. I couldn't think, I had no control over my emotions and I was losing my grip. Actually, I had *lost* my grip. Plain and simple. I was holding on desperately to what was left of my husband and the ragged scraps of our life. I had to face the facts: my husband was dying and I couldn't save him. I couldn't even take care of him anymore.

With relief and sadness, I prepared myself for our last days together at home. It was difficult for me to accept that Larry had deteriorated to the point where caring for him at home was no longer an option. He needed more than I could give him. In the end, love wasn't enough.

On a magnificent sunny morning in the summer of 2010, I left my husband in the expertly caring and genuinely loving hands of some very special nurses. More than four years after his death, I still have to hold back the tide of guilt for relinquishing him to the care of strangers.

I remained with him for most of that first day. I will never forget the sound of his voice following me out the front door that evening, "*Please*, Sonya-la, don't leave me here! I want to go home with *you! Please don't leave me!*"

I returned home alone, realizing I would never share a home or a bed with my husband ever again. The marriage as I had come to know it was over. Had been over for years. And the man I had been in love with for over twenty-five years was gone. It was the saddest day of my life. I felt like I had failed as a wife and a caregiver.

And now I understood why so many people said, "It can't be done, it's too much, it's too hard."

I visited Larry every day after he moved. Sometimes he searched his brain frantically to remember who I was. He didn't recall my name or that we were married, but he usually knew me as someone special. On the days when I was a complete stranger to him, he would become agitated, shout at me and order me out of his house.

One afternoon as I was helping him in the bathroom, I asked him, "Who is that handsome man?" as I pointed to his image in the mirror. We studied our reflections for a long time as we stood side-by-side in front of his bathroom vanity. He bent forward over the sink, wrinkled up his brow and moved closer to the man who looked back at him. "I don't know," he announced, looking completely perplexed.

"That's Larry," I remarked, pointing to him. "That man is *you*. The man I love. My husband." He gazed carefully at his image again and then turned his head to look at me. He didn't recognize the face of the man looking back at him. I wanted to scream and cry, all at once. What could possibly ravage a person's brain so badly that they couldn't even recognize their own reflection in a mirror? It is, perhaps, that one moment in which I knew that the end was not far off.

It was a genuinely understanding, sensitive and knowledgeable Hospice physician who was the first person to finally put his struggle into words. She felt Larry's emotional and cognitive pain to be just as much a torment as any physical pain, and treated it as such.

"The torment your husband is going through with Alzheimer's Disease is no different than the stabbing, aching pain of a physical illness." What Larry needed more than anything was to be released from the tortures of his mind. She prescribed Thorazine, a sixty-some-year-old and rarely used anti-psychotic medication.

Within the first week of treatment, the nightmares and

flashbacks disappeared. He was sleeping peacefully at night and resting comfortably during the day. His behavior had become more manageable. His memories of the Holocaust were laid to rest. The emotional pain had disappeared and he was finally at peace.

In the next few months prior to his death, I began to say goodbye to my husband. I held him close and whispered words of love to him. I thanked him for being the kind and gentle man he was. I shared my gratitude with him for being by my side during the years in which I rebuilt my life. I told him he could leave whenever he wanted to, and that I would never forget the love we shared. I think he knew that I was going to be all right. He was no longer a prisoner of his painful past. He was finally becoming a free man.

I still have to remind myself I wasn't weak. I simply had unreasonable expectations. I wasn't stupid. I just underestimated the enormity of his needs and the responsibilities brought on by the illness. And I wasn't selfish or cold-hearted. I should have listened to the professionals and placed him in specialized care sooner than I did. It would have been healthier for both of us. I ignored the signs that I was coming undone for far too long.

I didn't blame my husband; he was merely a victim of his degenerating brain. Searching for a way to explain it to myself, I would mutter, "Why him? A Holocaust survivor. Hasn't he suffered enough?

I will always have regrets, but perhaps in time the pain of those regrets will diminish. I will be forever grateful to Larry who enriched my life in ways I never could have imagined. He's still teaching me how to be more compassionate towards myself and others.

While I emerged from the experience of Alzheimer's Disease irreparably damaged, it transformed me for the better. Alzheimer's Disease was a "finishing school" like no other. It forced me to think about the meaning of life in all its fragility, to explore the consequences of those decisions I made for the better and those that didn't turn out so well, and to look at the people in my life with fresh eyes. If for no other reason than that, I owe my husband a great deal. But I owe him so much more. It was he who, with his support, helped me get sober and turn my life around.

Someday I intend to fill an enormous balloon with all of my guilt, regrets, self-blame and sorrows. On a warm, sunny day, blue sky overhead, and a gentle breeze drifting through the trees, the kind of day Larry would have enjoyed, I'll climb to the top of a mountain. Standing on tiptoe, I'll raise my arms high, whisper "Farewell" and release the balloon. It will be gone forever. Wherever my husband's spirit is, I believe he'll let me know in some way that it's okay to forgive myself.

Chapter 23

How Did Those Get Here?

Following that infamous Thanksgiving celebration twenty years ago when I lived my last day as a drunk, many such holidays came and went before I hosted another Thanksgiving. The Queen of Everything had long since passed on. She was still a queen, just not of *everything.*

Every Thanksgiving thereafter brought back the dark days of my addiction. It wasn't just the memories of my behavior that Thanksgiving that freaked me out; it was more the memories of my boozehound *life*, the squandered moments, missed opportunities, ruined relationships and years lost to the horrors of alcohol, recollections that will forever haunt me. My current life was a world apart from the past when the bottle controlled me.

I continued to work on putting to rest unhealthy and unproductive behavior patterns acquired through many years of heavy drinking. Knowing where I was and looking back on my drinking years made me sick to my stomach. *What the hell was I thinking?*

Slogging through the untenable stresses brought about by my husband's illness sometimes set me on the brink of relapse. The months before I placed my husband in residential care was the only time I even came close to drinking, but only in my thoughts.

I would imagine myself going to a bar and just having one, a single iridescent, amber-colored shot of something. Anything. To sip languorously, waiting for it to course through my veins and put my brain on ice. Relief, sweet relief.

Some days I would think, "It would be so easy to just drive to the liquor store, buy my poison and end the inexhaustible search for a "better" way. Swallow my beverage of choice and be done with it. Easy? Of course.

And deadly. Ruinous. Shameful.

"It's just temporary. Until the stress passes. Then I can pick up my sobriety where I left off."

Foolish woman. Drinking will only stave off a much worse fate. And besides, how would you feel about losing twenty years of progress?

I never relapsed. I had other coping mechanisms now and, for the most part, was able to step back, reevaluate and choose more effective ways to handle the tightrope of life. And sobriety. But I wasn't perfect. Some days were easier than others. And a few were downright terrible. It often seemed like I moved from one demanding challenge to another. With each one, I became stronger, smarter and more resilient.

I had a private clinical social work practice and a part-time consulting business, as well, presenting workshops on mental health topics to both mental health professionals and lay persons.

I was also an active volunteer. I was a field supervisor for Master's-level social work students and served on the boards of the local American Cancer Society and National Kidney Foundation. I never turned down a worthy *pro bono* client. I reviewed books for the Jewish Community Center. I loved to cook and was a skilled needlecrafter. I was very busy.

I was fortunate to have long-time friends whose friendship had survived the worst days of my alcoholism. And some new ones who entered my life with the onset of my husband's illness. Life was better in many ways, but the constant reminders of the destructive nature of Alzheimer's Disease would often bring me to my knees.

By Thanksgiving of 2012, my husband had been living at Greyswood for a year-and-a-half. The decision to place him outside of our home was the hardest one I ever made. I would never reconcile myself to the nature of our separation. I grieved fresh every time I saw him. But I had no choice.

His adjustment was lengthy and difficult. It took six months for him to settle in to his new home. Every week he experienced some physical, cognitive or emotional loss. Psychosis and Alzheimer's made him a caregiver's nightmare. He was difficult to manage and couldn't be left alone.

He was quite a handful for the staff at Greyswood. In his first year alone, he ran away from his residence, broke the security alarm, took off his clothes and got in bed with another resident, hit a nurse and another resident, and began pooping in the hallway. Greyswood purchased a camera that was trained on him wherever he was. There was no telling what he would do when he wasn't under the watchful eye of one of his nurses.

The nurses at Greyswood were outstanding, yet Larry often had his own private-duty nurse, Mila. During the times when he became violent or out-of-control, especially when he was "sundowning," she was usually able to calm him down. She was loving and gentle, but firm when she had to be. Larry was fond of Mila and called her "Sonya." He held her hand and kissed her frequently. He trusted Mila, and often called out for her when she wasn't on duty.

Once Larry was admitted to Greyswood, he never returned home. His emotional state was unstable, and those who were caring for him worried that coming home for a visit might trigger a meltdown. His meltdowns were psychotic in nature. As an observer, they were pretty scary. I can only imagine how difficult they were for him. It often took the staff hours to settle him down.

I was just as concerned that he wouldn't *remember* his home, and then I would have to accept, once and for all, that his memories of life with me were gone for good. That reality felt like someone had just unloaded a tray of ice cubes on my bare skin.

Larry had good days, a few, when he would be vaguely in touch with reality and others, when he was so delirious he required *two* nurses to manage him. There was no telling when he woke up in the morning whether he would be a ferocious tiger or a gentle lamb.

I knew it was selfish, but I wanted to experience his presence in our home one more time and figured Thanksgiving would be a good opportunity to do that. Given the unpredictability of his behavior and the frequent fluctuations in his physical health, Mila and I waited until several days prior to Thanksgiving to make a final decision.

When that time arrived, Larry was calm and quiet. We decided to move ahead with our plan for Thanksgiving. I prepared the meal and invited several people who Larry had known well and Mila's family.

Thanksgiving Day emerged sunny and mild. The red and white geraniums sitting in fat ceramic pots on the deck still bloomed profusely. The windows lining the back of the house were filled with vistas of the serene woodlands that Larry loved so much, the trees dressed breathtakingly in autumnal colors. Soon the branches would be naked, but today they were a glorious tribute to fall.

I cooked all the foods my husband used to enjoy. Similar to the Thanksgiving almost twenty years before, the table was set, the silver sparkled, the china shone and silver candlesticks graced the middle of the table. Subtle classical music threaded its way through the house.

All the guests arrived and were seated comfortably in

the living room awaiting the arrival of my husband, Larry. At precisely five o'clock the doorbell rang. I felt anxious. I had no idea what to expect. The part of me that wasn't prepared to let go of my husband *or* the marriage knew that as soon as he crossed the threshold it would all come back, all the lost memories and feelings.

As I rushed to the foyer to answer the door, I looked in the mirror one final time, wondering whether my husband would recognize me. I visited him daily, and it often took some time for him to figure out who I was. Other days, there didn't seem to be any hint of recognition whatsoever.

I opened the front door and was momentarily stunned. Larry stood at the entrance flanked by Mila, her husband and son. He looked so handsome and well-groomed. Mila made sure that his appearance was impeccable at all times. It was just what I expected. What I didn't expect was how much he had changed from the last time he stood in the same doorway a year-and-a-half ago. He was shorter, thinner and frail. I hadn't noticed the dramatic difference in his physical appearance until now.

Larry was holding Mila's hand. As I opened the door, he appeared startled, as if he weren't expecting to see anyone else there. *Did he recognize me? Was he trying to figure out who I was?* His facial expression was blank and he stood very still. The aroma of his cologne settled over me like a cozy afghan. How much I had missed him!

"Happy Thanksgiving," I said, holding out my hand to him. He looked at me as if he didn't know what to do or say. When he didn't respond, I added, "Welcome to my home. I'm so happy you could come for Thanksgiving dinner."

Larry extended his hand to me as he stepped into the foyer, guided by Mila. "How do you do," he said. With those words I knew he didn't recognize me. His head moved from side to side as he previewed the room. He didn't appear to remember his former home, either.

Mila removed his coat and hung it in the closet. As she

did, he moved closer to her and whispered, "This is a real nice place."

"Tell her that, Larry," Mila murmured to him.

Turning to me then, he said, "Your home is beautiful." He was so polite. Larry never forgot his social graces.

"Thank you," I responded. "I'm very happy you're here."

We moved into the living room, and I introduced the assembled guests, all individuals Larry had known for many years. He looked around the room; there wasn't anyone who triggered a spark of recognition. Every long-time friend was a stranger now.

Larry and Mila's family made themselves comfortable in the living room. Some of the guests spoke to Larry and he responded appropriately and politely, but not with any sense of familiarity.

"Would you like something to drink, Larry?" I asked. He looked at Mila, perhaps trying to make sense of my question or not knowing what to answer.

"How about some Johnny Walker?" I asked again, hoping the mention of his favorite drink would elicit a favorable response. Like most everything, the vacant look in his eyes told me "Johnny Walker" was no longer stored in his memory bank. He had no idea what it was. In the past, he would have perked right up with a knowing smile.

I was searching frantically for some connection. "You love Orangina, Larry. Would you like some?" He simply looked at me blankly.

Mila suggested a glass of water without ice. Larry looked at her and shook his head in agreement.

Several minutes later, I approached him and said, "Larry, would you like to take a tour of my home?" I wondered whether anything about where he'd lived would elicit a blink of memory.

"Of course," he said. Mila helped him up and I led the way. He was always so agreeable.

We walked into the kitchen we had both created from scratch not so long ago. I pointed to the photographs of familiar faces attached by magnets to the side of the refrigerator. He looked at them and nodded his head in response, but seemed oblivious. *How could he have forgotten their faces?*

As we walked down the hall, we stopped at what used to be *his* bathroom. "Do you like this wallpaper, Larry?" I asked.

"Very nice," he said, barely noticing it. We'd pored over book after book of wallpaper samples to choose the one with hazy images of birds that lined the walls of his bathroom. He used to pride himself on being able to correctly identify each of the birds. Today, nothing.

Further down the hallway was the bedroom we shared. Nothing about it had changed since he was gone. As he looked around the room, his face was expressionless. No flicker, no flash, no millisecond twitch of the eyelids. Not a thing.

From there, it was just a few steps into the library. This room was his favorite. With the sun pouring in from the floor-to-ceiling windows, this was where Larry spent the most time when he was home. He loved that room, sunny, cozy and comfortable.

One wall was lined with books and a large television, and another was covered with photographs of his family, most of whom were deceased. We had lovingly restored and framed all of the photographs. It was here in this room that he felt the most comfortable.

He looked around the room and as his eyes settled on the photos, a look of astonishment covered his face. More animated than I had seen him in months, he turned to Mila and excitedly said, "How did those get here?"

"What do you mean, Larry?" asked Mila

"Those pictures, those people. I know them."

"Who are they, Larry?" Mila inquired, pointing to the wall.

"Those are my family," he said with a strong, confident voice. He knew exactly what he was talking about. The connection was genuine. He moved closer to the photos as if he'd never seen them before. He could point out who most of the people were. "Why are these here?" he said, wondering why photographs of his family were hanging in *my* house.

"Well," Mila continued, "you used to live in this house with your wife, Sonya. Before you moved to Greyswood. Not that long ago." I remained silent as she pointed to me.

"Are you *kiddin'* me?" he said, his face contorted in a look of disbelief. "No, that can't *be*," he exclaimed. *"You're* my wife. I live with *you."*

Mila knew better than to try and correct him. He looked at Mila questioningly. It was clear he could not grasp the concept of me as his wife and the place he was standing as his former home. She could see he was struggling to remember his wife, the house in which he had lived and the photos of his family hanging on the wall. It was too much for him. He was becoming agitated so she quickly drew his attention back to the photos. "Who is *this* person, Larry?"

I left them in the den as they talked about the photos, returning to the kitchen to put the final touches on the Thanksgiving meal. Larry and Mila returned to the living room, with Larry still asking why the photographs were hanging in this stranger's unfamiliar home.

"Dinner is served," I announced. "Larry, would you like to join me in the dining room?" I asked.

Larry sat across from me at the opposite end of the table. Mila and her family seated themselves around him. During the meal, Larry didn't interact with anyone other than Mila. He never looked at me or any of the other guests. Before dessert, he turned to Mila, and grasping one of her hands in his and kissing it (he was always *so* affectionate), he whispered, "Darling, I love you. I'm very tired. I want to go home now."

As he rose, all of the guests bade him farewell. I walked him to the front door. Mila helped Larry with his coat. "Thank her for dinner, Larry" Mila whispered to him.

His voice was weak and tired. "Thank you very much for dinner," he repeated.

Perhaps this was too much for him after all. He looks so worn out. And sick.

"Thank you for coming, Larry. I hope to see you again soon," I responded achingly. My heart wanted to wriggle right out of my chest and embrace him eagerly. And never let him go.

With that, the genteel man with perfect manners held out his hand to shake mine in farewell and said, "Of course." There was not a speck of recognition.

Sadly, I closed the door on my husband's last visit home, grief cascading over me. I hesitated for a moment and allowed myself to sink into the moment. How different both of our lives were since that dreadful Thanksgiving twenty years in the past. For me, much of my life had changed for the better. For Larry, however, the man he had been was gone.

I was still profoundly in love with my husband, a man who had lost his past, had no future, and could barely live in the present moment.

He had become a stranger.

Chapter 24
Done With Him

The man and I sit caddy-corner from one another at the island in the middle of my kitchen. We're eating dinner together, a meal I've thoughtfully prepared to please him. Between us, resting in a rustic earthen bowl with a tawny-colored glaze, sits an appealingly pristine salad, lightly dressed with fresh herbs and a luminous drizzle of a pungent olive oil. The greens, some pale, some red-tinged, and others darker, lived happily in the ground this morning at Farmer Mac's.

A well-marbled, tenderhearted steak, steeped for hours in an herb-scented marinade, sizzles on a carving board in front of us, ready to slice. It's grilled just the way he likes it, mostly pink with a medium red center. Small multi-colored potatoes, slowly roasted with big chunks of fragrant garlic are piled in a sea green ceramic bowl. The kitchen is fat with the homey, almost sexy, aromas of simple food, well-prepared. The man has discovered a great deal of pleasure at my table.

He stands and carves the buttery meat and places it on a platter. His eyes are brimming with appetite. The dim light from the opal glass fixture hanging above the island casts a honeyed glow over both of us.

As we eat, the man and I talk, mostly about what we did during the day, what we'll do after dinner and our plans for tomorrow. He shares a funny story about a mutual friend, and I tell him something humorous one of my grandchildren recently said. Perhaps we talk about the weather, and his return to Chicago late the next day. He asks me about my husband, who is in the end stage of Alzheimer's Disease; the man is eager to hear about whether he had a good day or a bad day. He's interested in hearing how my husband's decline is affecting *me*.

"This food is wonderful," he says smiling, as he draws out the "wonderful" slowly and sensually. "*Won-der-ful*," he repeats.

"Thank you." I'm anxious to please him.

The man puts his fork down. His elbows are on the table and his hands are clasped. He's looking at me. He's not staring at me, but he's not *just* looking at me either; it's more like he's searching for something in my face. Or waiting. Perhaps he's simply choosing the most appropriate words to describe the meal.

Out of nowhere it comes. "I love you, Sonya," the man says.

The words are spoken clearly and carefully. Stunned, I feel as if I've just been slapped in the face. I'm not altogether certain I've heard him correctly.

He was just joking, of course.

A few seconds pass before I'm able to speak. "*What* did you say?" I ask him. The man continues to look at me, but I turn away. His startling confession has dazed me.

Brooding over the significance of the man's words, I begin to feel annoyed and angry. After all, from the beginning of our friendship, we had an "understanding." We were friends. School friends. Old friends. But the man isn't one to speak without thinking, especially about topics like love. He's not impulsive. He's not thoughtless or, least of all, manipulative. "Are you *kidding*?" I say incredulously, my voice rising higher with every syllable.

"No, I'm *not* kidding, Sonya. I love you," he repeats, just as calmly and confidently as before.

I permit each syllable, spoken in his deep and mellow voice, to gradually trickle over, through and around me. The words are electrifying, but untimely. Maybe at some future time or place my heart would perk right up at his words of love, rise joyfully out of my chest, and embrace the man. But not now. I stiffen my grip on reality; the pressure to push him physically and emotionally away from me is overwhelming. I'm suffocating on the sound of his voice.

"Please, don't *ever* say that to me again. *Not ever!*" Staring him down and speaking fiercely, I say, "I'm a married woman, I love my husband, and he needs me." His eyes are sharply, but not unkindly, focused on me as I lower my head in shame and embarrassment.

"You and I are just friends," I say, looking at him again, as I return to more rational thinking. "I like you, and we have fun together. That's as far as it goes. Nothing more. Besides, we had an agreement, remember? No serious relationship. There's no future in you and me. I'm here, and you're in Chicago. My husband is dying of Alzheimer's, and this is where my life is. Don't *ever* use the word 'love' again! *Please.*"

My soliloquy spoken, I wonder if the man will be convinced I'm sincere. He's still looking at me but saying nothing

Serene and composed, just as he always is, without so much as the slightest flinch or hesitation, he continues to study me thoughtfully. He's not insulted. He's not offended. He doesn't rise from his chair, raise his voice, and call me names or walk out. He doesn't say I'm an ungrateful shrew. And he doesn't back down, apologize or say, "I never should have said that to you." That isn't his style. I have never met anyone quite like him.

A moment or two pass where we simply look at each other. *I hope he'll say no more. I would like to pretend this scene has never happened.*

"Well," the man finally says, dribbling the "w-e-l-l" out

leisurely as if to prepare me for an even bigger shock, "You *may* be a married woman, Sonya, but you don't have a *husband*."

I'm speechless. *Did I just hear what I think I heard?*

The man resumes eating, oblivious to the epiphany his pronouncement has created. I pick at my food, wanting to dismiss what he's just said. I'm unable to think clearly. Bloated with guilt, I lower myself into the bath of despair.

How could I possibly justify having fun and feeling happy with another man when my husband has lost so much of who he is and has so little to look forward to? The man even sleeps in the bed where my husband used to sleep! What would people think if they knew? What could I have been thinking? I'm filled with disgust for how I've behaved.

"How dare you betray the vows you made to your husband," my demons shout at me. "You must be *crazy*. Put your big girl shoes on and deal with your life, selfish bitch," they yell in one ear, "Slut!" even louder in the other.

I'm not ready to think of myself as a widow yet. My husband is still alive. I love him. Life must go on for both of us. And I must remain free of any other complicated emotional attachments.

Right then and there, at that precise moment in time, I decide the relationship with the man must end. *Will* end. He didn't follow the rules. *He'll return to Chicago tomorrow, and I'll be done with him. I'll tell him before he leaves.*

As soon as I say these words to myself, I feel the scalpel-sharp tip of a saber puncture my guts, releasing a sorrow that gushes from my pores. It's an all-too familiar feeling.

The tumultuous years with my husband, a Holocaust survivor, the psychosis and Alzheimer's Disease which began to take him from me soon after our wedding, the marriage into which I poured so much of myself trying to make it right, the ricocheting intensity of emotion, the sheer exhaustion of those years, and now the end of the relationship with the man who sits next to me. It's all too much. Every cell in my body feels like it's being squeezed dry. I'm riding a rollercoaster draped from top to bottom in black crepe.

Over the last year, I've come to look forward to the easy conversation and comfortable companionship with the gentle man who sits next to me. We talk late into the night, he in Chicago and I in Bethesda. Our visits together are warm and plump with laughter. His relaxed nature, subtle sense of humor and easygoing temperament are a welcome relief from the turbulence of the last eight years. Perhaps, I should say, *my entire life*. Nothing seems to disrupt his Zen. Not even *me*.

His presence has become a surprisingly satisfying pleasure. He doesn't ask for much, and he doesn't take much. I believe he knows there's not much left in me to give. He doesn't condemn, and he doesn't judge. He knows how to reach me without words. I can tell him who I was and how I used to be, and his response is, "So what? That was then and this is now." He's not thrown off by my slightly wild and wacky side.

I'm not sure precisely what "happy" is, but sometimes I think I might feel it when I'm with him. It's something new. I've never had more than fleeting moments of happiness in my life. People tell me I look better, more rested and cheerful. My friendship with the man, in the midst of all the grief and chaos in my life, has created a cradle of peace I've never before experienced. I wonder if the end of our relationship will destroy all that.

I allow myself to daydream, and imagine I'm at the neighborhood pool. I climb up the two hundred and one steps to the high board. With all the poise and class I can muster, I spread my wings gracefully. I flex the muscles in my legs so I'm able to stand as tall as I possibly can and, balanced elegantly on the tips of my toes, hesitate at the end of the diving board. I close my eyes and pause for just a moment to center myself and, with great beauty and style, finesse an exquisite swan dive into the tranquil and steady waters of the pool.

In a millisecond, my lovely reverie shatters and I find myself shouting silently, "Don't do it! For God's sake, don't take another step forward! Move away from the board and you won't get hurt. Stop now before all is lost. You have a sick husband to care for."

I must peel the man off of me and remove any residue of *him* as soon as possible.

We finish dinner with dessert and small talk. I pretend the "I love you" never happened. He keeps me company while I do the dishes and then settles into a comfortable chair to catch up on the news. We watch a movie and slide into bed together. I sleep well when I'm with him. I've never enjoyed sleeping as much as I do when he's next to me. He says I purr before I fall asleep.

I think about the man all the time. I don't want him to leave. I miss him when he's gone. But I'm convinced that ending it now is the right thing to do. I'll eventually forget about him and the sadness will fade away.

"I'll tell him on the way to the airport tomorrow," I mutter glumly to myself.

Chapter 25

The Man In The Car

Time passes. I don't tell the man I'm done with him. There are many opportunities to do so, but every time I plan to say the words, I think tomorrow would be a better time. And when tomorrow comes there's always something about what the man says or does that makes me keep my mouth shut.

Perhaps my ambivalence about ending the relationship is what drives me. I like the man. A lot. And we have so much in common. But that's as far as I let myself go in mulling over my feelings about him. Yet, I continue to tell myself I'm determined to say "Goodbye."

But I don't.

The man's good natured lack of compliance with my request ("Please, don't *ever* say you love me again, *not ever!*") becomes part of our everyday banter. With a grin, he silently forms the forbidden words, writes love letters or draws pictures of hearts on my grocery list. When I remind him of my request, his response is, "You told me not to *say* it," he jests. "I assume you meant *out loud.*" Well, that's true, that's what I said. Most of the time I just smile and say nothing.

I look for every fault I can find in the man to convince myself I should finally end it. He lives in Chicago; he has a bird;

he's too quiet, too calm, too funny, too clean, too neat, too consistent, too helpful, too stable, too nice, too understanding, too kind, too accommodating, too agreeable, too handsome, too sensitive and too patient.

He's just not for me.

And, to top it off, he's a drinker. Or, I should say, he drank. Used to drink. He says that when he met me and discovered I'd been sober for years, it made him think about his *own* drinking habits.

"I knew I was drinking too much. When you told me you didn't drink and why, it got me thinking. I don't need alcohol in my life anymore." He wanted to stop, and says I gave him the motivation.

"Don't stop because of me; that's not a good reason to go sober. Because of somebody else."

"Maybe not. But I knew you would never tolerate having a drinker as a friend."

I think of the man as merely a temporary dalliance. A distraction. When I end the relationship, I don't expect to be that upset. After all, he lives 700 miles away. Besides, I'm probably just searching for someone to fill the void left by my beloved husband's illness.

But isn't it possible that our relationship is the real deal?

No, I don't think so. Rebound romances, especially long-distance ones, don't ever work out.

I'm prepared to tell the man goodbye (after all, he loves me, and nothing good can ever come of that).

Another six months pass. I don't break up with the man. We continue our long conversations deep into most nights. He flies back and forth for regular visits.

On one of those visits, we awaken one morning to a dazzlingly beautiful day in mid-June. It's the kind of day one doesn't see very often in a Washington, DC summer, otherwise known as a "tropical jungle." Cool, sunny and dry. A rare beauty.

The man and I are enjoying a few days together. He drives me to Greyswood, the private residence where my husband lives. The man is accustomed to my daily visits when he's in town. He understands my husband comes first. Before anything else in my life.

The man parks the car at the end of the street, like he always does. He sits there for as long as it takes me to visit with my husband and reads a book or does crossword puzzles until I return. Today, he parks in a warm patch of sun. When I open the door of the car to exit, he says the same thing he always does, "Take as much time as you need. I'm fine. I like sitting here and enjoying the beautiful day."

I always respond with the same words, "Are you sure?"

As I walk up the street towards Greyswood, I glimpse the colorful baskets of flowers hanging on the front porch. I hope their beauty will bring some small joy to my husband who had so carefully tended his rose garden before he became ill. Often, it's the most basic pleasures of life that bring him some meager happiness. *His world has become so small.*

I climb the stairs to the entrance and ring the bell. Almost immediately, the door is opened by one of the staff nurses. I enter the foyer, we exchange pleasantries, and I step into the living room where I see Mila. She's my husband's favorite nurse. She tells me Larry's having a good day today.

I've come to learn "a good day" means he's cooperative and calm; he didn't tear out the security alarm, break windows, rage deliriously, strike anyone, choke, poop in the hallway or cry uncontrollably. "He ate well, too," she continues, "but he's been calling for you again. He's sitting in his chair in the family room. He'll be happy to see you."

Donna and Rosaline, other nurses, step into the living room to join us. "But first," Mila says as she gently grips my arm and smiles, glancing at the other nurses, "there's something we'd like to talk to you about." Sensing my uneasiness, she immediately says, "Don't worry, nothing's wrong with Larry."

I'm not relieved. I don't believe her and expect the worst. *We've discussed the possibility of Larry moving to a facility that's better equipped to deal with patients who are as difficult to manage as he's been. Are they going to tell me Larry must leave Greyswood, his behavior so burdensome they can't handle him anymore? Will I have to find another place for him to live?*

"Well," Mila says hesitantly, "I'm not exactly sure how to say this to you, Sonya, um, well, you see," she says hesitantly, "we all know there's a man in your car."

What? No, no. It can't be. I've been so careful. This is awful. I was afraid this would happen. They know about my unseemly behavior. I'm so embarrassed.

"He sits in the car and waits for you whenever you visit Larry." All three of the nurses nod their heads in unison to acknowledge their agreement with this statement. "And he's sitting in the car now," Mila says.

The words are shattering. I prayed something like this wouldn't happen. I should have ended the relationship long ago. Before anyone found out what a tramp I am.

Stunned, I cannot give myself even a second to think for fear my hesitation will be seen as an admission of guilt. "What are you talking about? There's no *man* in my car," I rattle on with more than a fair amount of indignation.

My secret has been discovered. What am I going to do? I refuse to admit to anything. My initial reaction is to become defensive and cover up the evidence, just like a cat does after using the litter box.

"We've seen him sitting in your car parked down the

street!" Rosaline, the nurse manager, exclaims excitedly as if she's just discovered America.

I'm devastated. *I've worked so hard to keep the man a secret. Now everyone will finally discover that I'm not the loving and attentive wife they thought I was. How could I have been stupid enough to think I could carry this off? I should have been done with the man a long time ago, before my good reputation was dragged through the muck. The man and I cannot continue to see one another. It will be over when I leave here today. For sure. Look at the trouble this relationship has gotten me into. Today. Nothing will stop me!*

Seconds pass and I come to my senses. "Okay, okay," I say. "There *is* a man in the car, but he's just a friend. We went to kindergarten together and all through school. I've known him for decades. Just an old friend — that's all." I hope this explanation will satisfy them because I want this spectacle to end. They're all smiling.

Why on earth are they smiling?

"If he's just a friend, why haven't you introduced him to your husband?" Mila says. "Larry loves visitors."

"Oh no, no, no," I hastily respond. "I don't think that's a good idea. *Not* a good idea. He prefers to sit in the car. Really he does. He has work to do."

"Oh, come on, Sonya, we know you pretty well. You can't fool us. We've been aware for months that you have someone in your life," Donna insists, putting her arm around my shoulders and hugging me. "You're *so* much happier and more relaxed lately. You seem to be handling the ups and downs of Larry's illness much better. It shows on your face."

"He's *not* a boyfriend. Really, he's not. Just a friend."

I'm aware the nurses have known what I believed was well-hidden for quite a while. They're still smiling. "It would be a *very* good thing for you if you had a boyfriend, Sonya, in fact, *wonderful*, and we would be happy for you if you did," Rosaline continues, beaming at me, as if she has not heard anything I've said. "Larry would be happy, too. He *wants* you to be happy. Just because *his* life is ending doesn't mean yours should, too. The last few years have been terribly difficult; you deserve to be happy and enjoy your life. It's okay. It's great. But now's the time to bring the man in and let him meet your husband. Larry would like the opportunity to get to know him. So would we!"

My head is swimming backwards in an onward rushing current. I'm knotted up with indecision. There's no use in continuing to deny a clearly obvious fact. They know. "Go ahead," Mila says, pointing to the door. "tell him to come in."

Chapter 26

Who Is That Guy?

I walk out the front door of Greyswood, closing it behind me. I'm going to tell the man I'm done with him. "It's over. This is never going to work. Our relationship is complicating my life. That's all. Goodbye. Have a good life."

That's exactly what I'll say. Why would he agree to meet my husband? He would *never* want to do something like that. Of course not. It's ridiculous, but I couldn't argue with Mila. I'm sure the man will just blow it off or say, "Later," "Tomorrow," or "Next time." Or, "I didn't bargain for this. No way." Or, "Your husband is not my problem." Actually, I am not his problem, either.

As I walk down the street towards the car, I can tell he's reading. He won't like what I'm about to say. "I can't see you anymore," I'll announce. Maybe he'll say something funny or ignore it. Or maybe he'll blow up and drive off in a rage, screaming about all the time and money he's wasted on me.

That's it. That's exactly what he'll do.

No. He won't. He won't do any of that. That's not the way he reacts to things. It's possible that he'll just put me off. "I know how upset you are after seeing Larry. Let's go out for coffee and talk about it."

Yeah. That's it. That's what he'll say. Of course.

Or, I'll just get back in the car with the man like nothing's happened, ignore Mila's suggestion and go home. Then, on the way to the airport tomorrow I'll tell him to leave and never come back. I'll wash my hands of all this drama. Finally. Forever.

"Is Larry okay?" the man says as I open the door of the car. "You look worried. And you usually spend more time with him." I sit down on the seat, one leg in the car, the other on the curb. I'm staring at the floor of the car, lost in my thoughts. "What's wrong, Sonya?"

"Nothing. They think you should come in and meet Larry," I say in a barely audible voice. I'm trembling.

Why am I saying this? This is not how it's supposed to go!

"Who's 'they'?"

"Larry's nurses. They've seen you sitting in the car. They know about us. But I told them we were just friends. It's a terrible idea. I *knew* you wouldn't want to do it. And that's fine with me."

"Well, Sonya, I guess you '*knew*' wrong." The man is unruffled by the strange request. "I would love to meet Larry. I've heard so many wonderful things about him. I think it would be nice."

I turn around sharply and look at him. He's smiling. Sure of himself. Comfortable. "No. Really? Are you sure?"

I can't believe this.

"You don't have to do this," I say incredulously. "I don't think it's a good idea. Let's just go get some coffee and talk it over."

Is that my voice?

"C'mon," he motions to me, already out of the car. "Let's go."

That's so like him. He makes a decision and follows through. Is there anything at all that bothers him?

We walk up the front steps of the house. I'm nervous. The man is not.

How does he do it?

As we enter the house, my husband is standing in the living room holding Mila's hand, facing us. I walk over to him and say, "Hi Larry, my darling, how're you doing?" I can tell by his expression he recognizes me today.

"Sonya-la, my angel," he says with a smile, reaching out for me. My heart wants to melt with both love and sadness when I see him. He's losing weight and becoming weaker. I can't imagine what it must be like to be him.

What did he ever do to deserve this? Hasn't he been through enough?

Larry doesn't notice the man standing next to me. His world has become so small that when I'm present, he sees nothing but me. When I'm not around, he often calls my name endlessly. "Larry," I continue, "I'm so happy to see you today." I hug him tightly and whisper, "I love you" in his ear.

We stand there holding each other for a long time. "Larry, I've brought someone with me today who would like to meet you. The man moves closer to us. I'd like to introduce you to my old friend from school," I say. I point to the man standing next to me who smiles and holds out his hand.

So far, so good.

Larry's lost several inches of height during the course of his illness and his eyesight is impaired. The man is tall and towers over him by eight inches, at least. My husband is searching for the visitor at eye level and doesn't see him. I point towards the ceiling, directing his eyes upward. He sees the man then, and extends his hand in greeting.

"Thank you for coming," Larry says politely.

"I've heard so much about you, Larry," the man says

warmly, looking directly at my husband. "Thank you for welcoming me to your home. It's my pleasure to finally meet you. You know, Sonya and I have been friends since kindergarten. I want you to know that *you* are a very lucky man, Larry. Your wife is a wonderful lady."

These phrases, spoken so effortlessly by the man, touch me. His words are warm and sincere. The two men shake hands and I'm relieved. Larry hasn't lost his good manners. He seems happy to meet the man.

The worst part is over.

Larry and I cross the living room hand-in-hand. We sit down on the sofa. The man sits in a chair diagonal to us. Almost on the periphery, but not quite.

I put my arm around Larry and we chat quietly. He's gradually losing the ability to speak English, his last-acquired language. Sometimes what he says doesn't make any sense at all or sounds like gobbledygook, a melting pot of the eight languages he used to speak fluently. At other times, the brief clarity of his words simply stuns me.

I tell him some happy news and it makes him smile. We talk about flowers, animals and faraway places. I talk about my younger daughter. He was always intensely interested in her life. They had a good relationship. I show him some photos of family members. He responds as if he's never seen them before.

He asks me if I'm well, and I report that I'm taking better care of myself. He seems happy about that. Even though I may have repeated all of this many times, he doesn't remember that he's heard it all before. Every time I tell him something is just like the first time.

He complains about not having any money. "They stole all my money."

"Who stole your money, Larry?" I ask.

"The police."

"No they didn't," I respond. "You asked me to hold onto your money for you. You must have spent what I gave you last week." I open my purse and give him some bills that I've previously copied. He doesn't know the difference.

"Thank you," he says.

Larry asks me if I've seen his parents. They perished long ago in a concentration camp. "I just talked to them on the phone the other day," I report. "They're doing well. Is it okay if they visit you tomorrow?" Larry has lost all sense of time and place.

"Tell them to come and stay for a few days," he responds excitedly. "I haven't seen them in a while."

"I'll give them a ring later. That'll make them happy."

He cries now and then, expressing despair about his condition; he's aware that he is deteriorating. And he worries about me. He complains that he doesn't see me enough. He asks me to live in his house with him and I say I will. "I have a big house. There's plenty of room," he says trailing off into the unintelligible. He doesn't remember from one minute to the next that I see him daily. We sit there together, foreheads touching, whispering for a long time. He repeats over and over how much he loves me.

From where the man sits, he watches and listens. Every so often, I turn to him and tell him what we're talking about. He's paying close attention and looks interested, but doesn't join in the conversation. Larry doesn't remember that he and the man have just met, and says quietly to me, "Who is that guy?"

"Do you remember me, Larry?" says the man, "I'm Sonya's friend. I've known her since we were little kids. A long, long time." Larry looks at him and says nothing, and then looks quizzically at me. "Who is that guy?" he says again.

I can see that Larry is beginning to tire and believe it's time to say goodbye. The man notices that Larry needs help rising from the sofa and asks, "May I give you a lift, Larry?" The man gently helps him rise from the sofa.

"Thank you very much," he remarks to the man. Mila is standing by to escort Larry to his recliner in an adjacent room.

I hug my husband tightly and tell him I love him. Forever and always. I inform him I'll see him later, even if that "later" is tomorrow. He seems reassured by that.

"Where are you going now?" he asks. I always tell him I'm going to the grocery store to buy food for dinner and I'll be back soon.

"What would you like to eat for dinner?"

"Anything you want," he says. My husband has lost the ability to make even the smallest decision.

"Maybe I'll buy some salmon," I say. "It's your favorite. I'll make it just the way you like it."

"That sounds good," he adds.

"Why don't you rest while I'm gone? I think my friend here would like to say goodbye to you, Larry," I say pointing towards the ceiling again.

"It was such a pleasure meeting you." The man takes one of Larry's hands in both of his. "I hope you'll allow me to come back and visit with you later." And then, much to my surprise, the man, towering over my husband, asks Larry if he can give him a hug. The man puts his arms around my husband and holds him tight. I'm so touched. The tears rise from a painful place in my heart.

"Larry, I'd like to help Sonya with the groceries," the man says. "Would that be okay with you?"

"Of course," Larry responds, he looks like he's about to cry.

"I'll see you later then." The man looks my husband in the eyes and says to him, "If there's anything you need or anything I can do to make you more comfortable, you can always count on me. I'd like to be your friend. Is that all right with you, Larry?"

Tears are rolling down my husband's cheeks now as he says again, "Of course."

I kiss the tears away, tell him again that I love him, and the man and I walk to the front door. I turn around for one last goodbye. Mila's holding Larry's hand as she walks with him. "I love you," I call out to him. He turns around and looks at me and I wave.

♔

The man and I walk to the car. The day seems to have become even more exquisite. A gentle breeze, a brilliant blue sky and the fragrant aroma of newly mowed grass. What could be better? The abundant flowers that line Greyswood's sidewalk explode with a sweet-spicy perfume.

The man opens the car door for me. The inside of the car is sunbaked warm, still pungent with the aroma of the his amber-scented cologne. I settle myself on the seat, and as I reach for my seatbelt, I think, "That went well, very well. Much better than I expected. Now what?" I hope the man isn't mad at me for putting him through that ordeal.

Usually, when I leave Greyswood I'm weighed down by a heavy sadness. An emptiness that follows me for hours. Not today. I feel a sense of relief. I'm free, no longer burdened by an ugly secret. The kindness the man has shown my husband fills me with affection. I feel unexpectedly peaceful.

The man looks over at me as he buckles his seat belt. He hesitates, smiling, but doesn't say anything. Suddenly, I'm overwhelmed by the enormous gratitude I feel for the man's stunningly unselfish behavior. He handled the situation with such ease.

I turn around to face him. He's still looking at me. Staring at me. There's something palpable in the air between us, a barely detectable electricity that is increasing with every second. I can almost touch it. I realize then that whatever I'm about to do or say in the next few moments may move the earth and change everything about my life going forward.

Tears cloud my eyes, but I'm able to see clearly, maybe for the first time in years. It's as if I've completely lost all conscious control over my actions; the words just spill out of my mouth. "Thank you, Jim. Thank you *so* much. I truly appreciate your sensitivity towards my husband."

He starts to say something in response, but I hold up my hand to stop him. "I want you to listen to what I have to say."

"There's a part of me that will *always* belong to my husband. Forever. And when he dies, that part of me will die right along with him. It's something I can't ever give to anyone else. I can't even put a name on it."

"Before you say anything, I want you to know something. I'm in love with you, Jim. When I saw you with Larry, I realized that the feelings I have are real love. And I've had them for a long time." I move closer and reach out to hold him. He puts his arms around me.

I'm crying now. I don't know whether my tears are for the wretched state of my beloved husband's life, my love for Jim or both.

From that day on, I was in love with two men. Many of my visits with Larry also included Jim. When Jim moved from Chicago, he often went to visit Larry when he had a break in his work schedule. I believe he felt that to love me, he must also love my husband. I didn't have to tell him that. He just *knew*.

I doubt Larry was capable of understanding the true nature of my relationship with Jim, but he never expressed any anger towards either of us. It almost seemed as though Larry was giving me his permission to include Jim in my life and he was happy for me.

Whenever Jim and I arrived at Greyswood to visit, the two men would shake hands. Jim would always introduce himself to Larry as his "best friend." And when we left, he would give Larry a bear hug and say, "Larry, I want you to know I'm taking good care of Sonya for you and you don't have to worry about anything." When he was able to speak, Larry would always thank Jim.

In the months after I placed Larry in residential care, he would often wander around Greyswood and call out for me endlessly. This behavior ceased when Jim began to visit him regularly. I think Larry knew he didn't have to worry about me any longer.

As Larry grew more impaired, it became impossible for me to take him anywhere by myself. He would become agitated in the car which made driving with him hazardous. With Jim's help, we were able to go out. As long as Jim was along, everything went smoothly. Sometimes we would go to the doctor or dentist or out for lunch or ice cream.

On one such day, a good one for Larry, Jim and I took him to the mall. Larry used to love going shopping with me.

"Larry, what do you think about these shoes?" I inquired, slipping on a pair of glitzy royal blue sandals.

"I like anything you like," he said studying my impending purchase.

"Jim, what do *you* think?"

"I think Larry's right. If they make you happy, buy them."

"Larry, do you agree?"

"Of course."

Afterwards, we lunched at one of Larry's favorites, the Nordstrom's Cafe.

"Larry," I asked, when it came time to order, "would you like your 'usual?'" He didn't know where he was, had long since forgotten how to read and had no idea what the "usual" was.

"Of course," he replied. This seemed to be the standard

response to almost everything.

While we were waiting for our food, Jim and I chatted back and forth. We included Larry in our conversation but he was no longer capable of that level of communication. He watched us carefully as if he were trying to figure something out but he just couldn't get a handle on what it was. I was concerned about him.

"Are you okay, Larry?"

He looked at me intently for a few seconds without saying a word and then turned his head towards Jim, "I love my wife," he said distinctly. "She's my queen. She's my angel."

Jim looked at me and then glanced back at Larry. The two men sat there gazing at one another in silence for what seemed like a long time. I was prepared for the worst, yet I had no idea what that might be. I was extremely uncomfortable. Jim spoke first.

"I love your wife, too, Larry. And I'm taking very good care of her for you. You will never have to worry about her. Never."

Geez. Oh my. I didn't expect that.

My worst fears didn't materialize. Looking over at Larry, I knew it was going to be fine. He seemed relieved, relaxed and refreshed. "Good," he responded, smiling.

Months later, Larry and I were sitting together on the screened porch at Greyswood. It was a beautiful fall day. We were watching the squirrels climb up and down the trees, chasing each other. Larry's speech was more impaired. During the majority of the visit, he spoke in his own private language, and I responded in the best way I could. "Yes," or 'You're right," "I understand what you're saying," or "I love you." None of it made any sense.

Perhaps he knew what he was talking about, but I didn't. He was calm and we sat together for a long time, side-by-side. One of the nurses brought us some iced tea and cookies. Unexpectedly, he edged closer to me, touched my arm, looked me in the eyes and said in a whisper, "How are things going with, uh, um, the new man?"

I was astonished. His speech was clear as a bell. I had to take some time to think about my response. "Oh, you mean the *tall* man?

"Yes."

"Things are good, Larry, very good. He treats me well and we have a good time together."

"Good," he said smiling. "Don't fuck it up."

Did those words actually come out of my husband's mouth?

His unexpected comment brought a broad smile to my face. I assured him I was doing everything I could not to mess things up.

♟

One evening in particular I remember so vividly. Jim and I had just finished eating dinner when the telephone rang. It was one of the nurses at Greyswood calling to report that Larry wasn't doing well.

"He's out-of-control," she said, "and paranoid and violent. We can't manage him. He's already struck a nurse and I'm worried he might harm another patient or himself. We've given him the medicine the doctor ordered and done everything else we can to calm him down, but nothing's worked. We're going to have to call 911 and send him to the hospital. He's becoming increasingly disruptive."

"*Please* don't do that," I pleaded. "I'm coming right over. Ten minutes."

Jim and I entered Greyswood to find Larry pacing back and forth, screaming, delusional and more agitated and upset than I'd ever seen him before. He was yelling, crying and threatening the other patients. Everyone was afraid to get near him.

When he saw me, he ran to me and begged me to help him. "*Help* me," he cried. "I need to get away from here. They're trying to *kill* me! *Please* help me!" The psychosis was at work; he believed he was in danger of being harmed and needed to escape. I knew that reasoning with him was never going to work. He was lost in another world.

Jim walked over to Larry and took hold of his hands. In his warm and relaxed voice he said, "Would you mind if I gave you a hug, Larry?"

"Please *help* me," he wailed frantically.

"I will. Right now." Standing tall over my husband, he wrapped his long arms and sturdy body around Larry's frail frame and hugged him tightly. He began to rock him back and forth gently as he held him close. Larry cried and said over and over that he was afraid. Jim whispered to him softly, "You're safe now, Larry, you're safe. I'll take care of you and protect you. Nothing can hurt you now."

The two of them just stood there swaying back and forth rhythmically. It took less than ten minutes, but in that time, Larry gradually began to quiet down. His body became more relaxed, he had stopped crying and his eyes were closing. The medicine he'd been given earlier began to kick in.

"Hey, Larry, how about some ice cream," Jim suggested as he slowly released his grip on my husband. The nurse handed Larry a bowl of his favorite flavor of ice cream and encouraged him to sit down and eat. The meltdown had passed. He ate his ice cream and soon after, fell asleep.

How could I not love both of these beautiful men?

Chapter 27

Alzheimer's Is A Family Disease

"Alzheimer's is a family disease." I heard this phrase repeated over and over during my husband's illness. "Alzheimer's brings out the worst in some people and the very best in a few." That one, too.

"There is no other disease that can tear a family apart faster than Alzheimer's," so writes Gary Joseph LeBlanc, a Certified Dementia Communication Specialist and the author of four books on Alzheimer's, caregiving and families.

> Dealing with Alzheimer's can bring out many strong emotions. As the disease progresses caregiving issues can often ignite or magnify family conflicts. The reason for this may be due to the need of extensive care necessary to keep the loved one both safe and calm.

LeBlanc goes on to talk about how difficult it is to describe to the general public the hardships and stress that Alzheimer's patients and their caregivers must endure. Unlike cancer or any other terminal illness whose symptoms are more predictable and understandable, Alzheimer's Disease presents a more varied, confusing and often difficult-to believe-it's-happening picture.

Every patient who has Alzheimer's is different and the nature of symptoms and manner in which they present may be unlike any other patient. Some patients are more difficult to manage than others. Perhaps it has something to do with the individual's pre-existing personality traits, life experiences and mental health issues.

Alzheimer's is not simply loss of memory and the ability to think; there's many other behavioral, emotional and physical symptoms. Alzheimer's robs people of every single aspect of their *personhood*. And it's scary. So scary. If you haven't been there or known someone else who has, you're at quite a loss when it comes to understanding both the patient *and* the caregiver's behavior.

At the very least, Alzheimer's can set off many strong emotions in friends and family members alike. As the illness progresses, caregiving issues often become the focus of family conflict. Carole Larkin, a Certified Dementia Consultant in Dallas, Texas, estimates that 30-60% of families and friends of someone with Alzheimer's Disease experience severe conflict. Other writers suggest that the percentage may be even higher. Often, this break in family relationships is abrupt and permanent.

> Conflict is especially likely in families where people didn't get along previously, when the primary caregiver is not a direct family member (such as in a second marriage), and when some of the family members live out-of-town and only see the loved one for short, infrequent visits.

The conflict typically affects the primary caregiver more than other family members. It can be endlessly frustrating to have others make caregiving suggestions that are unreasonable because they're based on a lack of knowledge, understanding of the patient's condition and abilities, and an appreciation of the role of the caregiver. And even worse when they make judgments based on inaccurate information.

"Why can't I take Larry out to lunch?" someone asked

me.

"Because Larry chokes on his food, no matter what he's eating. Some days are worse than others."

"You're making that up. That's not a symptom of Alzheimer's. You just don't want to give up your control over him."

"I'd love to give up control. And I'm not making it up. I need a break more than you know. But, if he wants to go and you're skilled at the Heimlich, go right ahead."

The caller hung up on me.

Alzheimer's Disease impacts not only those living with the illness, but also has a significant impact on their caregivers. Nearly 80% of individuals caring for someone with Alzheimer's will develop a serious physical or emotional illness while they are caring for their loved one or within the two years following the patient's death.

In most family situations almost everything falls upon the caregiver. More often than not, the caregiver receives little assistance from other family members. I discovered early on that it was only a couple of people who could truly understand the predicament of the patient and the caregiver and provide some measure of help and support. Those people either had an Alzheimer's experience themselves or were mental health professionals.

Henri Nouwen, a Dutch priest, scholar and author, said it so well.

> When we honestly ask ourselves which persons in our lives mean the most to us, we often find that it is those who, instead of giving advice, solutions, or cures, have chosen rather to share our pain and touch our wounds with a warm and tender hand.

I was grateful to anyone who would simply listen and

understand, whose presence in our struggle gave us the strength to face another day. There were too many others who were quick to judge, criticize and unload their dissatisfaction with how I was handling the job of caregiving to anyone who would listen. And not one of those folks ever offered to lift a finger to find out firsthand what providing care to someone with Alzheimer's Disease was all about. Not one.

Put simply, it was like this: caregiving was a twenty-four-hour-a-day inescapable weight of responsibility, indecision and self-doubt that increased over time, and followed me wherever I went. For ten years I asked myself the same questions. "Am I doing enough?" "Am I doing it right?" "What do I do now?" "Did I make the right decision?"

At the same time, I was trying to do everything possible not to lose my patience with my husband and everyone who was working against me. And not break down from trying to manage it all.

Unfortunately, none of the rarely seen individuals who were generous with criticism were aware of the day-to-day trials of my husband or myself as his caregiver. After a phone call or a visit with my husband, more often than not, they would remark, "Larry seems to be doing fine. I don't know what all your fuss is about." Or, as one person so eloquently stated, "You signed your name on the marriage license, didn't you? Just do your job and shut up. It's can't be that difficult!"

These uninformed people weren't there after the visit or phone call to hear Larry say, "Who was that?" Or, when he swallowed a bottle of my medicine, fell and cracked eight ribs, had a meltdown, choked or pried up the wood floor in the hallway. It's almost impossible to describe to the general public the hardships and frustrations that the patient and caregivers endure. Most people had no idea of what was happening in our home and, thereafter, in the few years he was in a private resident. And didn't want to know.

Doubters, deniers and disbelievers often make the caregiving situation more complicated than it has to be. Their interference in every stage of Alzheimer's adds confusion, chaos and unnecessary drama to the life of the caregiver who has been there 24/7, often for years.

They come along, and with stinging critique make statements like, "Why in the world would you move him out of the house? He seems fine to me," or "What do you mean he's under Hospice care?", "Why do you have Power-of-Attorney?", or "How did you allow it to get to this point?" Or simply, "That can't be. You're lying."

One comment in particular shared by a trusted family member went like this: "I heard she moved her husband out of the house to make room for her new boyfriend. How could she mistreat him like that?" Those words came from the mouth of someone who never spoke to me or saw Larry during the entire illness.

It made me want to shout, "Maybe if you'd been around for the last few years, or taken care of him for a day or two, even a few hours, you'd be better informed!"

Maybe, maybe, maybe.

This is the time when lawyers often appear on the scene. One of the most common arguments brought to the table is, "She must be doing something to harm him," or "He wasn't competent when he made her Power-of-Attorney (or wrote his Will)," "She changed his Will," or "We need to extricate him from this terrible situation," or "He says she's taking all his money," or "She just wants his money" and "She's feeding him all kinds of medicines that are making him crazy."

I've heard it all.

The last thing a caregiver needs when coming to the end of this exhausting battle is to end up in court with his or her own family. Deplorably, these legal battles happen everywhere and every day. Alzheimer's Disease can tear families so far apart they never mend.

More than anything else I've written in this book, the following words spoken or written by people who thought they had all the answers, make my head spin. Back then, when I was in the thick of it, every single incident set me back and made it all the harder for me to care for my husband.

Of all the painful experiences of my life, it was those that occurred while I was caring for my husband that have hurt me the most. They hurt both me and my husband. They weren't the most damaging experiences of my life, but they were quite possibly the most distressing.

Had I not been in an Alzheimer's support group, as well as individual psychotherapy during the years of my husband's illness, I never would have believed that the unkind words I endured as a caregiver were fairly common. They were woven into the fabric of our experience and caused tremendous angst. Not to include them here seems coy at best, deceitful at worst. I haven't shied away from the truth in my stories. Why start now?

Most people don't understand Alzheimer's Disease. They can't possibly grasp how the person they love can gradually disappear and a stranger inhabit their skin. Whatever they had come to know about that person is gone. Forever. You can read or hear about this phenomenon all you want, but you must experience it on a day-to-day basis to fully understand what I mean.

My husband's struggle with Alzheimer's Disease was only part of his problem. He was a Holocaust survivor who, six years earlier, had been diagnosed with psychosis. His grip on reality was intermittently tenuous. Alzheimer's is what pushed him over the edge.

Long before Larry was ever diagnosed with Alzheimer's, the person he was began to transform. He looked like my husband and sounded like him, but he was losing his emotional control and the ability to think and behave appropriately. I attributed it to age. The Holocaust had just worn out his brain. But, in the end, it was the Alzheimer's that took down Larry, me and our life together.

In the weeks following the diagnosis of Alzheimer's, we shared the unfortunate news with our families and closest friends. Most people were surprised by the announcement. They didn't see it coming. Nearly everyone reacted with sadness and struggled to understand what that meant for Larry's future. Two or three others were aware he had been diagnosed with psychosis and, at the time, saw something even worse in his future.

On the other hand, there were those that said, "There's nothing wrong with Larry" or "Are you sure? Maybe you should get a second opinion." Except for a few who knew Larry well and had observed his decline over time, the majority had no idea anything was seriously wrong with him. But the diagnosis was no surprise to me. I saw it coming around the bend.

Larry wasn't shy about telling people of his diagnosis. Some people dropped us like a sprig of poison ivy as soon as they heard the word "Alzheimer's." Seemingly good friend, turned their backs on decades-long friendships and just walked away without so much as a backward glance. Others were concerned and interested until we asked them for help.

Some were unable to grasp just how sick he really was and found more than enough blame to load on my shoulders. They were the ones who created the most chaos.

In the first year or so after the diagnosis, Larry was often able to cover his deficits, some days better than others, but he relied heavily on me, especially in public. "You're my brain because mine isn't working too well," he would frequently comment.

At home when he was tired or stressed, the deterioration would be readily visible. For people whose only contact with him was by phone or infrequent visits, he might seem almost "normal," and some of the bizarre things he said or did, credible. Those individuals shut their eyes and ears to the symptoms of the illness and accused me of bringing harm to him. How else would you explain what was happening? I was a readily available scapegoat.

"What are you doing to him, Sonya?" someone demanded angrily after Larry, who wasn't in his right mind, said, "My wife has taken all my money, locked me in the house, abandoned me, hit me, poisoned me with pills and yelled at me. I want a divorce!"

The yelling part was correct.

"It's the illness," I responded.

"No, it isn't. You must be doing something to make him so upset," one person insisted.

Individuals who were familiar with Alzheimer's knew the peculiar things Larry said and did were illness-driven. But others took him literally and were unable to see the irrationality in his words. Or didn't want to. After all, he *sounded* normal. Who other than *me* would they hold responsible?

These same individuals couldn't understand that talking on the phone gradually became impossible for Larry. He couldn't dial, even in the early stages — the numbers and letters made no sense to him — and, later on, the voice on the other end was unrecognizable, even if it were someone he had known well. All of this added to his already confused state. And the more confused he became, the more out-of-control. The more out-of-control, the harder it was to manage him.

In time, Larry forgot what a phone was and what it was used for. He would look at it and say, "What's that?" Same with a toothbrush, bar of soap, comb and eating utensils. He was baffled by the unknown instrument in his hand, the unknown voice talking to him from an unknown place, in an unknown language. Those same people insisted that this just couldn't be and proceeded to condemn me for taking away his phone or not permitting him to talk on the phone.

As the illness progressed, Larry became more and more reluctant to leave the house with anyone other than me or his companion. Nothing was familiar to him any longer, and he feared becoming lost. Every place he went was new. Even if he had been there every day for years. At times, he was like a visitor from another planet, and at others, an astronaut whose lifeline was cut; every week he drifted further away from the mother ship.

He didn't like going to public places; the commotion was agitating and disorienting. If he became confused, that would often lead to delusions and paranoia. He would become filled with terror at the Nazis he saw lurking around every corner. And I was accused of not permitting him to go out with other people.

During this time, Larry and I were adjusting to a new normal every week. One individual e-mailed me saying:

> I want to spend some quality time alone with [Larry]. Take him out for the day. Run errands and have lunch together. Please let me know when this is possible.

I e-mailed the individual Larry's response:

> I don't want to go out with you. I want you to visit with me in my home. There is too much commotion at [name of place].

Danger was hiding in every new place. At home he felt safe.

Providing my husband with safety and security was a huge challenge, and I was often denounced when others thought I wasn't permitting Larry to leave the house with anyone other than me or his companion. Or being a control freak. But I refused to force my husband to do things he wasn't comfortable doing in order to satisfy someone else.

Not one of the people who condemned my caregiving ever witnessed Larry in the agony of a psychotic meltdown. Not one. Breaking windows, tearing out the security alarm, striking people and ripping steel handrails off the walls wasn't something that was easily forgotten. Larry offered the e-mail writer a reasonable alternative — you come to me.

Several days after the above e-mail, the e-mail writer's attorney called me and stated: "I had been asked by [my client] to attempt to make arrangements with you so that [my client] could visit with [Larry]."

The attorney's assumption via his client was that I was keeping Larry from seeing the client. What the attorney didn't understand was that Larry didn't want to leave the house. He was afraid. He wanted people to visit with him in his home.

My husband was very angry. He asked me to contact the attorney for whom he left an angry message: "*Nobody* is keeping me from seeing *anyone*. Don't ever bother my wife again." Later he scribbled the following note to him:

> [Your client] have (sic) sirious (sic) issues and [the client] is not telling you the trut (sic). . . . Please do not bother my wife.

I sent it to the attorney along with copies of the numerous e-mails I had sent inviting the client to visit in our home.

Several weeks later, I received another letter from the same attorney:

> I received [Larry's] phone call, as well as the letters and e-mails that were sent to my office. I extend my sincerest apologies to you and [Larry] for any problems that I may have caused in my attempts to remedy a situation that appears to have been misrepresented by my client.

> My client, [redacted] acknowledges that [my client] has seen the letters and e-mails. It appears that numerous attempts have been made to permit [my client] to visit [Larry] and that [my client] has no further need of legal representation at the present time.

During the same year, others challenged my role as his medical and financial power-of-attorney. "We're his family and we'll take care of him," said one person in a phone conversation. "After all, Larry belongs to us." And in other conversation, "If anyone's going to get Power-of-Attorney it needs to be one of us. We're blood."

If that were true, where was the "blood" when I needed help caring for him?

Another individual, a long-time friend of my husband's, vehemently denied Larry had Alzheimer's Disease. In telephone calls and letters to both me *and* my husband, he insisted it was I who was doing something evil to harm my husband.

My husband reported to me the following conversation: "I know Alzheimer's Disease, and you don't have it," the friend shouted at my husband. He encouraged Larry to pack his suitcase and move out. "Don't listen to your wife," he said, "she's trying to kill you. You don't need doctors, you need a lawyer." He offered to make an appointment and drive Larry to a divorce lawyer.

Later, in a letter addressed to me in 2010, the friend stated:

> I have made a number of attempts to pick Larry up and take him to a restaurant or out for the day. I do not accept Larry's or your explanation that he is afraid to leave the house with anyone but you or his companion. Neither am I willing to accept that he chokes when he eats. Neither are symptoms of Alzheimer's. Make sure that you tell Larry this. I want him to know what a liar you are.

I could hardly believe what I read.

A year later, still beating the same drum, he wrote me another letter:

> You have thwarted every effort for us all to have a normal and caring relationship with Larry!! Even if he does have Alzheimer's

(which I doubt) it isn't as bad as you say. He said you were feeding him medications that were making him crazy. I think you are a delusional and hateful person!

This "friend" visited Larry several times before and after he entered residential care, and had observed his condition first-hand. He addressed this final letter to *Larry* several months prior to his death. At the time, Larry could not read, write, speak, feed or care for himself in any way:

It has been quite a long time since we have talked. The major reason for this problem is your wife. . . . I do not understand why you accept this. Also, you have <u>lost</u> your phone! Why can you not be a free person and do as you please?

When I opened the letter, I didn't know whether to laugh or cry. *How* could this be? The writer had visited my husband several months earlier when Larry's condition wasn't much better than it was that day. When I recounted the experience to my therapist, her response was: "Some people are capable of considerable denial and significant cruelty."

My husband was not the same person, and his friend couldn't accept that. It had to be *somebody's* fault. Mine.

In 2012, I had minor surgery and wasn't able to drive or visit my husband for a week. In an e-mail to a family member, I asked the individual who was planning to visit him in residential care to pick up a few things Larry needed on the way. I sent this e-mail:

Would it be possible for you to purchase some personal care items for [Larry]? Your assistance would be greatly appreciated. If you have a Costco membership, that would be the best place to purchase these: Toothpaste, body lotion, mouthwash, (alcohol-free), shampoo, body wash.

It would be great if you could bring these items with you when you visit on Sunday. Thank you.

I had every intention of reimbursing the individual for the items, of course.

I transcribed the phone message I received in response:

I got your e-mail and I'm very, very confused as to why [Larry] would run out of so many products all at once and why you don't just go out and buy them yourself and why you would want ME to stop and buy these for him? Why do I have to do that?

I don't have a Costco membership and I'm NOT gonna go and buy generic products that you would just throw in the trash because of your high tastes. I honestly believe that if [Larry] really, really needed these things that you would go out and buy them yourself and not ask ME to buy them for YOU, or you would write me down specifics – Kraft, Colgate, whatever things he specifically needs, and you didn't write anything down specific, and because of your caviar tastes you wouldn't allow me to pick the different, cheaper things that I would because you have caviar tastes and would throw them in the trash or give them away because they're not the high tastes that you have. So, I'm just wondering what is this all about? Why are you asking me to go out and buy things?

I'm not going to buy something that you should go out and buy yourself or you're going to throw in the trash or give away to somebody because it's not your champagne tastes, what you or [Larry] would need or want, and if things are just OK as you stated in your e-mail with the pants that gives me a clue as to what your feeling is about me and what I would buy so I'm not buying anything for [Larry] at all. You'll have to buy them yourself.

NO, I will not get these things for [Larry].

I could *not* make anything like that up. I never asked the individual for anything again.

Before I placed Larry in residential care, a report to Adult Protective Services was made charging me with abuse and neglect. Unannounced, a nurse and social worker came to our home and insisted upon interviewing Larry in private. Larry's nephew was staying with us at the time, and he and I were directed into another room. The APS workers weren't aware that Larry had Alzheimer's Disease.

Larry was less confused and disoriented that day. He was embarrassed and angry, and fiercely denied that he was being abused or neglected in any way, as per the complaint. After the APS workers left, Larry asked me over and over, "Why did they come? Who sent them? Why would they ask me those questions?" It was hard for him to accept that someone had reported *me* to Protective Services because they believed *I* was neglecting and abusing my husband. Both of us were deeply saddened.

Larry's nephew, an attorney, spoke to the agency director that afternoon. The charges were dropped as unsubstantiated, but not after it had seriously rattled both Larry and myself. Believe it or not, this very same thing happened to *several* of the other women in my Alzheimer's support group!

I'm sure the complainant(s), well-meaning or mean-spirited, felt they were doing what was right for Larry.

Larry's psychiatrist saw him every few weeks. One day

he sent me this e-mail:

> Hi. I wanted to make you aware that I received yet another angry call from [a family member] again today . . . [The family member] was very inappropriate and it sounds like [the individual] has some serious problems. . . .

He received calls from others, as well. I suppose they thought Dr. K. needed to understand the situation the way *they* saw it. In response, Dr. K wrote a letter to all the people that had contacted him saying,

> This letter is in reference to [Larry] who is currently under my care for Alzheimer's Dementia. [Larry's] depression has deteriorated substantially over the past several months. He has often described himself as significantly depressed, hopeless and distraught.

> During my extensive and lengthy conversations with [Larry] during this time he repeatedly cites an ongoing situation with [a family member] as his primary stressor. . . . He further associates the numerous, persistent and inflammatory telephone calls from [other people] to both himself and his wife in recent weeks . . . with his current incapacitating emotional state.

> Further, he [Larry] clearly retains his ability to make grossly informed judgments in terms of his interpersonal affairs and is fully capable of expressing his opinion in these matters. . . . and I am fully confident in saying that he is not under any undue influence by any other parties, including his wife which apparently has been suggested.

> Finally, I cannot state strongly enough the impact that this current situation

has had on his mood and overall ability to function under these terrifically stressful conditions. . . . Without question, he requires immediate respite from this conflict for any pharmacologic or therapeutic measures to have a chance for success.

It didn't do a bit of good.

One night over dinner, not long after I placed Larry in residential care, a long-time friend dressed me down in this way: "When you signed your name to the marriage license, it was for better or worse. Your husband's illness isn't about you. Can you imagine how much suffering your abandonment of him has caused? Sounds pretty selfish to me."

She made up her mind without ever seeing Larry. Not once. She never talked to me again until more than three years after my husband's death. Her own husband had been diagnosed with Alzheimer's, and she e-mailed me to apologize because she was finally beginning to understand what I went through.

After I met my current husband, another friend cautioned me repeatedly, "You better be careful. What if Larry finds out you're seeing someone else?"

"*What?*" I responded incredulously. "Larry doesn't even know who I am anymore!" I never heard from her again.

It was hard for me to understand how some people could be so critical and judgmental. Especially those who saw him seldom or not at all. Another individual, one who visited Larry twice during his illness, would ask me over and over in regular phone calls, "Does he ask about me?"

"Does he ask about *you?*" I replied, unable to believe what the individual was saying. "He doesn't even know who *he* is! That person simply couldn't accept the severity of the illness and how it had transformed my husband into someone else.

Several months after Larry was admitted to residential

care, I received a letter from the same individual's attorney:

> [My client] has requested that I write you to discuss [my client's] concerns about the welfare of . . . [Larry]. [My client] states that [my client] used to talk to [Larry] by phone every day. That is no longer occurring and [my client] believes that you are not permitting him to use the phone. On the few occasions that [the client] does talk to him, [Larry] complains that his wife has taken all his money and is poisoning him with medications. [My client] states that [Larry] has told [my client] that he wants to move [to my client's city] and live with [my client] and that his wife is preventing him from doing so. [My client] is not aware of any physical or psychiatric problems that might explain [my client's] concerns.
>
> [My client] assures me that [my client] will take further action if we do not hear from you within one week of the signed receipt of this letter.

Larry's nephew, an attorney himself, knew the attorney and was very familiar with Larry's condition. He contacted the attorney to tell him he had been conned. I never heard from the attorney again.

What does it take to convince someone that the person they used to love is gone forever?

Armed with inaccurate "information," these same people became self-appointed "experts" about Larry's condition, and particularly about my role as his caregiver. The "facts" they shared with one another were flagrantly false. The truth wasn't easy to face, and it didn't happen to fit their perception of reality.

Another individual visited Larry in his residence one

evening. Larry had gone to bed for the night and the staff turned the visitor away. The visitor was angry because he was sure it was *my* "rules" that prevented him from visiting Larry. He didn't realize how sick my husband was.

The individual simply couldn't understand why informing me or Larry's nurse that he was planning to visit might prevent him from turning around and going home again. But the individual just wanted to show up, like he was dropping in on an old buddy for a beer and a few laughs.

It didn't stop there. And nothing I could say or do would convince the party that "the rules" about visiting weren't mine, that they were imposed by the illness itself.

Several months before Larry died, that same person sent me an e-mail after having compared notes with other individuals who had no more accurate information than he did. He had neither seen Larry or talked with any of the individuals involved in Larry's care in over two years. He asked me to "resolve my concerns, which are as follows:"

> How and why was Larry's will changed?

> Why did you have trouble finding a lawyer to write the new will?

> How and why did it evolve that [redacted] came to be disinherited?

> Why did [redacted] refuse to be the executor of the will?

> Did you take Larry's cell phone away from him and give him one with only your telephone number?

> How did Larry end up in a nursing home with no prior notice to anyone?

> Who filed complaints against you with the Montgomery County Adult Protective Services, and what were the allegations?

. . . when was the last time [redacted] and [redacted] visited Larry?

I do not accept your other explanations for this behavior. . . . It is therefore apparent to me that despite your various explanations, your need to monitor who sees or speaks to Larry is not out of any concern for him, but simply out of your own need to control.

I don't expect an honest response from you to the above concerns, but I also don't want to waste time meeting with you and listening to your practiced rationalizations for your selfish behavior. Perhaps I am wrong, and I and the other people who have been complaining about you are simply misunderstanding you. If so, you are welcome to respond specifically to my concerns, and I will keep an open mind. If not, I will try to spend my time with generous, loving people and you may spend your time the way you wish.

My therapist advised me to steer clear of the individual. "You're being set up and scapegoated. The writer is a coward. That person has no other way to explain away what he's heard from unreliable sources, so you *have* to be wrong."

"I recommend that you tell the individual to walk in your shoes for about twenty-four hours. And until then, he has no basis whatsoever for judging you."

Where in the world have common sense and empathy gone?

♚

Like every other complex situation, there were no simple or "right" answers to the writer's concerns. And the individual wasn't interested in them anyway. He and his cadre of "experts" had made up their minds and didn't want to be confused by the facts. And yet, all they had to do was speak to his doctors or the nurses who were caring for Larry. Or, better yet, spend just *one* day with him. Even *half* a day. Simply observing. Did they not realize the illness was eating away my husband's brain and body, and destroying his life? I think not. I answered the e-mail truthfully, but that's not what the writer wanted.

When I shared my experience of the situation in my support group, other members shook their heads knowingly. This too, was a common scenario among family and friends of the patient. In fact, in one situation the caregiver was one of the patient's adult children. The caregiver's sibling took the caregiver to court because the caregiver was forced to place the patient in residential care. Apparently, the other sibling believed that the caregiver was spending the patient's money frivolously and wanted the court to intervene and "force" the caregiver to care for the patient at home. He wanted desperately to preserve his inheritance.

In another situation, a second marriage, the patient's family members entered the couple's home while the caregiver was out and cleaned them out of all the valuables that had belonged to the patient prior to his marriage to the second wife, his caregiver. "After all," they protested, when they were arrested, "the patient's property really belongs to *us,* not his wife."

In one more circumstance, a decades-long second marriage, the caregiver was accused of altering the patient's Will by the patient's family. The case eventually got to court where the judge determined that it was the patient who, before he lost the ability to make decisions, eradicated the trusts that would have prevented his wife from accessing enough money to finance his care. The Judge chastised the family in open court.

In his decision, the Judge ruled against the family because the changes the patient made in the Will were legal. He stated that the family of the caregiver should be lucky the patient had such a caring and compassionate caregiver, otherwise they'd have to be providing care themselves. "This family should learn something from the behavior of the caregiver. I hope each and every one of them understands that Alzheimer's Disease has a strong genetic component and they should pray that they're not the next victim."

♜

The weeks after my husband's death didn't bring the peace I anticipated. Within days of the funeral, an individual called asking me for the framed photographs of my husband and his family that had hung on the walls of our home for over twenty years. And still do, over four years after his death. This person had the same photographs, but they weren't framed quite as beautifully. "We're his family, and those pictures belong to us," the individual stated confidently.

And who am I? Chopped liver?

Months later there was another, even harsher request from another person. "I want those framed pictures! Send them back *now* with the rest of his things. COD. He was part of *our* family, not yours," the caller ordered.

"Larry and I gave you copies of those pictures a long time ago," I countered. "In fact, I saw a couple of them hanging on the walls of your home."

"I want the ones that belonged to Larry. And anything else that belonged to him, too. His clothing, mementos and jewelry. You have no further use for them."

Did I hear that correctly? Thirty years of loving my husband eradicated in one tongue lashing?

A couple of months later, the same individual called again offering to *buy* the photographs from me. "No, thank you. You have all the same photos," I responded politely.

♜

Within the first few weeks after his death, several individuals called or e-mailed me about Larry's Will. One of those e-mails stated,

I was wondering what the status [sic] of reading of [Larry's] will? I have not heard from you since I gave you my info. I am not sure how long it takes or what the process is to get a will read.

I addressed the individual's concerns by phone a few days later, and the conversation, to the best of my recollection, went something like this:

"There is no 'reading of the Will,'" I stated.

"Why not?"

"Because there's nothing left in his estate."

"What about my inheritance?"

"There is no 'inheritance,'" I said as calmly as I could.

"What? He told me he was leaving me a lot of money!"

"When was that?" I asked, annoyed.

"Before he met *you.*"

"You mean thirty years ago?"

"Yes."

"Was that before or after he bought you a lovely home?" I inquired.

"After."

"And didn't my husband give you a large gift of cash every year since? Including $10,000 after he was diagnosed with Alzheimer's?"

There was no response.

"Did he promise you the money *before* he was diagnosed with Alzheimer's Disease and needed 24-hour residential care for over three years?"

"Of course," was the reply.

"Your inheritance was used to provide care for Larry.

The same with *my* inheritance. Almost one million dollars in ten years from his accounts and mine. There isn't any money left."

The individual was irate. The long-anticipated windfall was not forthcoming and the individual couldn't understand how that could be possible.

Larry's attorney sent the individual a copy of the Will and explained the circumstances of Larry's estate. There was virtually nothing left. It had all been used to finance his lengthy illness.

Not long after, the individual sent me the following e-mail:

> ...You very conveniently maneuvered to take as much money as you could from [Larry's] estate. . . . You canceled the one thing that [Larry] prepared for me and told me about -- his life insurance policy. I already know what you will say "it was his choice to cancel the policy because [I] would not tell him how much money he gave [me]". Horse hockey!!!!

Martin Luther King, Jr. summed up our ten-year experience of Alzheimer's better than anyone else: "Nothing in all the world is more dangerous than sincere ignorance and conscientious stupidity."

None of the folks who were involved in these vignettes are bad people. Uninformed, misinformed and in denial, perhaps. Even ignorant and arrogant. In their defense, it takes tremendous courage to face something as perplexing and terrifying as Alzheimer's Disease *and* psychosis.

When we come face-to-face with a situation or a person's actions which defy credibility, it's normal to want to find a way to explain it to yourself. Or find a scapegoat.

But, sometimes, trying to see past our own blind spots

can cause whiplash.

My role as caregiver meant taking over every aspect of Larry's life. Yes, *controlling* his life because he could no longer do it for himself. I suppose that may be impossible for some people to accept.

There have been some redeeming qualities for me in this hideous drama. I've learned more about my strengths and weaknesses. And just as much about other people, too. Hopefully, if I ever have to wear those caregiving shoes again, I'll be able to avoid much of the conflict that permeated my husband's illness.

I've learned that some people don't *want* the facts. Or perhaps it's that they can't *come to terms* with what's real. They would rather come up with their own definition of reality. One *they* can control.

And I've learned that I can't assume that just because something is crystal clear to me that it will be the same for everyone else. Given their limited perspective of the situation, the doubters, deniers and disbelievers thought they were protecting Larry from a fate much worse than Alzheimer's.

One more thing I've learned. If I don't hear something first-hand, read it or see it with my own eyes, it didn't happen or it may be gossip. I will try to refrain from making things up in my mind and then sharing them with my mouth. I've experienced directly how very hurtful that can be.

It's been a challenge to me as a memoirist to write honestly and compassionately about people, whether they were members of my family, my late husband's family or friends. I've struggled to understand why people behaved the way they did, and what their actions or words said about *them*. But even more, I've wrestled with understanding what my own behavior may have contributed to the above situations.

Each of the above persons has been a victim of having crappy things done to them in the past. They're human beings, flawed and limited, whose life events informed who they became. And given those experiences, it is no wonder they reacted as they did. A background of pain and loss may cause good people to behave badly. It did to me.

I can't assume what each person was thinking about or experiencing when they said the things they did. I present the experiences here as a way of understanding *my* place in the situation. Perhaps it may prepare some other unsuspecting caregiver. Alzheimer's Disease can be a minefield of unseen hazards and conflicts.

My sense of each of the people here may not match anyone else's experiences. And *they* may view themselves quite differently. But since this is the story of *me*, I have to own my truth. Their humanness shows in their comments and behavior and describes the vulnerability and insecurity behind their words and actions. And fear.

When faced with a similar situation, would any of them act in ways similar to mine? Probably. God knows, I wouldn't wish that experience on anyone.

Chapter 28

Let It Go

In the years since my late husband's death in January, 2014, I've challenged myself to understand and make peace with the emotional chaos that accompanied our shared experience of Alzheimer's Disease.

There was an overabundance of drama, and a substantial part of it was "man-made." In the early days of the illness, when Larry was still aware, he was disappointed in the people who created the distress. Thankfully, the illness eventually wiped his slate clean of every who, what and where.

Looking back, I believe I was meant to learn something from the turmoil, something that would inspire me to become a kinder, gentler person and possibly even share what I learned with others as I moved forward through life. There *had* to be some good that came of it. I was determined to root it out.

The man who was my husband died long before he took his last breath. I grieved for ten solid years prior to his death. I figured the funeral would finally bring some peace; Larry was free and I could move on. What I found was that I was just as hurt and angry as I'd been in the years preceding his death. I felt more like fighting than forgiving.

It was the women in my Alzheimer's Support Group,

some of whose experiences were similar to mine, who pulled me through. They told similar stories of mean mail, gossip, Protective Services complaints, hurtful and condescending conversations with people who didn't get it and being ganged up on by angry folks who wouldn't and couldn't believe the caregiver. They told stories of lawyers and court cases in which children, step-children and siblings challenged the caregiver's right to care for their loved one, fought over what was left of the estate and then fought even more when there was nothing left.

I wondered if people were born doubting things they couldn't understand or if they were cast that way by their life experiences? Was it against human nature to question the essence of situations too outrageous to believe, or would they just go with the flow? Sociologists say, in general, people go with the flow.

It took me a long time to understand that most individuals (even medical professionals) can't comprehend the impact of Alzheimer's Disease on a person, a marriage or the healthy spouse. I certainly didn't. On the other hand, denial can be a marvelous thing. It protects us from getting cozy with a painful truth, from feeling the discomfort and grieving the loss. When it comes to Alzheimer's Disease, sometimes it's just too demanding to face what is real and true.

When people come face-to-face with something that is painful or beyond their experience they may behave badly, especially if it goes against everything they believe. I was just as guilty as anyone. I had no baseline for understanding the incomprehensible combination of Alzheimer's, psychosis and the Holocaust.

Those who hurled criticism my way may have found it easier to find a scapegoat than accept the harsh realities of the illness or the responsibilities of my role as caregiver. They created just as much havoc as the disease itself. Trying to tune out the needless commotion made it harder for me to care for Larry, harder for him to die in peace and even harder for me to let go.

The misinformation that spread from one person to another bore little resemblance to what was actually going on. And it always resulted in finding fault with what *I* was doing, did, should have done, shouldn't have done, was going to do or might possibly do!

If one were to trust all the tales that were told, one might believe me to be a woman who purposefully made her husband sick, neglected and abused him and then spent all his money on doctors, medicines, aides, companions, nurses and residential care!

There were many things I wish I had done differently. Perhaps the result would have been less turmoil.

I should have taken better care of *myself.* I should have placed my husband in residential care *earlier* than I did, like his doctors suggested, *before* I broke down from the stress of it all. I should have worried *less* about my husband's well-being. I should have felt more secure about the decisions I made as a caregiver. I should have been less reactive and not taken so much of the mean things people said to heart. But most of all, I should have *expected* and been prepared for all the negative and unfavorable responses I received.

What I discovered from this experience, if I'm ever chosen to fill those caregiving shoes again, will help me *never* make the same mistakes twice.

During the years of my husband's illness, I learned what made me tough and what knocked me down. As a result, I've become smarter and wiser about myself. Loving my husband through his illness made me a more compassionate, generous and grateful individual. Coping with unkindness has taught me to be less judgmental and more forgiving.

I learned what makes other people strong and what makes them weak. I learned about respect and disrespect. I learned about courage and cowardice. I learned about how far some people will go to be right. I learned about the power of true friendship and the pain of discovering those that weren't. I learned that some of the people I thought weren't up to the challenge came through with the most heroic behavior. I learned that being part of a family doesn't mean people will be there for you, and sometimes it even means they turn on you and cause tremendous pain. Most of all, I learned who I could count on and who I couldn't.

Some people were always there for us to the very end, no matter how difficult the situation became. They did more than I could ever have hoped for. They took time off from their *own* lives to be present in ours. They were with us when we were both at our worst. They tried to understand even when I didn't. I will always be grateful for their fearlessness.

A year after my husband's death, I was still feeling outraged from all the drama. A conversation with a close friend about how I felt went something like this:

"How much longer do you intend to hold on to your anger?" my friend asked.

"Forever," I said, not even knowing why. "Or until it goes away on its own."

"Well," she said, "then it looks like you're not going to live very long."

"What do you mean?"

"Don't you know that lack of forgiveness is like drinking a toxic substance and expecting the other person to die? It rots you, slowly but surely, from the inside out. I see cancer, heart disease or a stroke in your future."

"I know, I know," I replied. And then I remembered other times in my life when I held on to anger long after it had served no purpose.

"Well, if you *know*, why aren't you doing something about it? Your wrath isn't hurting anyone but *you*," my friend continued. "Anger is far more dangerous to your *own* heart than to theirs. It has a corrosive effect. But, it's your choice; either you allow your soul to be tied in knots, angry and gnarled, or you let it go."

"I'm not sure I'm ready," I responded truthfully. "I know I can't do anything to change things. People believe what they want to believe. Maybe my anger allows me to feel righteous, or have a reason not to deal with those people again, or keeps me on the side of good vs. bad, right vs. wrong."

"Maybe, but who *cares*?" She was raising her voice now. "*You* can rise above pettiness, anger, and divisiveness. They can't and won't, but *you* can!"

"*Can* I?"

"Look, all those painful words spoken or written by people you knew happened in your 'long ago.' This is now, today. It's time to let go of all the bullshit and move on, girl. You're giving those people too much power over you."

"Well," I responded, startled by her frankness, "what shall I do? Just forget all about it?"

"You don't have to forget what happened -- you can't -- but you *can* let go of the negative feelings attached to the memories. Those folks believe they're right and *nothing's* going to change that. Larry could rise up from the grave and scream the truth in their faces! They. Will. Not. Change. But *you* can."

"Okay, maybe you're right. Sometimes the anger does get in the way."

"You *know* it does. You're a shrink, for God's sake!" She was a bulldozer now. "You have a happy and peaceful life now. You're madly in love with a great guy who adores you. You have a lovely home, some devoted family members and wonderful friends — some of them for almost *seventy* years! And you have *purpose*. Purpose! Why do you need to hold on to that garbage?"

"Because the wounds were deep," I cried. "They spoke to who I was as a *person*."

"*They did not!*" They spoke to *who the other people* were! Don't you see? Their cruel words reflect how badly *they* were handling the situation. Not *you*. They had to find someone to *blame*. That's the only way they could explain it to themselves. You did the best you could do. Save your life and get over it already!"

At that moment, I realized that if I didn't find a way to forgive and let go, I would continue living in the past.

And that's what I'm working on. Forgiving *myself*, first of all. And then being generous enough to forgive others. It hasn't been easy. I'll never *forget*, but at least it'll be behind me.

I can live with what I've discovered about myself and other people. That doesn't mean I'm happy about it, though. I suppose those people had their reasons for doing what they did. I can only learn from it, let it go and move on. Those experiences have become just another part of me and my story.

I wish it had been different, but I'm learning to be okay with the way it's unfolded.☐

Not every Alzheimer's situation is as difficult as my husband's. Larry's manifestation of Alzheimer's disease, coupled with psychosis and his background as a Holocaust survivor, made his illness a management nightmare. And not everybody behaves the way some of the people in our circle did.

If there were any words of wisdom I could pass along to another caregiver, it would be the following:

1. Take care of yourself. Do whatever you can to get a break from caregiving once a week, at least. Recharge your batteries. As they say on an airliner, "Put the oxygen mask over *your* face first." If you don't find a way to restore yourself you'll burn out. You have to be there for the long haul. I've heard too many stories of the caregiver becoming a patient. Realize your limitations.

2. See an attorney as soon as possible after the diagnosis. If you don't already have it, you must obtain both medical and financial powers-of-attorney while the patient is still *legally competent.* Once the individual is diagnosed, interviews of the patient by attorneys and healthcare professionals will be necessary before any documents can be executed. The patient's ability to make healthcare decisions and manage money will deteriorate quickly. He may cancel insurances, give away large sums of money and purchase unneeded luxuries that can't be returned (my husband did *all* those). Often, these transactions cannot be reversed (that happened, too).

If yours or your spouse's assets are in tied up in trusts, annuities, or insurance policies that will be passed on to other individuals upon his death, you must determine, while your spouse is still *legally competent*, whether or not you may need these assets to provide care for him. He <u>must</u> be legally competent to be able to give informed consent in order to release these assets. *No one can change anyone else's will except the person who wrote it as long as that person is still legally competent.*

After the diagnosis, my husband contacted his attorney about changing his will. The attorney wouldn't discuss the change with him until he had a letter from his psychiatrist attesting to his competency as determined by a battery of tests, and an extensive interview by his psychiatrist and a second psychiatrist. I was not present for either. When he actually made the changes, it was in the presence of three attorneys and two psychiatrists. I was not present for that, either.

Alzheimer's is a long and costly illness. Nurses, nursing assistants, companions, residential care and some equipment and supplies are *not* covered under Medicare or any other medical insurance. Many of the medications needed to alleviate the symptoms of the disease are either partially covered or not at all. Over a ten-year period, my husband's life savings were almost completely depleted.

3. <u>*Look into long-term care insurance.*</u> It won't pay the majority of expenses related to the illness, but it will pay *something*. Unfortunately, my husband cancelled his without my knowledge not long before he was diagnosed and, when I discovered what he'd done, it couldn't be reinstated.

4. *At least once a month, provide every family member and close friend of the patient's with the same information* about the patient's condition. Of course, that's no guarantee that they'll all believe you, especially those who live out-of-town or infrequently visit. Or, those who just want to stir up trouble. Never assume that because one person knows the facts, the rest will, too.

Share factual and concrete medical information that is supported by the patient's care team. Consider doing this via a conference call. Everyone will hear the same thing at the same time and have an opportunity to ask questions and share their concerns. This may eliminate *some* of the misinformation surrounding the illness. As your loved one passes from one stage of the illness to the next, let everyone know what that means and what to expect. Let them know how they can access additional information on the web.

5. *Send a follow-up e-mail or letter* briefly stating what you've just covered by phone. There will still be those who will twist, pervert and distort what you've said (or what they've observed or heard from others) when they compare notes later.

6. *Tell those who are interested in visiting how best to relate to your spouse*. That means when to visit and how to interact with the patient. They can see firsthand how your spouse is faring. Since choking is a troubling issue with Alzheimer's Disease, visiting at mealtimes and sharing food is *not* a safe plan. Photo albums, newspapers, walks, music, massage and simple games are all good ideas. If your pet is well-behaved, bring him along.

7. *"My spouse took all my money, had an affair, abandoned me, mistreated me,"* are phrases spoken by many Alzheimer's patients. If you tell people this in advance, they won't be as surprised when they hear it. And a lot less likely to take the patient at face value.

8. *Don't be shy about asking people to help.* Let everyone know by e-mail exactly what they could do to provide support to you or the patient. It won't take long to find out who

you can count on and who you can't. The leader of my support group said over and over, "Lower your expectations and raise your acceptance level."

9. _You do not need anyone else's permission to place your loved one in residential care_ if you are the caregiver and medical and financial power-of-attorney. You are the one doing the hands-on care. It is _your_ decision, not your children's, siblings', or step-children's, about how best to care for your spouse. If anyone objects to your decision, invite them to take over your duties for a few days.

10. _Don't feel guilty about placing your spouse in residential care_. Alzheimer's Disease is a twenty-four-hour-a-day, two-man-at-a-time job. You are the only one who knows the toll the illness is taking on you and your spouse. No matter how much you love him and want him to remain at home, most people just can't keep up the grueling day-to-day caregiving, even with full-time help. If you break down like I did, you're no good for your loved one. Placing him outside of your home means you can be a spouse and not a nurse.

11. _You don't owe anyone any explanations about the decisions you've made as a caregiver._ That's no one's business but yours. There will always be people who think what you're doing or saying is illegal, immoral, unethical or an outright lie. Ask them to care for the patient for a few days, and then see what they have to say.

12. _There will always be those who will find fault with whatever you say or do_. Just because _they say_ you've done something unacceptable, doesn't make it so. Have faith in the decisions you make for your loved one. Stand up tall against the bullies who haven't walked in your shoes. Of course, you'll make mistakes. It's all part of the story. Suck it up and forgive yourself. It happens to everyone.

13. _Finally, when it's all over, get down on your hands and knees and kiss the ground on which all the people who helped and supported you walk._ Whether they were friends, family, volunteers or paid professionals, they're truly remarkable. Larry used to call them "angels." Without them,

Alzheimer's would have killed us both.

14. *Forgive those who coulda,' shoulda,' woulda', wouldn't, didn't, and shouldn't have.* *Why*? Because you *can*. Open your mind and heart with loving generosity. Forgiveness is not forgetting or building something new, but letting the old anger wash away. An ancient Jewish ethicist, Eleazar Ben Judah said, "The most beautiful thing a man can do is forgive."

It's over. Let it go.

Chapter 29

The Best Years Of My Life

Dear Larry,

I know I should have written you a lot sooner. It's not because I didn't want to. It took me a long time to collect my thoughts after you died. I needed time to sort everything out and find a way to make sense of it all. And then another few years to put it down on paper. I wanted my words to be an honest reflection of where I am *now*. You know how I am — I had to rewrite it over and over again. I hope you'll forgive me for the long delay.

It's been over four years since you left and I think about you all the time. I used to replay the most difficult days of your illness over and over in my head searching for what I could have done differently or better to make your life easier. I don't do that as much anymore. I try to remember the happy days.

I had a conversation with an old friend recently. She told me "It's time to let go of your life with Larry and the difficult years of his illness. Every time you get hooked on rehashing the past, you lose your focus on the present."

I'm making progress, Larry. Really, I am. I've been rebuilding from the inside out. I think the hardest part is over.

Since you've gone, my search for closure has led me every which way. I've spent so many days turning myself inside and out, creeping all over the nooks and crannies of my soul and tiptoeing through the rubble of my heart. I needed to find the answers to some important questions and close the book on ten years of caregiving.

I wanted the process to be easy; to ask some guru to give me the answers and then spell it out in big black letters that stood tall and confident on the page. It wasn't so simple, of course, and it took a while (a long while, really) and some effort (more like hard labor), but I've arrived at an answer I can live with.

I'm ready to say, "I did the best job I could," accept it and move on. I'm not going to torture myself anymore with what I should or could have done. The story of *your* illness has become a huge part of who we were as a couple and who I've become as *me.*

Over twenty years ago, I sat mute with you as the doctor said, "Your husband has a depressive psychosis." I told myself, "He'll take the prescription drugs, get some therapy, avoid stress and things will improve." That was 1998.

Six years later, another doctor spoke even more frightening words, "Your husband has Alzheimer's Disease." On that day, I discovered why our paths crossed in the first place. Perhaps, it's the reason I was put on this earth. During the ten years after the diagnosis, nothing would matter more to me than you.

At first, I thought I could outsmart the illness by caregiving alone. Or love. I was always on the lookout for new drugs, treatments, herbal cures, vitamins, anything to alleviate your suffering. *There must be a way to prevent the inevitable from happening, or at least not in the way I heard it would.*

I learned what you needed to be comfortable, safe and secure. I advocated for you in any way I could. And pissed off a lot of people in the process. It made me feel I was contributing to your wellness and *my* need for hope. I was never going to give up on you. Caring for you was my job.

It took me time to understand you had no control over your behavior. I apologize for the moments I assumed you were doing or saying things on purpose to irritate me. Now I know that wasn't so. I hope you'll be able to forgive me. God knows, I'm trying to forgive myself.

I worried I wouldn't survive to tell my story. At least not in my right mind. And that's the truth. There was no instruction manual for handling Alzheimer's Disease or the crazy situations that plagued us non-stop. The days of constant watchfulness and worry, sleepless nights and new challenges became almost more than I could bear.

The times I regret most were when I failed to meet your needs, or when I was lost, helpless or running amok. Or, when my words or behavior added to the drama. I wish I could go back and do it over again. I'm so much wiser today. On the other hand, no. Neither of us would *ever* want to live through that again.

After six of the ten years I spent as your caregiver, when I finally came undone, there was no longer the illusion that, by some miracle, love alone would save you.

Honestly, there were some days when I prayed you wouldn't wake up the next morning. You asked me over and over to end your life, and if I could have done it without causing you more suffering or going to prison, I would have. I'm so sure of that. I hope you don't feel any resentment towards me. I only wanted you to be at peace. But that's all behind us now.

After you died, I considered the ten years of the illness as the worst years of my life. Really. I was so sure of that then. But now I know they weren't. In fact, in many ways they were the *best* years of my life. But I don't mean they were the *happiest*. Or the most *tranquil*. Not at all. I realize now that your illness was a gift you gave me. I was meant to learn from it. And grow.

Caring for you taught me to be more open,

compassionate and grateful. Less judgmental, more generous and more forgiving. Every good day you had, every time you remembered a name, or smiled in recognition of my face, when we would walk outside and smell the flowers, enjoy visits from family and friends, when you slept well, and ate your favorite flavor of ice cream, every time you told me you loved me, I was grateful. Or other times when some small joy gave you pleasure, and I would swell with happiness.

Aren't those the things that really matter in life, anyway?

Alzheimer's Disease forced me to learn about life. And about love. And even more about the *people* in our life -- how some disappointed, and others rose to the occasion in the most stunning of ways.

I can only imagine how you suffered. You fought so hard to be brave and not appear weak; you didn't want others to think you had given up or given in. You called it "rusting." When people asked how you were doing, you always told them you were "fine." Even when you weren't. You rarely complained or found fault.

Perhaps that is the domain of those who feel their time is infinite.

You, more than anyone, didn't want to leave this life. You fought a courageous battle against death. In fact, you lived several years longer than your prognosis. All those years of surviving during the Holocaust wore out your brain, but etched their mark in your DNA. Living was programmed within you; dying wasn't.

No matter what else I had done, or whatever I would do from then onward, nothing in this life would matter more than what we shared when you were dying. *Nothing*. I wouldn't trade those years for anything.

I don't think there was anyone who didn't love you, Larry. I will always remember your kindness, generosity, exuberance and loving heart. And many other qualities that took me so long to understand. You loved children, animals and the underdog. You felt everyone's pain, especially the emotional kind. You were hilariously funny, irreverent and wise. You could talk up a stranger and in ten minutes you'd be best friends. You were a good judge of character and you were *never* wrong. Your greatest need was to be needed. And loved. There was, and never will be, anyone like you.

The day you died, you left behind a transformed woman. I had grown up and matured in a way I never expected. I discovered what mattered and what didn't. All the pettiness of day-to-day life paled in comparison. And I am a much better person for it. I wonder if I will ever have such a lofty purpose again. I hope not.

How do I thank you for all the times you freely shared your love with me, whether it was with words or actions. People have asked me, "Were you ever sorry you married him," knowing what obstacles stood in my way and what I was up against. "Never," I said confidently. "From the moment I met him, my life was forever changed."

If it weren't for you, perhaps I wouldn't be where I am today. As you were dying, I was learning how to live. You had the courage to give me strength to confront my demons and begin my healing odyssey. When I despaired at the task before me, you would say, "People can survive much more than you think. You can too."

We had some difficult days together, yours, mine and ours. But we both stuck it out. You saw me through to sobriety and a much healthier state of mind. I know now how much my drinking affected you and our relationship. It must have been so difficult for you to watch while I slowly self-destructed.

You told me over and over again, "You have a drinking problem," but I didn't believe you any more than I did anyone else. The problems that we had from my drinking, I blamed them on you. I thought you were driving me to drink heavily. But it wasn't you, it was me.

I truly believe that when I stopped drinking I would never drink again. That's just how solemn and serious was the promise I made to myself. I know how you worried that I would relapse, but that never came to be. I was true to my word. I haven't wrapped my hand around a glass of anything more harmful than water in over twenty-five years.

I'm not completely healed, though. Is anybody? Just a work in progress. But I believe you would be proud of me.

I'm happy now. I married my boyfriend from kindergarten two years ago. We were both by your side on the day you died. He's a fine man, and a wonderful husband, gentle, funny and loving. His calm and quiet disposition has rubbed off on me, and my high spirits have infected him. We laugh all the time.

He was proud to have become your friend, and often talks about what he learned about being a "mensch" from your example. Thank you for welcoming him into your life during those last years, Larry. He was genuinely honored to have shared them with you.

I retired soon after you died. I miss the work sometimes; I helped many people turn their lives around. I couldn't have asked for a more fulfilling or rewarding career. I'm very busy now, and take great pleasure in nurturing my creative side.

Thank you for being a caring friend and support to my younger daughter. She's working hard and making her way in the world. You would be proud of her.

I feel your presence while I'm sleeping. For months after you died, you would visit me almost nightly with so much anger. Sometimes I would wake up crying. You blamed me for your death.

I'm sure leaving this world was hard for you. I know you didn't want to go. But I sense you're at peace now. I still dream about you frequently, but you're not angry. I suspect you've found the serenity you always longed for.

Often, the dialogue in my dreams between the two of us goes something like this:

"You died," I say to you.

"No, I didn't," you insist.

"I was there with you when it happened, Larry; you stopped breathing!"

"No. I *did not* die! You're wrong. I'm not dead. I'm here with you. I'll always be here."

Sometimes when I'm awake, I suddenly become so exquisitely aware of your spirit that I believe I could reach out and touch you. And you would be there.

The wonderful folks at Capon Springs planted a tiny sugar maple tree on the grounds in front of the tree swing in your memory. I wish you could see how strong and healthy it's become. It's practically twelve feet tall now! Underneath the tree rests a bronze plaque that reads: "If love could save you, you would have lived forever." You would love that.

We were lucky, weren't we? Even though we had some truly difficult times together, there were many beautiful days and happy moments. Even when you were sick. I tried to imagine life without you then, and I just couldn't. The way you looked at me. It's as sharp in my mind now as it was then. The music of your laughter, so full of vivaciousness. You loved life and it showed.

Do you remember when we visited the Louvre in Paris? And your hilarious jokes about the Mona Lisa? Your smile was better than a thousand of hers. I can see you now, your wide grin and then the belly laughs rising all the way up from your toes.

When I began writing this letter to you, I was sure I could never forgive you for dying. At least, not for dying in the manner you did. But I don't feel that way any longer. You died the only way you knew how — in the same way you lived your life. Struggling and surviving the best you could. I've accepted that it couldn't have been any other way.

I'm certain when my life ends, we'll meet again. I simply can't believe this is all there is. I hope your soul has finally found the peacefulness you deserve.

Actually, I'm working on the same thing myself here in *this* life! I'm not running away from *me* anymore. Perhaps it took somebody like you, someone who was no stranger to suffering, to take me by the hand and say, "It's time to change your life." You didn't give up on me and, for that gift, I will be forever grateful.

Rest in peace, my love.

Chapter 30

That Explains It

I sat on a comfortable sofa across from the new doctor, a young psychiatrist. It was my second visit. I liked him. He was professional yet personable. I had already shared so much with him as he did his best to obtain a complete history and arrive at a reasonable evaluation of my mental health.

I've taken antidepressant medication since before I stopped drinking. It didn't do much good until I was sober. Then, everything changed. Within a week I was sleeping better than I ever had. Within two weeks my anxiety had decreased substantially, and I was considerably less irritable. A month into treatment, my mood improved. Over the next few months, I finally realized what it was like to wake up in the morning and look forward to the day. Whenever someone asked me to compare myself before and after medication, I would usually say, "Until I took Prozac, I didn't know trees had leaves!"

Any health care professional who's ever treated me in the past knows I like to play doctor. No, no, no -- it's not what you're thinking.

Every few years, I would begin to worry about the effects of taking psychotropic medication for such a long time. Decades. Usually I would tell myself to just leave well enough alone. "Don't mess with something that works," I scolded. And whomever my therapist or psychiatrist was at the time would second that. Sometimes I didn't heed their advice, and I weaned myself off.

Generally, I wouldn't notice much difference. "You see," I'd say, "I'm fine. Cured. No difference between my medicated and unmedicated self."

A week, two weeks and more passed. Sometimes months. And then came the crash. The old feelings would return, the dour mood, sleepless nights, the anxiety I couldn't control and the irritability at just about every*one* and every*thing*. I didn't want to go anywhere or see anyone. I didn't have the energy.

"I feel bad and I don't know why," I would say to myself.

And then it would hit me. It's the antidepressant -- or lack of such. My brain is half-starved, gasping for the serotonins which it can't produce enough of on its own!

And so, I would re-start the antidepressant again, wait for it to kick in, and always feel better. Much better. And then I would wonder why I ever stopped in the first place. My doctor would remind me that if I stopped taking the antidepressant again, it would be like going scuba diving without my oxygen tank!

Somewhere, sometime, somebody in a high-up position (don't know whether it's the American Psychiatric Association or the insurance companies) decreed that any individual who takes a psychotropic medication must be seen by a physician or psychiatrist every so many months. I'm fine with that. Maybe the individual doesn't need the medication any longer (not me), or needs more of it (sometimes me), or it's just not working and that person needs some other medication. Or perhaps they're abusing it. I get it. So, every few months, I go to the psychiatrist for a medication check-up.

Having recently moved to the South, I was in the process of finding all new doctors. This particular psychiatrist came highly recommended by an individual whose opinion I trust. I didn't expect much because, by and large, most psychiatrists are a pretty wacky bunch. Maybe all mental health professionals are attracted to this field in order to work out our own problems. And some have and some haven't. Dunno. But it sounds reasonable.

As a mental health professional myself, I've worked with a lot of psychiatrists and had a few as my own. The ones whom I would consider outstanding I could count on the fingers of one hand.

But after all, I wasn't in crisis and all I needed was a medication evaluation a couple of times a year. What the hell. Any psychiatrist that can certify that I'm reasonably mentally healthy and will renew my prescription for Prozac for another few months will be just fine.

I made an appointment with the new psychiatrist but, frankly, wasn't prepared for much. The same questions. The same concerns about my sobriety, family history, and am I going to kill myself.

This time, however, I was pleasantly surprised. No, *more* than that. My new psychiatrist is probably one of the best ones I've ever personally or professionally known. Over and above any that *I've* ever seen in the past, for sure.

His office is well, uh, *normal*. Like a homey living room. It's not a blank slate and it doesn't look like a medical office. He even has a few pictures of his family around. At least I guess they're his family. And some art on the walls. And lots of books about mental health. They're not just medical textbooks either. Some are popular books about a variety of topics related to mental health. A few are bestsellers. The books a person reads tell something about the person who reads them, don't you think?

The office is clean and cozy. A wall of windows looks out onto a wooded area speckled with sunlight. He has some personal effects on his desk, some from his travels, perhaps, and others, maybe an award. I feel comfortable here. I can let down my defenses. I want to trust him.

The most distinguishing feature of his office, the one item I saw just as soon as I walked through the door that first time, placed strategically at eye level, left me feeling that he was a good guy, down to earth, grounded, someone who would set me straight if I needed it in plain English. It was the boxed canvas poster on his wall.

"Yesterday is history. Tomorrow is a mystery. Today is a gift. That's why it's called the present." That's exactly what it says. No psycho-mumble-jumble.

"I like that poster a lot," I remarked during the first visit. "It's meaningful to me."

"What touched you about it?" the doctor responded.

"Well," I began, "it means that I'm not *now* who I was then. *That* Sonya is gone. She no longer exists. It's hopeful. I'm not a prisoner of the past. I don't have to keep going back to ancient history to recapture or remember a part of me that's dead. I am who I am *now*. Today. I need to live in the present, enjoy how far I've come and cherish what I have. And receive the gifts that every new day brings. No more wishing, hoping or pining for something better down the road. Today is here and it's good enough."

"Well put," said the doctor. "I wish all my patients would think like that. They'd be a lot happier."

The doctor asked me numerous questions about my alcohol addiction. "It's very unusual for an alcoholic not to relapse, even once."

"Yes, I know that. But the morning after that Thanksgiving I saw myself more clearly than ever before. I hated who I'd become. I couldn't, wouldn't live another day as a drunk. I was so deeply affected by the images that swirled around in my head, by the mess I'd made of my life. I vowed I would never drink again and I didn't. I've definitely thought about it, though, but I didn't. My 'relapses' were of a different sort."

"What do you mean?"

"They were *behavioral* relapses. The kind of behaviors I engaged in when I was actively drinking. I was sober but acting like a drunk. Particularly in the beginning years of sobriety or during those times when I was incredibly stressed. Making bad choices, poor judgment, going off, losing control, not thinking, behaving like the only thing that mattered was me. Thoughtlessness, anger. I didn't like myself very much when I acted that way. It took many years and countless therapy sessions for me to lose my dry drunk persona."

"It sounds like you've been successful then."

"I have. But I'm not perfect. I will never aspire to perfection any longer. Even now, twenty-some years after I had my last drink, I still find myself thinking about acting like a drunk now and then! But, these days, I can usually stop myself."

"We're all dragging a lot of excess baggage behind us. Some of it is so weighty that it's hard to heave overboard," he says, chuckling at my choice of words.

I liked him. I liked his approach. I liked that he was transparent. Human. Laid back. Understanding. And kind. I *wanted* to talk to him.

He suggested that I remain on my current antidepressant. It seemed to be working. I didn't have any symptoms of depression.

"I guess I'll see you again in a few months, then?" I said, thinking the session was over.

"I have one more question for you before we end."

Uh-oh, here it comes. He's going to ask me if I know how terribly mentally ill I am? How truly crazy!

"Has anyone ever suggested that you might have PTSD?"

"You mean Post-Traumatic Stress Disorder?"

"Yes. I know it might sound odd because the term often applies to the survivors of war and disasters."

"No. No one has ever suggested it. Why?"

"Well, if you take a look at the Diagnostic and Statistical Manual, you'll notice that you have many of the symptoms that are consistent with PTSD. In fact, for you, PTSD is probably a better fit than clinical depression or anxiety because it includes some symptoms that aren't necessarily characteristics of either of those, like a heightened startle reflex."

I could *really* relate to that one. "Well, I do seem to have exaggerated reactions to situations much more so than other people do."

"And the hypervigilance and anxiety you've mentioned. And guilt and mistrust."

"Well, I've never thought about myself as anything other than a clinical depressive in remission," I joked. "But I'm familiar with the symptoms of PTSD and, in fact, have treated a few clients with it myself."

"You've had a pretty traumatic life, haven't you?" What you've told me about your alcoholism, upbringing and your late husband's illness is traumatic, don't you think?"

"I've never thought about it that way. But indeed it is."

My brain went to work then. In a period of seconds, I reviewed events that might be considered a "trauma" and realized that I certainly had many agonizing experiences I could look back on, ones that have affected me for decades.

"You're not a Vietnam War vet where extreme trauma may occur over a short period of time. Rather, you've experienced many traumas over a much longer period of time. Every time you're traumatized in the present it brings up all the unresolved traumas from the past."

"You mean like when my mother left me by the side of the road and drove away? Or when I was attacked by the dogs?"

"Exactly. Those are significant, life-changing events. They may cause much more damage to an individual's physical, cognitive and emotional functioning over the long term than depression. And it's often a lot harder to manage some of the manifestations of the illness."

"How about my husband's illness and the harsh treatment I endured when he was ill? Or going to jail? Or getting a divorce?" I was on a roll now. It was all beginning to make sense. Finally. "But why does the diagnosis matter so much?"

"You're a therapist and you know the answer to that. The treatment focus is different. We often treat the psychobiological responses, identify triggers and try to separate the traumatic memory from the debilitating emotion associated with it.

Once you identify and change maladaptive coping behaviors, you can do some cognitive restructuring. And lastly, develop trust and personal relationships. It's a long process and takes many years. But it sounds like you've done quite a bit of that in working with your own therapists in the past."

"I have. But this puts a whole new spin on my mental health and some of the symptoms which have troubled me."

I was excited. PTSD explained so many things about me that I've never been able to figure out before. It fit. In fact, it was a *great* fit. Now, when I tried to figure out my occasional over-the-top reactions to present situations, I could understand what happened in the present to trigger the emotional reactions rooted in the past.

"It's something we can discuss further," the doctor suggested. "But let's get back to your sobriety. You've been in recovery for a long time now without a relapse. Do you think there's anything that might cause you to start drinking again?"

"Nothing, never," I assured him. "I have a mental list of all the bad things out there that *could* happen but haven't. Each one is terrible, painful and traumatic in its own right. But I feel like I've already been through the worst part of my life and I haven't relapsed. Whatever is yet to befall me might crush me emotionally for some time, but I would *never* drink again. That part of my life is over. If all the craziness around my husband's illness didn't make me drink, nothing will!"

"Based on what you've told me about those difficult years, your assessment is probably correct. Perhaps the worst is over."

As I rose to leave, the doctor asked, "How do you feel, Sonya, about this new diagnosis?" He was smiling.

I felt relieved. He had taken the fifty-pound sandbag wrapped around my shoulders and hurled it across the room.

"That explains everything. Finally. I think I can wrap my head around it quite well. Thank you."

Chapter 31

The Photograph

Tacked precisely in the middle of the bulletin board over my desk is a recent photograph of me standing in front of the home in which I grew up. Before the picture was snapped, I jumped around on the front lawn like a silly kid, as my childhood friend, Penny, camera in hand, tried to capture my image for all time.

"Stand still!" she yelled at me. Obligingly, I did as I was told. "Smile, Sonya. Remember how happy it made you to win when we played Monopoly together!" Sixty-some years earlier, Penny and I had spent many afternoons together playing board games on the floor of her bedroom or holding secret meetings in the clubhouse in her backyard where she was the president and I was the secretary.

Penny and I grew up on the same street, two doors from each other. I spent a lot of time in her sandbox. We liked to peek through the bushes and spy on the neighbors. She had a big dog and we would nibble on his dog bones with her sister, Candy. They actually didn't taste too bad — except when they were mixed with sand.

Our favorite outdoor activities were jump rope, tag and Kick the Can. We shared so many secrets, gossip and stories on our mile-long walks to school every morning. Other kids in the neighborhood joined us as we walked. The years of our childhood friendship bring back fond memories.

I unpinned the photo and held it up for a closer look. I imagined myself standing on the front lawn the day Penny took the snapshot. The air was cool and thirsty; brilliant sunlight scattered warmth over my skin. The royal blue sky vanished into the green land in a spectacle that occurs only on the flat landscape of Northwest Ohio.

I wanted to preserve the memory of that day forever; just tenderly fold the moments up in soft powder blue tissue paper, secret them away in a velvet-lined box and then, whenever I wanted to remember the beauty of a cloudless day in June, gently unfold the memories and let them sail on a breeze.

In the photo, I wore a blue and green tee-shirt that didn't flatter me. It pulled across my chest and was too tight under the arms. I peered at my image and decided to give the tee-shirt away. A lime green sweater was tied casually around my waist. Both pockets of my favorite jeans held water bottles. My hair was untidy; I recall how the top layers rose and fell in perfect cadence with each ripple of air.

The house I grew up in was a pleasant looking place, but it wasn't welcoming. It didn't shout, "Come in, come in, within these walls live happy people having good times!" There was nothing to reveal even a hint of who might dwell there now. No car, no "Go Green Bears" pennant, no bicycles, soccer balls or yard tools. Nothing. It's just as I remembered it. Cold and barren. There was no life in that house. There never was.

I can almost feel the spongy patches of dirt that speckled the lawn as I looked at the photo. I was holding my flip-flops in my left hand. I pictured myself digging my toes into the familiar loamy soil like I did as a child, provoking the plump earthworms that rested just below the surface. I could almost smell the sweet musky fragrance of rich earth and succulent blades of grass.

On the left side of the photograph stood a rotting

stump where the disfigured oak tree in the front yard used to stand. Once healthy and full of life, the tree became worn out and decayed by the time I left home. I imagined its death may have mirrored the struggles of the people who lived within the walls of that house. The naked stump which remained was a harsh reminder of the losses that have swept through my life.

The blood-red brick of the house was re-painted snowy white. I stared at the photo and remembered the shiny black mailbox with a red flag that once stood at the end of the driveway. After a heavy rain, the mailbox would tilt precariously as if to say, "All I want is to lie down and rest for a moment."

I loved that mailbox and the daily ritual of waiting for the mailman. The anticipation of long letters addressed to me from far-away friends and pen pals promising friendship and love filled me with excitement. The mailbox and the joy those letters brought is gone now. I'm living in different times and no one writes letters any more.

I reached across my desk for a magnifying glass and gazed into the face of the adult woman who was once the child who lived in that house. I recall the jumble of emotions she often experienced as a youngster. Sorrow bubbles up from the pit of my belly. I have the unsettling sense that I am searching for answers about the young girl's life, without even knowing what the questions are. I could still feel the tattered remnants of pain and sadness that haunted that little girl.

I studied the photograph even more closely, looking for signs of life in my former bedroom over the garage. Unevenly hung curtains at the window obscured my view and hid what lay beyond.

I closed my eyes and pictured my room, large and high-ceilinged. The carpet and walls were pink and the floors sloped. There were windows on three sides, and it was always chilly. At night, I dressed in many layers and burrowed down under the covers to stay warm. I hid a flashlight under the bed, reading books in my toasty cocoon.

Sometimes I would lie there on my back and shine the flashlight on the ceiling, watching the tiny spiders as they constructed sophisticated webs extending from one wall to the other. I followed their progress from night to night, pretending I was part of the community they were building. I pictured myself as a tiny spider, living in a loving family surrounded by hundreds of other itty-bitty sister and brother spiders. We traveled joyously day after day along the narrow filaments of our web looking for spider playmates.

Every so often, the intricate handiwork would be swept away, only to be renewed by the same tired spiders in the same tedious manner. Nearly invisible myself, I felt a close kinship with those minute creatures.

I tacked the photograph back onto the bulletin board and stared at the image of my house. The air around me pulsed with the sensation that I was waiting for something to happen but I had no idea what it was. It was so quiet I could hear the rhythmic pulse of blood as it coursed through my body and the reliable tick-tock of my heart as it echoed against my rib cage. But most of all, I could hear myself think.

I couldn't help wondering who lived in that room above the garage now. Was it a girl? Was she happy? Did she love books as much as I did? Did she long for a different life? Were there any traces of me and my life remaining in my old room? Did the walls still harbor the legacy of my pain? Did the child who lived there now sit alone in her room, unseen and unheard?

Certain that I was the last invisible child to live in that room, I tacked the photo back on the bulletin board and silently said goodbye to my childhood.

Chapter 32

Finding My Voice

During the years I spent writing this book, I struggled with what to say about my first marriage. I spoke lovingly about my late husband, and happily about my new husband. But what to say about the man I married when I was little more than a young girl myself?

We separated twelve years after the wedding, and spent the next few years yo-yoing back and forth in various states of ambivalence. And even more years filled with open hostility.

"I'm stuck," I remarked in a writing class one day. "Shall I simply pretend he and the marriage didn't exist, or act like a snarling, mad dog of an ex-wife who, filled with revenge, can't see or write anything about the relationship except the parts colored by the end of the marriage and the aftermath of an unhappy divorce?"

"That's not a voice in which I'm comfortable speaking. Not any longer." I continued. "It doesn't feel right to me. He's a decent person and he *is* the father of my children, a good father. He never wanted the marriage to end in divorce any more than I did and tried the best he could to make it work."

"Were there any happy times?" one of my classmates

asked.

"Of course. We got married, didn't we?" I replied laughing. "There were many tender, loving and peaceful moments. I remember them well."

"Then why don't you write about those? You must have hoped the marriage would last forever, didn't you?" asked another classmate.

"I don't think I ever thought about 'forever' when I married him. I guess I thought that once I was married, the rest would just take care of itself."

My writing teacher reminded me of what I had learned about being "stuck." "When you're writing in a voice that doesn't feel comfortable or sound like you, don't continue. It won't be authentic. If it's not the real you, what you're feeling at this very moment in time, it won't sound real. Push your mind in another direction," he suggested, "towards your true feelings. How you feel now."

"Write the story in your words and with your voice, not someone else's. If you write what you think the reader wants to hear, or what you believe might sell more books, your story won't be honest."

"And if it's not honest, why bother writing it," another student chimed in.

"Why shouldn't she talk about how she felt a long time ago?" someone else asked.

"Because," the teacher continued, "she has to end up in the here and now. Hers is a story of going from bad to worse and, ultimately, to better. What purpose would be served by speaking now with her angry, drunken voice from long ago?"

"Exactly," one more student noted. "In the first year or two of the relationship, young and in love, how would you have described your husband then? And what about when you became a parent? And what if your husband had died when you were still married, how would you have remembered him?"

"I think I know what you mean." I interrupted. "I should talk in my voice *today* about my feelings right now, rather than in the enraged, boozy voice I used then."

"And later," the teacher added, "when you separated and were still taking vacations together with the children, what did you experience? How would you describe the man and woman who didn't want to let go of the marriage?

What would you feel today if the marriage had worked out and you were still together? Write it all down," he advised, "and then come back to it a week or two later and see how it sounds. Ask yourself this one, important question -- Am I speaking in yesterday or today's voice?"

I decided to give it a try. I liked to change things up and this was a good opportunity.

I began to write about my first husband as a perfect specimen of mankind and me as his lowly unequal. My family couldn't believe that someone like *me* snagged someone like *him*. One of the more negative members of my family said, "How did you do it? He's going to be a lawyer, for God's sake!" I guess they expected that someone like me would bring home some stupid schlub.

No siree, not me! I'd been trained well. *Go to college and find a nice Jewish lawyer or doctor to marry and live happily ever after.* And I did just that. Without any thought at all as to how to make the "happily ever after" happen. I figured that all one needed to do was make that legal commitment and the rest would be easy.

Not so much, I discovered.

My friends considered him flawless. He was good at school; I wasn't. He had a happy family; mine was not. He smiled a lot; I didn't. He was comfortable in social situations; I had no self-confidence. He was handsome; I didn't think much of *my* looks. He excelled at most things; I didn't know where to begin, let alone finish, anything.

Our early relationship was riddled with tremendous

highs and terrible lows mostly caused by my increasingly excessive use of alcohol and worsening depression. I was drunk on my first date with him. I cast him as a model man and me as a whiny, drunken slag.

When I thought about him later in the marriage, I saw him as frozen and distant, an unemotional, WASP-y, workaholic, prince of a Jewish boy. I saw myself as an imprisoned, emotional, out-of-control loser, who couldn't manage my own life, let alone a marriage.

In reality, though, it was *I* who was frozen and distant -- hysterical, reactive and controlling, too. A princess who wanted things her way, and who drank to excess to blunt her growing emotional problems.

I wrote it all down, but it still didn't seem right to me. It felt like I was blaming or casting him and I into black or white, good or bad. It sounded harsh and critical about *both* of us. I wrote as if we were diametrically opposed. Completely at odds. Enemies. He sat on the side of perfect and right, and I sat on the other. In reality, though, we both wanted the same thing. To be happy. To grow a good marriage. To raise contented children.

I was still stuck.

I returned to class later that week. My classmates listened to what I had written and agreed, "It's more of the same. You're not there yet." They suggested I force myself in yet another direction.

"What were your dreams about the relationship when you were dating?" one asked. "After you were married, how did you imagine your future with your new husband?"

"You don't need to glorify him as he stood on his pedestal, or make him out to be the frost-bitten and unfeeling person he wasn't," my writing teacher interjected. "After all, Sonya, I know *you* wouldn't have married someone like *that*. And you, you must have had some warm and wonderful qualities, didn't you?"

Sonya Braverman

It was obvious now. None of the words I'd used to describe him or the marriage so far had touched me. They didn't make me *feel* anything. They weren't spoken from my heart. Today. They came from the angry feelings that dulled the pain and sorrow, emotions I thought I had let go of years before.

I left class that day determined that I was going to speak in my present voice about the years in the past. I wasn't going to get lost in the years it took me to process the divorce. Or whether or not I even wanted a divorce. Or how I beat myself up about not knowing what to do to make things better.

I had to accept that the person I was *then* couldn't make that happiness ever come about between us. *I* wasn't happy, and my need to blame someone other than myself for my unhappiness was greater than my need to keep the marriage together.

Even though I wanted to communicate those feelings to him time and again, I just couldn't find a way to express myself. I needed to let go of it all. All the negativity and old feelings. That's not who I am today.

Sitting in writing class the following week, I listened to a story written by another classmate. The author was an older woman, in her mid-seventies, and she prefaced her story by telling the class that for many decades, she had a quarrelsome and antagonistic relationship with one of her children, her oldest daughter. She acknowledged that she had failed her daughter as a Mom.

Those years were heartbreaking, and she didn't want to think about them, much less write about it. Even though she still had many negative feelings and unpleasant memories about her relationship with her daughter, she couldn't put those words down on paper and include the story in her book. She knew she needed to take another approach in order to write honestly about her firstborn child.

One afternoon, as she was sitting in her family room and sifting through old photographs of her daughter as a baby and, later, as a young girl growing up, she was choked up by feelings of a different kind. She embraced the pictures of her lovely daughter with her eyes and thought about how easy and effortless were the years before their problems started, and then in all the years since they had begun to heal. And that's what she wrote about. A touching tribute to what she cherished most about her daughter. She cried as she read the story aloud in class.

I was exquisitely touched. Her words brought me to tears. They were deeply affecting. My eyes were open in an entirely new way. The author stated later that writing about her daughter in such a loving manner was freeing. It permitted her to focus on what was good, not what wasn't. How I hoped her story would provide some direction for me!

It had become easier to make amusing remarks about what a crappy wife I thought I was, or what a shitty husband I thought he had been. Writing about the emotions that led us away from the path of loving each other into blind alleys, cliffs and courtrooms was more familiar, but it just didn't feel right any more. Those words were no longer consistent with where I was in my life and who I had become.

One day, flooded with vivid memories about my relationship with my former husband, I didn't allow the hands of grief or anger to push the memories away as I had done countless times before. I allowed them to flow freely.

An attractive couple, young and in love, walking hand-in-hand in a clear mountain stream looking for treasures. Dancing. Hanging out at college parties, picnics together, studying in the library, kissing, anticipating the birth of their first child, vacations, holidays and looking lovingly at their newborn daughter. So happy. A beautiful pair.

How innocent and new we were. How warm and affectionate. Loving and kind. The memories brought a stab of emotional pain that was almost physical -- I'd avoided thinking about the good things we had and focused instead on the *bad*. All the unpleasant details that contributed to the end of the marriage.

I continued to write about how in love we were, lives filled with hope, aspirations and dreams for the future. It was gut-wrenching to think about these things, and harder by far to see the rawness of my words on paper in black and white. They were real. And powerful. They reflected who I am *now*, not who I *was*, and my sorrow over what was irretrievably gone.

And on it went. I continued to write about the happy times, a honeymoon in Jamaica, holidays at the beach, watching our children at play, Christmas, Thanksgiving, visits to family, evenings with friends and our first home. And remembering the look on his mother's face when she discovered I was pregnant.

It felt better that way. Much better. I was more comfortable. I had finally found my voice.

Chapter 33

Healing

The late afternoon sun squeezes through the shuttered windows and throws long speckled shadows on the wall next to the bed. The deepening veil of October blankets the bedroom in dreamy shadows, an ambience well-suited to snuggling.

The man and woman lazily disentangle from one another. The air is charged with the electricity of a relationship which is intensely emotional, and the easy laughter and loving companionship only shared backgrounds and years of commonalities can create.

Her body hums with a contentment she's never known. In the few years since they've been a couple their love for one another has deepened and intensified. They've come together after lives which have left both of them crushed and broken. They can feel the other's sorrows and understand how their respective lives have transformed each of them. She believes their meeting was destiny; they've been brought together to help each other heal.

She's remarkably relaxed, yet wildly awake. Turning on her side to look at him, she studies his face. She explores the sleepy-eyed man's ruggedly good-looking face. His smooth skin is covered in weekend salt-and-pepper stubble that only adds to his masculine appeal. She loves how his gray-white curls hug his neck and coil around his ears.

"You're *so* handsome," she says, leisurely drawing out each syllable as if it she were slowly pouring a thin stream of a golden liquid into a tall crystal goblet.

"I know," he says playfully in his deep velvet voice, "that's what all the ladies say." They both enjoy the humor in this statement. He's discovering greater confidence in who he is, and enjoys the good-natured banter.

She trusts him and plays along. "They could never love you as much as I do," she jokes. Their relationship crackles with the fireworks of amiable teasing.

She inhales the spicy-sweet fragrance which arises from his skin. "Mmmm, I love how you smell," she sighs.

"I love *you*," he whispers as they lie next to each other. Both of them have been married before, but neither has experienced the kind of intimacy that permits them to lay skin to skin, lips touching lips, with complete comfort. They share an awareness that even when they're not together, they're together.

"I think about you all the time," she murmurs, her words lingering honeysuckle-like in the air as she carefully traces the deep creases in his face with her index finger. His appearance is immensely appealing to her.

"Mmmm," he sighs drowsily. He burrows his face into her neck in the way she likes. She feels a profound enjoyment thinking about how satisfying her life has become. She suspects that he's painfully vulnerable, and that arouses a tenderness in her she hasn't felt since the days when her children were small. She cares passionately about his happiness.

The warmth and security of his embrace is a sanctuary she's come to depend on, just as much as her need for food and water. He's an anchor, a steady voice-of-reason and complement to her incompleteness.

"I sit by the garage door and wait for you to come

home," she jests, "every day." She misses him when they're apart and delights in the anticipation of his return home after work.

She rests her head on his chest, warm, sweaty and salty with spent excitement. "You worked hard today," she says smiling. She's a contented woman.

"I didn't let you down this time," he says with pride. "It's my duty to serve my Queen in any way I can."

"No, you didn't; you stood up straight and tall today," she reports appreciatively.

"I hope I made you happy," he says as his hands travel over the still smooth contours of her well-rounded torso, hesitating at the hollow in the small of her back. His eyelids gently close in the seductive manlike way they do when he's falling into slumber. He's a happy man; his exclamations of pleasure still ring in her ears.

Astonishing. The room is so still, yet I can actually hear him smiling.

There's a subtle, intangible feeling, an almost mystical sensation that hangs in the air between them like a lazy harvest moon.

She's in love with a fierceness that's frightening. For with every loving in the past, there's been a leaving. Sometimes she wants to inhale the whole of him, all at once in one enormous deep breath. She yearns to keep him warm and safe and free of pain.

He's sleeping now. She watches him breathe, preserving for always the image of the healthy and untroubled man she wishes him to be.

She wonders what course her life would have taken had he been in it all along.

Chapter 34

Breaking News

*Reprinted with permission from the *St. Kitts-Nevis Observer*, April 22, 2016.

On the magically beautiful island of Nevis, a tropical paradise hanging lazily in the southern West Indies, after a frenzied day of sipping virgin pina coladas, snoozing under gently undulating palm trees in the shadows of towering Mount Nevis, soaking up the blush of a nearly equatorial sun, and frolicking in the shimmering turquoise waters of the Caribbean Sea, Sonya Webne Braverman and James Hamilton Cooper, both 71, indiscriminately and wantonly, in a moment of pure abandon, without reason or forethought, having carelessly surrendered the capacity to think logically about what they were about to do, resolved to spend the rest of their lives in the care and comfort of one another and became husband and wife.

At five o'clock in the afternoon on Thursday, April 21, 2016, the happy couple stood side-by-side in the center of a heart created by thousands of hibiscus petals, under a canopy of sheltering fronds on the majestic Avenue of Palms at Nisbet Plantation Beach Club, a former sugar mill, and finally closed the circle of their sixty-six-year friendship.

Born just two weeks apart in February, 1945, the bride

and groom grew up in Ottawa Hills, Ohio. They lived less than a mile from one another, and attended kindergarten through high school together.

According to Sonya, "Jim was sweet and shy as a little boy. He was adorable. He didn't smile or talk much. I don't think he was very happy. His hair was dark and curly, and he wore suspenders and plaid shirts. I often dragged my rug next to his at nap time; he was my best friend."

"Jim was the strong silent type, but I always knew he loved me. In middle-school he never missed an opportunity to kick the back of my chair, pull my hair or make farting sounds! The older we grew, the more he tormented me."

"That little girl I knew in grade school was quiet and well-behaved," Jim mused. "She wore pretty dresses and her long brown braids were gathered on top of her head with big colored bows. Gee whiz, she was a cutie!"

The groom claims the bride is neither quiet nor well-behaved today. "In fact, she hasn't closed her mouth once since I've been with her! And, just for the record," he added. "I still fart. Whenever and wherever I damn well please!"

Today, the bride's long brown hair is blonde and Jim's dark curls are pearly white. Jim smiles all the time now and seems pretty happy. However, when his new wife does something to irritate him (which is pretty regularly, he adds), he's in her face with a whole lotta powerful words. "She's a wildcat," he adds, "and I got the battle scars to prove it," he says proudly.

With a lustful twinkle in her eye, the bride admits, "we sleep on the same rug every night now, and he's still my best friend."

♚

Sonya, a retired Clinical Social Worker, says she'll spend her time after the wedding organizing her drawers and arranging every one of her possessions in alphabetical order. "I intend to die with everything neat and tidy. I wouldn't want my children to see what a mess I've become."

Jim, on the other hand, plans to continue working twelve hours a day, six days a week -- "More if I can get it. I have no interest in organizing anything except maybe my stash of sedatives."

The bride affectionately refers to Jim as "Coop" or "Coopie," except when he relapses into his "inner bachelor," which is pretty frequent.

"That's when Sonya calls me 'James' or 'Mr. Cooper,' and a whole lot of other unflattering names. Her pretty face knots up, her pleasant voice becomes an ear-piercing screech, she bares her fangs, and starts foaming at the mouth. She's a bossy old lady! Those are the times I hanker for my bachelor days."

"'Do you think your laundry is going to grow legs and walk itself into the washing machine?' she shrieks, gesturing wildly, when she spies my collection of dirty clothes on the bathroom floor."

"I don't argue because I like being alive," Jim grins. "I try not to annoy the Queen too much."

Sonya fell in love with Jim's gentle nature, subtle sense of humor, and unflappably calm demeanor. "Nothing much bothers him. Oh, except for *me*, that is," she declares.

"Hey, don't forget to mention my astonishing good looks!" Jim shouts from across the room.

As a former Marine, Jim's motto is: "I do what I want, and I answer to no one." He hopes marriage won't change that.

"How about 'one team, one mission'," Sonya says sharply with a hint of a wink. "If that doesn't work for you, you'd better re-enlist in the Marines and pray they send you somewhere I can't find you!"

The groom refers to his bride as "Old Lady," (that will *not* win him any points) and describes her as affectionate, kind and intelligent. "Sonya can be prickly and stubborn, too," Jim admits, "but she's not the *colossal* pain-in-the-ass she once was."

The couple believe they fell into each other's lives for a reason. Sonya desperately needed someone to keep her in line, an achievement no one has ever been able to pull off. Jim boasts he's the only person in modern history who can fearlessly shout, "Silence!" to the bride and she obligingly complies. "If that doesn't work, an old sock and duct tape will usually keep the peace between us."

Jim acknowledges that Sonya makes him happy and nobody has *ever* done that before. "I work long hours and she always makes me a hot dinner and keeps my bed warm. Or maybe it's the other way around: she keeps my dinner warm and makes the bed hot? Whatever."

Jim and Sonya enjoy being together and laugh all the time. Mostly at each other. They have similar backgrounds and like books, movies, travel and theater. When the duo was asked if there were any major differences between them, they both jumped up and down excitedly and shouted, "Gender!"

Although the newlyweds seem to be dragging a lot of excess baggage behind them, it doesn't seem to have affected their relationship that much. Jim's first marriage went belly up years ago, but he hasn't turned sour on the ball and chain. In fact, he says, "I'm going to do this marriage thing until I get it right."

Sonya's working on her third marriage and hoping Jim's a keeper because she's never doing marriage again. "You have no idea how hard I have to work to get 'em ripe and ready to marry! It's exhausting."

For her wedding costume, the bride chose white linen slacks from Target and a pink tee-shirt from Chico's. Her bejeweled flip-flops from DSW were uber-elegant. The red, orange and fuchsia shawl draped over her shoulders coordinated perfectly with her painful sunburn. The fragrant purple Bougainvillea blossoms woven through her upswept hairdo were a splendid accompaniment to her ensemble. That is, until her head started itching and she discovered the flowers were crawling with ants.

The groom wore cuffed and pleated khaki trousers from L.L. Bean and a pink, Ralph Lauren button-down shirt he bought on sale at Lord & Taylor for $21.64, including tax. Allen Edmonds shoes graced his aircraft carrier-sized feet; his impeccable Gold Toe socks were from Costco.

Thanks to the blazing sun, high humidity, and gale-force ocean breezes, the bride's hairstyle and makeup were gone-with-the-wind in about two-and-half minutes. The groom had his hair cut (what's left of it, anyway) at the local barber in Nevis, the same person who works part-time at the butcher shop. The bride didn't look one bit happy with his coiffeur.

Jim wore his adored Ray-Bans atop his head and his beloved Rolex on his wrist. As he delicately patted his barren pate, he stated that he used to have a lot of hair -- before he met his bride -- and it's been falling out at a steady pace since then. Several of the guests commented that the final photographs of the wedding couple would require a great deal of retouching.

The background music was provided by Mother Nature herself — gentle sea breezes whispering through the fronds of the stately palm trees, the rhythmic rush and retreat of the ocean waters, and the harmonious chirping of tropical birds dancing overhead.

Mother Nature was also responsible for the coconut that fell dangerously close to the bridal pair, the spits of lightning that came out of nowhere, the gritty sand that covered the wedding cake, and the dollops of bird poop which dropped out of the sky onto the joyful couple's shoulders.

Pastor Davidson Morton of Eden Brown Church of God in St. James Parish officiated. The couple held hands during the ceremony. The bride wiped away tears of happiness when the groom, looking longingly into her eyes, touchingly promised he would remove the used tissues from his pockets before tossing his clothes into the washing machine. In return, the bride swore she would stop saying, "*What* did you say?" and finally buy those hearing aids she needs.

As the pastor pronounced the twosome husband and wife, the groom seized the bride's face in his hands and kissed her with seemingly endless passion. To everyone's surprise, Sonya's hair caught fire. "Happens all the time," she said blushing, as she excitedly fanned herself. The amorous groom had to be subdued with a tranquilizer gun.

Following the ceremony, the newlyweds entwined arms and toasted each other with sparkling cider accompanied by the rowdy cheers of the assembled guests, most of whom started drinking the good stuff two hours before. The handsome groom was overheard asking his beautiful bride, "Are you going to stop nagging me now that we're married?"

To which his lovely bride replied, "Are you going to clean up your desk?"

The bride gave the groom a special look that could only mean the answers to both questions were a resounding "No!" and "Never!"

After a beach barbecue at which the newlyweds dined and danced long past their bedtime, they returned to their cottage and changed into their wedding night attire. The bride wore an elegant OHHS Green Bears tee-shirt from 1963; based on the groom's behavior during the wedding ceremony we suspect he wore nothing at all.

The newlyweds said they didn't sleep much on their wedding night; they were kept awake by the tree frogs who serenaded them from the hibiscus bushes outside their cottage. The hotel manager was overheard saying that the bride created quite a commotion that night by threatening the tiny lizards creeping innocently around their cottage.

"If you ask me," the manager muttered, "the love-struck groom has married a total whack job." The next morning, when the dazed and confused groom was asked to comment on the racket coming from their cottage, he looked around furtively, lowered his head and whispered, "*Well,* people tell me she's always been a little off."

Upon their departure from Nevis, Jim and Sonya Cooper planted a tiny coconut palm on the grounds of the Nisbet Plantation Beach Club in honor of their marriage. Their fondest wish is that they will live long enough to see the itty-bitty palm tree grow up happy and healthy and produce big nuts -- just like them.

*Although this interview with Mr. and Mrs. Cooper didn't really show up in any newspaper, the content is accurate and true.

Chapter 35

Coming Home

I can still hear my teenage brother's excited words as he slammed the front door of my home and bounded noisily up the stairs two at a time. It was 1976, and he'd been living with me and my family for the past year. Such a show of animation was unusual for him. It was late on a Sunday night in mid-June, and he'd just returned from a weekend in West Virginia with his girlfriend's family.

"You have to go to this place in West Virginia," he shouted, out of breath. "It's Paradise! There's no locks on the doors; everyone eats the same thing at the same time; there's a curfew, bingo, a Saturday night campfire and sing-a-long, and a flag-raising ceremony every morning. They play music through the trees, too. The whole place is in some kind of weird time warp. It's awesome. And kinda corny, but I had so much fun! Here, I brought you a brochure. You *gotta* go!" He pressed the brochure for Capon Springs Resort and Farms into my hand.

There was a picture of a white clapboard building trimmed in green on the front. I read the first paragraph and then tossed it aside.

> First and foremost, we are a family operation. Owned and operated into four generations, we experience our everyday lives

right alongside our guests. So, if you need anything, we are right there. This creates an atmosphere of caring, trust and security.

And the moon is made of green cheese. What garbage.

Five stress-filled years passed and, desperate for a break from the frenzy of work, graduate school, single parenting and an impending divorce, I pulled out the Capon Springs brochure again. Why I kept it I'll never know. My brother was no longer living with me, but I could still feel his enthusiasm years later. "Capon Springs is your escape to recreation and re-creation," the words proclaimed, "once you've made your first trip to Capon, you are considered an old friend."

Uh-uh. Sure. Liar, liar, pants on fire!

Come home to Capon Springs, West Virginia. Experience a vacation retreat where you can completely relax and leave the outside world behind. A place where you, your family, and friends can enjoy great food and outdoor fun while making lasting friendships.

That's what it promised.

The gall of those Capon people! Who are they anyway, and why are they so, I don't know, dishonest?

I was hungry for a break and more than a little curious about that place. On the very slim chance my brother had discovered Nirvana, I made a reservation at Capon Springs for the following weekend.

Once you are here, our all-inclusive meals and activities create a stress-free getaway, especially for mom and dad! You don't need to worry about shopping, cooking, cleaning or where to go and what to have. Everyone eats together around the table three times each day. In between meals, kids experience a freedom to explore and play that they can never have back home. Unplugged from their electronics, they rediscover the wonder of nature, developing friendships among kids of their own age. Multiple childcare options also provide the opportunity for adult alone time.

This unscrupulous crap made me so mad. I couldn't wait to tell those people to stop making up stories!

My daughter understood that if we didn't like Capon, we'd just pack up and leave. We'd only be two-and-a-half hours from home. I'd find someplace else for us to stay for the weekend. *After all, what did my seventeen-year-old brother know about hotels?* Feeling like Alice before she fell down the rabbit hole, I wasn't sure what I would find when I arrived there.

Fairy tales. Hokum. Yuck.

The following Friday, I loaded the suitcases and my younger daughter in the car, and set out from my home hoping I would be able to follow the complicated set of driving instructions the nice man at Capon Springs had given me. "Turn right and then left, and then make the hairpin turn near the cemetery, a quarter mile from the white church with the green spire, where you follow the winding road around the river, and then turn right again at the dirt road up the mountain. And be careful," he added, "the road's not paved."

Oh, my goodness gracious. What have I gotten myself into?

I was worried about how this new adventure would unfold. Very worried. I couldn't help but be pessimistic. The brochure made this place sound like the Elysian Fields. Paradisiacal. I was prepared for the worst because nothing, *N-O-T-H-I-N-G*, was too good to be true.

The road was choked with traffic, worse than usual due to an early morning downpour. The smog, fog, and clog of the city enveloped us on all sides. I groveled my way west from the Beltway to Route 66 and the outskirts of the Washington, D. C. suburbs.

Gradually, the topography of the flat land, gaudy with an unattractive mishmash of residential and commercial structures, interspersed with the usual mega-shopping center, began to transform. The further west I drove, the more the vista became a rollercoaster of green hills, lush farmland, a smattering of houses and few cars. The ash-colored cloud cover dissipated, and the late morning sun hung motionless like a yolk suspended in a dazzling sapphire sky.

"Look at the cows," my daughter exclaimed from the back seat. "White horses, Mom, and goats!" All uncommon sights to this trendy suburban kid.

As we continued our journey, the hills grew higher and rockier, the meadows and farmland more wooded and signs of human life sparse. We drove for miles without seeing anything more than a lonely abandoned barn.

In time, a large sign announced we were driving through the pristine beauty of the Shenandoah National Forest. *Nature's Calling*, the sign read. "You're in big trouble if nature is calling you out here in this wilderness," I chuckled to myself. "Not even a gas station!"

The road drove fast -- picture-postcard scenery of small checkered farming villages buried in a backdrop of deep woods, peppered with a randomly situated log cabin perched on the top of a mountain, or a ramshackle hovel buried in a thicket of trees.

Civilization existed somewhere as evidenced by a sign for a diner and feed store in Marshall, and a tractor pull and sheep shearing fair in Delaplane, Virginia. Oh, and signs for brown eggs and baby chicks. I imagined farmers in overalls plowing the land and white-haired ladies in housecoats churning butter. I almost expected to see a sign for moonshine.

It seemed like we had been transported to another planet.

At the minuscule green sign for Route 274, less than a mile after the even tinier signs for Bear Creek and Duck Run, I turned right, just like the nice man at Capon Springs had instructed. The two-lane, paved road became a one-lane gravel trail. Worming circuitously upward around the mountain, we were tightly enfolded on both sides by dense woods. The sun disappeared behind the trees and the area became masked in the somber, silent gloom of the deep green and dark brown of ancient forest.

"There's two baby deer," my daughter said, pointing out the window as if she had never seen an animal in the wild before. "They're so cute. Stop the car, Mom! Maybe we can get out and pet them!" The deer stood motionless, looking in our direction. I stopped the car in the center of this no man's land in the middle of some godforsaken wilderness to watch a gaggle of deer who were watching us watching them.

I could swear I heard the banjos from "Deliverance" playing somewhere off in the distance. I expected a group of masked bandits to suddenly emerge from the trees with bows and arrows pointed in our direction, block the road, commandeer our car and hold us hostage in this isolated backwoods. We would disappear off the face of the earth. How could I have allowed this to happen?

God help me and my child. Where in the devil am I, and where am I going to end up?

As we reached the summit of the mountain and crossed the state line between Virginia and West Virginia, a huge billboard proclaimed, *West Virginia -- Almost Heaven, Wild and Wonderful.* "It was certainly wild," I thought, "but the heaven and wonderful part — not so sure."

I can't wait to return home and position both of my hands securely around my brother's neck!

The funereal trek through the thick foliage of a primeval wood lining the rugged mountain road rewarded us with spectacular views at its summit. I imagined the very same road once carried horses, wagons, or covered carriages. Mile after mile of mountain peaks, verdant meadows filled with fits of colorful flowers, rich farmland, deep green clumps of trees and a few primitive cabins polka-dotted the land.

We slugged down the other side of the mountain, my foot pumping the brakes gently, fearful one of my tires would be pierced by a sharp rock lying in the road. We would all die here, never to be found.

The road continued to slope downward and eventually the landscape gentled-out. A stream coiled serpentinelike down the mountain and turned into a cascading waterfall. The natural beauty of this place was spellbinding.

The final stretch of our journey took us up one side of a mountain and down the other — twisting roads and exquisite summer scenery, with not another car or human in sight. As I gently eased out of a hairpin turn near the foot of the mountain, the gravel road gradually gave way to pavement and widened slightly. The dense wooded terrain pushed back on both sides of the road as if it were a curtain opening on the first act of a play.

As if I had just opened my eyes after a long sleep, the sun broke through the heavy cover of forest and shone an unblinking eye on the 19th century, white clapboard buildings lining both sides of the road. Out of nowhere they appeared. We had arrived. Capon Springs. I'd never seen anything quite like the sight before me.

What on earth is this?

The green-trimmed buildings, all decked out with wide porches and comfortable chairs, were situated in a town square layout around a wide expanse of lawn. Inviting hammocks suspended between mature trees were scattered over the grounds. A gazebo, fountain, playground, tree swing, shuffleboard court, pool, ping pong house and more beckoned us to play. As I drove up to the Main House, where the nice gentleman said I should check in, people of all ages were sitting on the front porch in rocking chairs, talking, laughing and reading.

Appealing. But I'm not getting my hopes up about this place. No way. Not a chance.

I checked in. Everyone was so nice and helpful. We climbed back into the car to drive to our accommodations in a separate building backing to the trail around White Mountain.

Our room was old-fashioned, simple and clean. Being a Ritz-Carlton kind of girl, the accommodations didn't measure up. Not at all. Except for the view. And the sounds of nature. Trees and lawn, flowers and hills — we were surrounded on all sides by the splendor of nature. Singing birds, leaves rustling against one another in the breeze and the ripple from a brook right under our window.

I'm sure the truth of this place will make itself known. And soon, I suspect. I give it an hour, at most.

My daughter was excited. She wanted to go swimming in Capon's spring-fed pool and join the other children she saw on the playground. There were no locks on the doors, no fancy hotel safe in the wall, and I was concerned about leaving my belongings in the room unattended.

Holy crap. What will become of my clothes and jewelry?

I crammed everything of value into my already-too-heavy purse and out we went.

I found a comfortable lounge chair on a wooden deck hanging precariously over a gurgling stream. I pulled a book out of my bag and read under a shady oak tree. My daughter swam and played. She was "making friends," the hallmark of a good time for a kid. The children followed each other from the pool to the shuffleboard court, the playground, sandbox and back to the pool. They were having fun.

At five o'clock, much to my surprise, gentle music began pouring out of the trees. "What's that?" I asked of no one in particular. A teenager lounging nearby said, "They play music one hour before breakfast, lunch, and dinner. It's kinda like a wake-up call telling you to get ready to eat." It reminded me of when I was a kid and the neighborhood mothers stood on the front porches ringing cow bells to call the kids inside for a meal.

We went back to the room and dressed for dinner. The music followed us. I figured eating dinner at Capon Springs wasn't much different than at any other hotel. We ditched the swim- and casual wear and dressed up. I wore jewelry and worked on my hair and makeup. I didn't want to be embarrassed or out-of-place. My daughter looked lovely in her party dress. By the time we were ready to leave the room, the music had stopped and someone was ringing the loudest cow bell I'd ever heard.

As we walked across the square to the Main House dining room, I could tell our attire was, uh, "a little" over the top. Everyone was dressed down, *way* down: shorts, tee shirts and flip flops. The two of us were "dolled up" and exquisitely out of place.

If this is such a nice place, why is everyone dressed like they're going to a picnic?

Dinner was served in a large sunny room looking out over the grounds. The room was flanked by windows on three sides, each dressed with old-style ruffled curtains. Our waitress seemed genuinely happy to see us, introduced herself as Pauline and welcomed us to Capon Springs.

"Could we see the menus, please?" I asked Pauline, who was dressed in a crisp white uniform and a flowery apron.

"Ma'am, this must be your first visit to Capon Springs. We don't have menus here. Tonight's dinner is fried chicken with all the trimmings. We serve family style, and if you want seconds, just holler."

Easy. No decisions. Eat what's put in front of you. Nice. Real nice.

I later learned the menu was the same every week. A few minor changes, but essentially, what is served at meals has remained the same for the thirty-seven years I've been visiting

Capon Springs. My daughter loved the predictability and wanted me to replicate it at home. Her favorite day was Saturday — hamburgers for lunch, Thanksgiving at dinner, and later, a hotdog roast around the campfire.

After dinner, I expected the two of us would return to our room and entertain ourselves. We strolled through the living room in the Main House, and discovered people reading, talking, playing games and doing puzzles. Others were sitting outside on the porch, or just meandering around the grounds. Or playing shuffleboard. My daughter spied her "friends" from the afternoon, and wanted to go outside and play.

I located a cushy sofa and took out my knitting. It wasn't long before a another woman sat down beside me and asked what I was making. Then she showed me what she was crocheting. We talked about our love of yarn, and she offered to teach me how to crochet. Several other ladies joined us and we gabbed about needlework. Suddenly, my daughter ran into the living room out of breath and trailing a posse of friends. "Guess what, Mom? At nine o'clock they have cake! Can I have some?"

"How could you be hungry after all that fried chicken?"

"I'm not. But I want *cake*. I have to have it. *Pul-eeeze?*" She didn't wait for an answer, as she ran out the screen door chasing after her new friends, "We're going to play ping-pong now. 'Bye."

At nine o'clock we were starving for cake, and at eleven the lights were turned off in the living room. Curfew. I'd never gone to camp, but I imagined Capon Springs wasn't much different.

I slept with the window open next to my bed. The smell of the cool mountain air washed away the day, and the trickle of water tumbling over the rocks directly underneath our room cushioned me into the best night's sleep I'd had in months.

We awoke the next morning to now familiar music winding its way through the trees, a slice of sun barely rising over the mountains, and a hearty appetite. We arrived at the Main House for breakfast in time to see the raising of the flag, say the Pledge of Allegiance, and sing the Star-Spangled Banner. I was greeted warmly by the owners of Capon Springs and my new friends from the prior evening. Even the waitress seemed happy to see us again! And everyone knew our name.

Astonishing. Is it something these folks are eating? Or maybe drinking? Yeah. That's it, they all drink! A lot!

The whole glorious day stretched lazily before us. My daughter wanted to play with her friends, but acquiesced to a nature hike with her Mom after breakfast. We walked for miles. The trail curved under the forest canopy, over mountain streams, through meadows blossoming with color, through a Christmas tree farm, and to the top of a mountain, where we looked down upon all 4,700 acres of Capon Springs property. The scenery left me breathless.

On our trek back to the Main House, we stopped at the pig farm, where we laughed at the **piglets'** sloppy habits and disharmonious grunts. After hamburgers, mac and cheese, salad, stewed tomatoes and apple crisp, we went fishing (bait, poles and boat provided), and toured the pond in a rowboat. My urban child and her worn-out mother were about as far away from the real world as possible.

I looked around me, remembering more from the Capon Springs brochure.

The days at Capon flow around made-from-scratch meals with ingredients fresh from our farm, which begin with the ringing of the dinner bell. In between meals, Capon offers plenty to do – golf, swimming, shuffleboard, badminton, tennis, hiking, fishing, reading, 'porching', or napping in one of our hammocks....

I had to admit it. Maybe the brochure was telling the truth. Maybe. Just maybe.

Capon Springs isn't for everybody. There's no alcohol and no smoking; no fine Italian linens on the bed or down-filled comforters; no thick, cushy towels or heated towel racks; no turn-down service or chocolates on your pillow; no air conditioning, wake-up calls, rainforest shower or whirlpool tub. No dressing up or artisan-created cuisine and no well-known chef. There's no in-room TVs or Wi-Fi, no locks on the doors and everyone lives by the good old-fashioned honor system.

Capon Springs wouldn't suit people who want complete privacy, or for those who don't enjoy nature. Or for others who require room service or candlelight and stringed instruments at dinner. Or for those who want to stay up late and party. And it surely isn't for people who like changing things up or who think variety is the spice of life.

That first weekend at Capon Springs left me with a sense of well-being that was altogether new to me. I had never experienced such a carefree few days. Perhaps it was the lithium-laced spring water, a natural mood enhancer, known for centuries for its healing qualities. Or just nature's gifts of woodlands and meadows, clean air, a night sky full of stars, the birdsongs at dawn and the evening chorus of tree frogs and cicadas. Maybe it was the atmosphere of friendship and love.

Am I hallucinating? No. It's real. I have to return.

In the early years of my visits to Capon Springs, I wasn't sure what it *really* was that drew me to that unfashionable, old-fangled resort. Decades later, I finally explained it to myself: Capon represented coming home. To something I never had -- a welcoming mother, a happy place and a loving family. I felt peaceful, confident and calm there. I was able to think. And *find* myself.

I held my breath from one visit to the next. I expected Capon to change, to become modern and impersonal, to put an end to the hugs when I walked through the front door. I was ready and waiting, even *expected* Capon to become untrustworthy and deceitful just like the family in which I grew up. To finally show its true colors.

But, it never did. It's just the same today as it was the day of my very first visit. Well, not exactly. But the things that matter haven't changed one bit.

And I came to appreciate my time at Capon Springs as one of the truly beautiful experiences in my life. It's remained consistent, reliable and predictable. Of course, it's changed, but only in the small ways that make it homier and more appealing. I've come to know that, from one year to the next, coming home to Capon is just what it's always been. Worlds away from the home of my youth.

When my late husband died, a man who loved Capon just as much as I, the Capon family planted a tree on the grounds in his memory. It stands proudly in a sunny space near the rope swing and not far from the pool. When it was first planted, it was a spindly little sugar maple, just short of four feet tall. Today, that tree is filled with my husband's exuberant spirit and love of life. It is healthy and robust, standing nearly twelve feet high. It is here in this place that I most keenly sense his enduring presence.

Since that first weekend, Capon Springs has become my haven. It's where I retreat to when I need to re-focus on what's most important in this life. It's effect on me has been almost magical.

A place as comfortable and familiar as my own home. The Capon family has welcomed me back time after time with the same happy smiles and caring words. I look forward to the informal **atmosphere** and warm hospitality. I haven't romanticized Capon; it's spirit is real, and transformative.

And just as authentic is the feeling that I've somehow stepped back in time to a quieter, gentler less complicated era.

Lift up your eyes to the mountains. Breathe deeply the crisp sweet air. Listen to the murmuring water. The spirit of peace is there.

There is nothing that can compare to the feeling of coming home.

No lie.

Afterword

I'm sitting on the front porch at Capon Springs Resort in West Virginia as I record the final words of my memoir. I've come home again. The stress muddling my thinking just a few days ago is gone. My mind is free to lose itself in yesterday.

I imagine the pristine day of my birth. I came into the world delicate and intricately detailed, a fine and unfettered tiny human. I was a clean slate onto which my passage through time would inscribe its memories. Imprinted there would be all the experiences of my days, the ones I cherish and those I would like to forget. So, too, the paths of all the people who have come into my life, and those who've gone.

When I embarked on what has become a five-year writing journey, it seemed like many of the stories I composed weren't connected in any logical way. Yet, the more I wrote, the clearer became the common threads in the fiber of my life. They wove themselves through my days and nights, year after year, and created the complex pattern in the fabric of me. And opened my eyes to what drove me to begin writing in the first place.

I wondered if my memoir would have meaning for anyone other than me.

At this moment, I realize it is *I* who have benefited most from giving life to my words, for adding images to feelings, wisdom to insanity, and understanding to chaos. Writing has permitted me to order and organize the experiences of my life. To capture the essence of one event which led to another; to make sense of those situations which were painful and others which brought great joy; to appreciate the people who shared my journey; and say goodbye to those who didn't.

Writing this book has shown me that coming face-to-face with yourself is actually much less exhausting than running away from it. And the people and situations which have haunted me -- they've finally lost their power over me.

In the process of drafting each chapter, my words came alive in a process far more painful than psychotherapy could ever be. Immersed in the drama, every word and every page transported me back to another time.

Surprisingly though, rather than tying me up in knots, writing has enabled me to unravel the mysteries of my life. Moving backwards has helped me understand the turmoil. But, most of all, writing has helped me heal.

In fact, the act of placing words on paper has been more liberating than anything else I've *ever* done in my life.

Several of the individuals who reviewed this manuscript prior to publication have asked me, "How will you forgive so-and-so or the person who said this-or-that?"

Actually, the person I must forgive first and foremost is *me*. Even though I'd like to believe my actions in the present might somehow undo my behavior from the past, that's ridiculous. And irrational. I found that the only thing I really have control over is taking responsibility for myself. Then and now.

I've stammered and struggled and foundered and faltered through more than seven decades, some days less gracefully than others. As I approach the end of my life, my feet are dancing, my eyes are smiling, my voice has mellowed, my words are gentler, my heart is open and I'm learning to love who I am. I've rummaged through my insides, turned myself inside and out, let go of what's been dragging me down, reorganized the rest and decided I can live with what's left.

♕

Someday I'll leave this life knowing that my presence on the earth has meant something. I've left my mark on some people in a positive way and on others in an unfavorable way. And some both. I can't undo anything. But I can understand it, learn from it and move forward in a healthier direction. Happy or not, pleasant and unpleasant, my experiences and memories are part of who I am.

To those who read this book and, perhaps, come face to face with the parts of themselves they would rather forget, you're not alone. If you should decide to make a clean sweep it'll be scary, but life on the other side of the bottle is better.

Or on the other side of whatever might be holding you back.

To my family and those who follow, I hope to leave a less troubled footprint on this earth. I hope my story will encourage those who read it to look inside of themselves *first* for the answers to their troubles.

Happiness is no longer as elusive as it once was. And I don't look to anyone other than *me* to make it happen. I've finally discovered how to be happy, not just for a moment or a day, but for an extended period of time. Sure, there are times when I may find myself immersed in the suffering of the past or lolling around in the old feelings of not being good enough. But now I can ruminate for a minute or two and then let it go. I usually don't let the feelings get me down.

In one sense, the past is behind me; in another, it's right where it's always been — it's just that the view from where I'm sitting now is much different.

Sonya Braverman
Capon Springs, West Virginia
June, 2018

Sonya Braverman

Addendum
Childhood Alcoholism

Not much is written about childhood alcoholism, that is, children under the age of twelve who drink alcoholic beverages. Few novels, movies and hardly any memoirs discuss the experiences of prepubescent drinkers. The body of knowledge that exists to define or explain this phenomenon is slim and there is even less scholarly research about children who drink. Those who desire more information about childhood drinking either personally or professionally are at a genuine loss.

As a Clinical Social Worker for over thirty years, I never treated anyone who began drinking below the age of twelve. That is, a child who savored the taste of alcohol, anticipated the effects and used it routinely.

Everyone knows that alcohol use among teenagers is a huge problem in the United States. However, a thorough search of any material about alcohol abuse among children under the age of twelve revealed scant literature in this area.

One of the individuals who has done some research about childhood alcoholism, John E. Donovan, Ph.D., Professor of Psychiatry and Epidemiology at the University of Pittsburgh has studied the problem. He writes that, "The study of alcohol use by children ages 12 and younger [grades 6 and lower] has been very limited."

There are few research studies of alcohol use and alcohol-related problems among children and preadolescents, a situation that makes estimation of the alcohol burden in this age-group problematic. The available data indicate that although the rates of alcohol use are relatively low in this population, substantial numbers of children do, in fact, have experience with alcohol.

Donovan writes that,

> Chief among the factors inhibiting the estimation of alcohol burden in children and preadolescents is the absence of ongoing national surveillance data. The prevalence of child alcohol use can theoretically be estimated from either adolescents' retrospective recall of their alcohol use in childhood or from survey research with children.

Retrospective reports of the age at first drink are not reliable sources of data among adolescents and, although direct surveys of children can be a more appropriate approach for capturing such data on childhood alcohol use and alcohol-related problems among children, no such formal surveys include children younger than twelve.

One of the limitations of this kind of research is that the surveys originally developed for use with adults have been modified for use with college students; then modified again for use with adolescents; and, finally, modified for the assessment of children. Reliance on such hand-me-down data has resulted in limited research into sipping and tasting of alcohol despite the fact that this is the most common form of children's experience with alcohol.

There is also a lack of consensus on the definition of the various levels of alcohol involvement for both children and adolescents. Drinker status was defined variously as consumption of more than a sip, more than a few sips, or a whole drink.

Donovan postulates that, nevertheless, a substantial number of children have had some exposure to alcohol. According to the 1999 Partnership for a Drug-Free America which surveyed elementary-school students, 9.8 percent of 4th graders, 16.1 percent of 5th graders and 29.4 percent of 6th graders had had more than just a sip of alcohol in their life. The data indicate that although the rates of alcohol use are low in this population, substantial numbers of children do drink alcohol.

That study was completed almost twenty years ago. With the alarming data that we currently have about the frequency and quantity of adolescent drinking today, we could probably safely assume that the percentage of children under the age of twelve who drink has risen likewise.

"Increased research in childhood drinking is needed," suggests Donovan, but there are barriers to conducting this kind of research. One barrier is that few children drink. A second is the difficulty of gaining approval to access elementary school children. A third barrier is the concern that parents will be reluctant to consent to their children's participation in alcohol research.

Parents contribute to the alcohol burden of their children in several ways. First, they model drinking behavior. Children initially learn about alcohol from observing their parents or hearing them talk about their drinking, as well as from their exposure to drinking in the larger social environment (relatives, peers, TV and radio, magazine ads, the internet, social media and movies). It is common knowledge that children whose parents drink are more likely to initiate early use.

Second, parents actively teach their children about alcohol. Children are first introduced to alcohol use by parents or other relatives in a family context. Such socialization into alcohol use can reflect either cultural beliefs regarding the role of alcohol as food or as a necessary adjunct for celebrations, or the belief that introducing children to alcohol use as part of family dinners or events serves to inoculate them from later involvement in problem drinking.

While it may be presumed that learning to drink within the family context serves to protect children from developing later alcohol problems, longitudinal research suggests that prior supervised drinking *increases* the likelihood of later unsupervised drinking and increased alcohol involvement and drunkenness over time.

Third, the home environment is the most popular source of alcohol for children. Among 6th-grade students, 32.7 percent obtained the alcohol from a parent or parent figure. As children move into adolescence, other adults become an important source of alcohol. Greater access to alcohol in the home and outside and greater parental and other adult provision of alcohol are associated with greater alcohol intake and problems in the future.

Although more work is needed in this area, what data is available on children twelve and under supports the belief that early-onset drinking of alcohol predicts involvement in alcohol problems, alcohol abuse and alcohol dependence in adolescence and adulthood.

Sonya Braverman

Made in the USA
Lexington, KY
13 November 2018